Willis King

Stories of a country doctor

Willis King

Stories of a country doctor

ISBN/EAN: 9783743376151

Manufactured in Europe, USA, Canada, Australia, Japa

Cover: Foto ©ninafisch / pixelio.de

Manufactured and distributed by brebook publishing software (www.brebook.com)

Willis King

Stories of a country doctor

To meet the almost universal demand for a safe, reliable and elegant liquid laxative, we offer to the medical profession our

SYRUP OF FIGS
(SYR. FICI. CAL.)

which is an agreeable and effective laxative or purgative, according to the dose or manner of administration. It is delightful to the taste, is perfectly safe, does not debilitate, hence may be given to patients of all ages, even the very young and very old. We utilize in its manufacture the delicious

BLUE FIG OF CALIFORNIA

After a thorough study of the results to be accomplished and of the best methods to be employed to produce a perfect laxative, which would always be pleasant to the taste and as safe to

One or two teaspoonfuls act as a

LAXATIVE

when given at bedtime or before breakfast

One-half to one tablespoonful acts as a

PURGATIVE

and may be repeated in six hours, if necessary

administer to infants as to adults, we began the manufacture of SYRUP OF FIGS (Syr. Fici. Cal.) by adding to the Blue Fig of California an excellent combination of carminative aromatics, pure white sugar and the juice of

TRUE ALEXANDRIA SENNA

which represents all the purgative principles without any of its griping properties.

SYRUP OF FIGS (Syr. Fici. Cal.) is now prescribed by prominent physicians everywhere, and is giving them general satisfaction. We devote our entire attention to its manufacture, have complete facilities especially adapted to the purpose, and thus we are enabled to make this perfect laxative, which though so simple in itself has not been produced in all its excellence by others; therefore, we trust and believe that physicians will not allow imitations of our syrup to be substituted when they prescribe **SYR. FICI. CAL.** (Syrup of Figs.) which is manufactured ONLY by the

CALIFORNIA FIG SYRUP COMPANY

LOUISVILLE, KY.   SAN FRANCISCO, CAL.   NEW YORK, N. Y.

IT IS SOLD IN BOTTLES OF TWO SIZES ONLY, THE SMALLER BOTTLES CONTAINING FULL FOUR OUNCES AND THE LARGE SIZE ABOUT TEN OUNCES.

The American Antipyretic, Analgesic and Anodyne

1-OZ. PACKAGE, $1.00, PREPAID

Antikamnia

OPPOSED TO PAIN — A SUCCEDANEUM FOR MORPHIA.

Valuable in Neuralgia, Sciatica, Acute Rheumatism and Typhoid Fever; also Headache and other Neuroses due to Irregularities of Menstruation. Exhibited in Asthma, Hay Fever, Influenza, La Grippe and allied complaints, it secures the desired results.

☞ Further information and samples sent free on application.

Antikamnia Chemical Co.
St. Louis, Mo.

For $3.00

No. 2. Size, 7½ x 3⅞ x ⅞ inches Price, 3.00.

We will send a handsome, double morocco pocket case, containing 24 vials, filled with the following complete assortment of

Tablets and Triturates

Hypophos. Quinia comp. Creasote.
Acetanilid, 2 grains.
Morphia Sulph., ⅛ grain.
Zinc Sulpho-carb, 1 grain.
Dover's Powder, 2½ grains.
Fever, (Dr. T. G Davis).
Hydrarg Iodide Virid, ⅛ grain.
Iron, Arsenic, and Strychnia.
Paregoric, 10 minim.
Strychnia, 1-60 grain.
Quinia sulph., 1 grain.
Corros., Sublimate, 1-40.
Ammon, Mur. comp.
Calomel, 1-10 grain.
Calomel, 2 grains.
Calomel ipecac and soda bicarb, No. 1.
Tr. aconite, ½ minim
Tr. belladonna, 2 minim.
Nitro Glycerine Comp. (M. & Co.'s).
Cascara comp. (M. & Co.'s)
Acid Arsenious, 1-60 grain.
Four Chlorides (Univ. Hospital).
Bismuth et Cerii Oxalat.
Kermes Mineral Comp.

All vials in this case are fitted with screw-caps.

We would call especial attention to our TABLETS, HYPHOPHOS. QUINIA COMP. CUM CREASOTE, which are superior to syrups and solutions, owing to absence of sugar and free acid.

H. K. MULFORD COMPANY,

Factors of Compressed Goods and Pharmaceutical Preparations,

2132 Market Street, Philadelphia.

Write for Complete List.

STORIES

OF

A COUNTRY DOCTOR.

BY WILLIS P. KING, M. D.

First Vice-President of American Medical Association, Ex-President of the Missouri State Medical Association, Assistant Chief Surgeon of the Missouri Pacific Railway Co., Formerly Lecturer on Diseases of Women in the Medical Department of the Missouri State University, and Professor of Diseases of Women in the Medical Department University of Kansas City; Lecturer on Orthopedic Surgery and Clinical Surgery in the University Medical College of Kansas City, Member of the Jackson County (Mo.) Medical Society, Ex-President of the Pettis County (Mo.) Medical Society, Formerly Assistant Physician and Surgeon to the Pettis County (Mo.) Jail and Poor House, and Ex-Physician and Surgeon to the Branch Water Man, and his Folks.

WITH ILLUSTRATIONS BY T. A. FITZGERALD.

Price, One Dollar, in Cloth.

PHILADELPHIA:
HUMMEL AND PARMELE, Publishers,
612 Drexel Building.
1891.

Entered according to Act of Congress, in the Year 1889.
BY WILLIS P. KING, M. D.
In the office of the Librarian of Congress at Washington.

Dedication.

TO THE
PROGRESSIVE, GOOD, CONSCIENTIOUS AND TRUE
MEN OF THE MEDICAL PROFESSION
OF THE UNITED STATES,
AND TO
THE JOLLY GOOD FELLOWS EVERYWHERE,
THIS 'BOOK
IS AFFECTIONATELY DEDICATED, BY
THE AUTHOR.

W. B. OUTTEN,
   Chief Surgeon, St. Louis, Mo.
W. P. KING,
   Ass't Chief Surgeon, Kansas City, Mo.
D. J. HOLLAND,
   Ass't Chief Surgeon, Atchison, Ks.
R. C. VOLKER,
   Ass't Chief Surgeon, Ft. Worth, Tex.
J. W. JENKINS,
   Dep't Purveyor, St. Louis, Mo.

The Missouri Pacific R'y Co.,

LEASED AND OPERATED LINES.

HOSPITAL DEPARTMENT.

KANSAS CITY, MO.,
July 12, 1890.

THE ALE & BEEF CO.

DEAR SIRS—Answering yours of 8th inst,, will say that I have used the Ale and Beef, "Peptonized," in both hospital and private practice, and am much pleased with it. My house surgeons (Drs. F. R. Smiley and Geo. F. Hamel) inform me that it agrees with the stomach in cases where food can not be retained, and this agrees with my own experience. *I had one case of a delicate lady with a forming pelvic abscess* which involved the ovary. There was constant vomiting and retching. She retained the Ale and Beef, "Peptonized." This, after I had tried a number of things which had failed. She drank it steadily for a month, and it seemed to be, in her case, food, medicine, stimulant and lodging—all in one. It is an excellent thing. Keep up the good quality of the preparation and it will readily sell.

                Very respectfully,
                    WILLIS P. KING, M. D.,
                Asst. Chief Surgeon, Mo. P. Ry.

Dr. J. R Walker
 Fresno, Cal
Mar. 6, 1933.

CONTENTS.

CHAPTER I THE WEST.

The Pioneers—Causes that Move Men into a New Country—Character of the People who Settled Missouri—Their Simple Honesty and Hospitality—Dealing with a Dishonest Neighbor—Helping a Neighbor—Athletic Sports—Settling a Controversy—Old Gill R. and His Tangled Shirt—A Joke on Judge H................................. 13

CHAPTER II—EDUCATION AND PIONEER SCHOOLS.

Disadvantages as to Education—The Pioneer School House—The old Irish Teacher and His Terrible Discipline—Text Books—Examining the Teacher—Turning the Teacher Out—Stimulants—Joe—The Mad Teacher.. 32

CHAPTER III—OLD TIME DANCES AND PARTIES.

Country Dances and the Dancers—Female Critics—Three Stories of Three Generations of Men.. 47

CHAPTER IV—CIVILIZATION AND PIONEER WEDDINGS.

Good Fellowship and Hospitality—Effects of Civilization—Dancing Parties—A Conspiracy, and What Came of It—Tom's Appetite Works Havoc—Weddings—The Preacher's Two Stories................ 62

CHAPTER V—PECULIARITIES OF PIONEER PEOPLE.

Influence of Education on the Conformation of the Body—Some Specimens—Story of the Old Linen Coat and the Masonic March—Col. Jack's Story of His Only Love.. 83

CHAPTER VI—THEN AND NOW.

Hardships of the Pioneer—The Way They Lived—Muscle and its Environment—The Result of Education and Wealth—C. Augustus and Arabella—A Contrast—Why?.. 106

CHAPTER VII—SUPERSTITIONS, TRADITIONS AND FOOLISH IDEAS.

Antiquity of Superstition—Man a Superstitious Animal—"Signs"—Crowing Hens, Bellowing Cows, Etc.—Losing Her "Cud"—McGee's Diagnosis—Bible Witchery—Raising the Palate—The Silver Plate, Etc.—Passing the Handkerchief—Negro Superstitions......... 119

CHAPTER VIII—PREACHER DOCTORS, MIDWIVES AND NURSES.

Reasons Why the Profession do not Like Preacher Doctors—The Nurse and the "Nuss"—Stories about "Nusses."............ 142

CHAPTER IX—THE BRANCH-WATER MAN.

His General Character and Habits; His Dog, Team and Wife—Stories of Keesecker and Old Darling............ 157

CHAPTER X—THE UPS AND DOWNS IN EARLY PRACTICE.

The Country Doctor—The Young Doctor's Dream—Obstacles—My First Case—Laughing Down Her Throat—The Widow B. and the Night I Slept with the Cat—A Blood-Curdling Incident............ 182

CHAPTER XI—UPS AND DOWNS, CONTINUED.

A Contrast—How to Tell When Your Patient is Dead—Cupping the Old Lady—Smart People—The Sick Horse—Fighting Fire—The Prairie Mirage—Home Again............ 200

CHAPTER XII—BENEVOLENT DESIGNS.

Wanted to be a Millionaire—A Trip to Colorado—The "Phœnix" and the Tree Oyster—Natural Phenomena—"The Lightness of the Atmosphere"—A Tenderfoot's Failure—The Grandeur of the Mountains—The Good of Desiring to do Good............ 219

CHAPTER XIII—DEATH BED REPENTANCE AND CONFESSIONS.

General Considerations—"Cause of Bill Simpson Going to H——!"—The "Colonel" and the Meteoric Shower—"Uncle Mike" and the Story of the Stoning of Stephen............ 237

CHAPTER XIV—SHAM SUICIDES.

A Startling Statement—The Young Wife—The Jilted Girl and the Deadly Flour—Dr. Eggslinger—Story of the Widow Minor—The Rejected Lover—How to Detect the Fraud............ 255

CHAPTER XV—LIARS AND THEIR LIES.

General Observations on Lying—Classification of Liars—Bill Whittington and a Sample of His Lies—Sim's Unfair Trick—The Story of the Bullies—Jack, the Barber, and Rafferty's Funeral—A Great Shot and a Fast Trotter—Do Doctors Lie?—Several Samples which Answer the Question—An Asylum for Liars............ 272

CHAPTER XVI—CONSULTATIONS AND THE CODE.

Reasons for the Code—Relations of Doctor and Patient—The New Comer and the Emergency Case—Smith and the Cat Skin Poultice—Jones' Hot Corn and Burnt Feathers—" Old Pill Garlic " and the Dying Girl.. 297

CHAPTER XVII—PEOPLE WHO ANNOY DOCTORS.

Patients, Hotel Keepers, Etc.—The Homely Crank—" The Hon. Mrs. Skewton "—Mr. Gutzweiler—The Sick Girl, the Deaf Landlady with the Trumpet, and the Milliner.. 319

CHAPTER XVIII—DID HE KILL HIS WIFE?

Helping the Doctor, or Otherwise—A Second Marriage and a Motherless Child—The Result of Developing One Side of the Family—January and May—" Did He Kill His Wife?".................................. 346

CHAPTER XIX—GOING BACK TO COLLEGE.

Necessity for More Education—The Southwest—My Own Trip—My Ill Fitting Clothes—My Plug Hat and the Old Maid—My Revenge—The Oyster Supper with Observations on the Heathen...... 363

CHAPTER XX—QUACKS AND QUACKERY.

The True Physician—The Different Kinds of Quacks—The Gentlemanly Quack—The Smart Pretender—The Professional Buzzard or " Jim Crow " Doctor—" Abdominal Digitalis and Aortic Regurgitation "—Dr. Connecktie and Dr. Gullus................................... 378

Gardner's Syrup of Hydriodic Acid
IODIDE OF HYDROGEN

This is the original preparation of Syrup of Hydriodic Acid, first brought to the attention of the medical world in 1878, by R. W. Gardner. Its use has established the reputation of Hydriodic Acid as a remedy.

Indications: Hay Fever; Rose Cold; Poisoning by Lead, Mercury or Arsenic; Rheumatism, Acute or Chronic; Asthma; Chronic Bronchitis; Catarrh, either Respiratory, Uterine, or Intestinal; Sciatica; Scald Head; Vaginitis; Urethritis; Congestion of the Lungs in Children; Adenitis; Eczema; Lupus; Chronic Malarial Poisoning; Lumbago; Acute Pneumonia; Psoriasis; Scrofulous Diseases; Goitre; Enlarged Glands; Cold Abscesses; Indolent Sores; Obesity; Fatty Degeneration of the Heart; to Absorb Non-malignant Tumors; in the latter stages of Syphilis; Syphilitic Phthisis; Pleurisy with Adhesion; Pleurisy with Exudation, etc.

This preparation has been successfully employed in the above-named diseases, details of which, written by the physicians who have used it, will be sent to the medical profession, without charge.

Gardner's Syrups of Chemically Pure Hypophosphites

Prepared strictly in accord with Dr. Churchill's views, representing single salts; enabling the physician to follow this eminent authority in the scientific methods which his experience of thirty years has proven the most efficient.

Copies of the third, seventh, and eighth editions, issued by the undersigned, containing copious quotations from Churchill, upon the scientific aspects of this treatment; physiological and therapeutical doses; toxic or poisonous doses; indications and contra-indications; auscultation; complications; relapse; phosphates and hypophosphites compared; other and antagonistic remedies; theory of Tuberculosis, etc., will be mailed **without charge to physicians.**

It is worthy the study of any physician, and accidents, relapse, and failure may be the result of its non-observance.

Prepared by R. W. GARDNER
Pharmaceutical Chemist

W. H. SCHIEFFELIN & CO., 158 William Street, New York
NEW YORK, SOLE AGENTS.

PREFACE.

> "When a person knows a story that he thinks he ought to tell,
> If he doesn't get to tell it why, of course, he don't feel well."
> —*Eugene F. Ware.*

Every book must have a preface, and so, "yielding to an imperious custom," I write one for mine. The preface usually tells why the author wrote the book;— "there was a demand," "a crying need," "a long felt want," etc., etc.

Now, I can scarcely tell why I wrote this book. There were many reasons that impelled me to the task. My friends urged me to write it—friends who had seen me, with my great capacity for enjoyment, gallantly wrestling with poverty year after year and generally getting thrown the "three best in five." They thought I had a fortune within my grasp if I would only put my ideas and my stories into a book.

They desired that I should grow rich so that they could borrow my money. I desired to grow rich so that I could refuse them. I can't refuse them so long as I am poor.

I found a niche ("a long felt want," you see, reader) which has never been filled by any writer, and so occupied it.

I desired to give the world the benefit of what I had learned of humanity in a quarter of a century's practice. I desired to give the praise due the honest, conscientious and hard working men in my profession—the noblest and most unselfish humanitarians that grace the earth with their noble deeds—as well as to put on record the good, the beautiful and true in human nature which we find in connection with our life work.

I also wished to hold up before the calcium light of public scrutiny and to properly excoriate the quacks and scoundrels who infest our communities and, by their falsehoods and frauds, bring disgrace on a noble calling : and, I desired to properly characterize and satirize those who hinder our work by their ignorant superstitions, their selfishness and vanity.

I also wished to go down in history with that noble army of the world's benefactors—the book writers, as a man who had written a book. I hope that the book may be the means of affording amusement and giving pleasure to both my overworked professional brethren and the community at large.

And last and best of all, dear reader, I desired to make something out of the enterprise. If I do there will be rejoicing at our house when the receipts come in. There will be a feast in which the timbrel and the hewgag will be sounded, and I promise you that the widow and the orphan shall not be forgotten.

Complaint may be made that the personal pronoun "I" has been used oftener than it should have been. This may be true. My friends say that I have a plenty of that very necessary faculty called self esteem. To this I also "plead guilty and put myself upon the country."

As a defense, however, I desire to say that most of the things written about in this book have a personal relationship to myself, and, being too modest to put myself on an equality with the editors and the Lord, by saying "we," I was compelled to say "I;" so "the 'I's' seem to have it."

The publishers are instructed that, if the font of large "I's" runs out, to put in little "i's" and go on with the book, so, "the 'i's' have it."

       I bow, W. P. K.

KANSAS CITY, MO.

Chas. Truax Greene & Co. ✻ MANUFACTURERS OF Artificial Limbs OF ALL KINDS

Deformity Apparatus AND Appliances   Artificial Eyes   Crutches Trusses Supporters

The opposite engravings are from photographs of John Langfeldt, of Rock Rapids, Iowa, who lost both hands and both feet in the great blizzard of Jan. 12-13, 1888.

He was fitted with both hands and feet in September, 1888, when he came to Chicago with an attendant, utterly unable to do anything for himself—had to be carried from a carriage into our store. Within an hour after completing the feet he walked to his hotel, several blocks distant, and thereafter walked all about the city. Within a few minutes after fitting his hands he took a pencil and wrote his own name quite plainly.

The following letter was written in April, 1891:

Charles Truax, Chicago, Ill.:

Dear Sir: In reply to yours of the 10th inst., I will state that Dr. Wallace amputated all four of my limbs on January 27, 1888, and in September, 1888, you put artificial limbs on me, and almost ever since I could walk well, and now I am following a plow all day, and also can walk up and down stairs with perfect ease, and have been seeding or farming all spring,

Yours respectfully,

(Signed) JOHN LANGFELDT.

Hearing Instruments, Rolling Chairs, Etc.

CORRESPONDENCE SOLICITED

CHAS. TRUAX, GREENE & CO., Chicago, U.S.A.

Reed & Carnrick will never add any new preparations to their list unless they possess important points of superiority over those in use by the medical profession for similar purposes.

We are confident that the following preparations for the purposes described are superior to any therapeutic agents known to the Medical Profession, or are presented in more elegant form for administration.

Zymocide (Antisepsine) — For **Leucorrhœa, Catarrh** of the nasal organs, stomach or bladder, and **all diseases** of the **mucous Surfaces**, or whenever a non-toxic, antiseptic and detergent preparation is required.

Pancrobilin — For **Intestinal Indigestion, Constipation** and to **increase fatty tissue.** The price of Pancrobilin has been reduced 33 per cent.

Cordial Analeptine — For **Rheumatic and Gouty Diathesis, and excessive Urates.**

Corrigent Pills — For **imparting tone to the system, increasing the appetite,** improving the digestion, enhancing the **functions of assimilation and blood-making** and removing **malarial** and other **taint** from the blood.

Sulpho-Calcine — For **dissolving** the diphtheritic membrane and for treating diseases of the mucous surfaces. Valuable in parasitic skin diseases.

Lacto-Preparata — For the **feeding of Infants from birth to six** months of age. The only **All-Milk Food prepared for** Infants.

Carnrick's Food — For **Children** from **six months to fifteen months** of age.

SULPHUR-TARTRATE TABLETS — For **Biliousness, Torpid Liver, Skin Diseases, Pimples** and **imperfect growth of the nails and hair.**

Cod Liver Oil and Milk — For all purposes where **Cod Liver Oil** is indicated. The most palatable and digestible preparation in the market.

Velvet-Skin Soap — For making the skin soft. It is a **perfect Soap for Infants** and all **Toilet Purposes.** It is made only from Vegetable Oils.

Velvet-Skin Powder — For **Infants and all Toilet Purposes.** It excels all others in **delicacy** and **fragrance.** Contains no starch or deleterious substances.

Send for pamphlet giving minute formulas and full description of each preparation.

Reed & Carnrick

P. O. Box 3042   NEW YORK

CHAPTER I.

THE WEST.

THE PIONEER—CAUSES THAT MOVE MEN INTO A NEW COUNTRY—CHARACTER OF THE PEOPLE WHO SETTLED MISSOURI—THEIR SIMPLE HONESTY AND HOSPITALITY—DEALING WITH A DISHONEST NEIGHBOR—ATHLETIC SPORTS—SETTLING A CONTROVERSY—OLD GILL R. AND HIS TANGLED SHIRT—A JOKE ON JUDGE H.

"GO West, young man, and grow up with the country." What is "the West?" At one time western New York was "the West;" then Pennsylvania was "the West;" then Ohio and Tennessee; then Indiana, Illinois and Missouri; afterwards Minnesota, Kansas and Nebraska; then Colorado, Nevada, Oregon and the territories; and now—*there is no West.*

Immigration, capital, railroads, the telegraph, newspapers, and all the arts of civilization have penetrated to the Pacific Ocean, from Puget Sound to the Bay of San Francisco; and everywhere, where only a few years ago the wild Indian, and the wild beasts of the forests and the prairies held sway, and where the deep silence had never been broken by civilized man, now on the prairies, in the valleys, and on the mountain sides, cities, towns and villages stand, and in place of the yell of the untutored savage, the prattle of civilized children on their way to school, or the plaintive voice of prayer is heard. Instead of the screams of the wolf we hear the bay of the faithful watch dog; and instead of the rush of the great herds of buffalo we hear the peaceful low of the Short Horn, the Jersey, the Hereford and the Polled Angus, as they quietly graze in meadows of clover, blue grass and timothy.

This is a wonderful change to have been wrought in less than a century. How, and by what means, has this change been wrought? By the energy, nerve and pluck of man. By the indomitable courage of Americans; of men who were tired of the restraints and forms of older communities; of men who desired and sought a wider and better field for themselves and those dependant upon them.

It is a fact that in all communities there is a tendency toward an accumulation of money—the wealth of the commuity—in the hands of a few. The brainy, the crafty, and the stingy men; the men who starve themselves in order to hoard money; the men who always have something to sell; or, who, if they do purchase, always do so when a thing is cheap, and never sell except when it is high; the men who loan money at twenty-five per cent; who take "cut-throat" mortgages and sorrowfully sell their neighbors out when the mortgage is due.

This man you will find everywhere, a man who seems to have been born with a dollar in his hand, and that dollar crying for ten per cent. secured by a deed of trust. These men are often ignorant, but always know how to accumulate and keep money. They are sometimes religious, but never let their religion get between them and ten per cent. interest. They often express and seem to feel an interest in their fellow man, but when you probe the matter to the bottom, *it is ten per cent. interest or more.*

I have seen a man of this type go so ragged that you wouldn't have thought of using his suit for a scarecrow, and wearing a hat that a decent, thoughtful hen wouldn't deign to make a nest in. They are always poor and always hard up, if you will believe them; but, when the opportunity of a good bargain offers they can always go down and get out an old pocket book filled with bills pressed so tight that it is difficult to open them, and with twenty dollar gold pieces whose luster is dimmed by the sweat of their stingy groins.

I am neither an anarchist, nor a communist, but with all the power of an intense nature, I contemn and despise the man who gets money through selfish motives and purely and solely for selfish purposes.

Well, these are the fellows who cause immigration; these are the men who compel other and better men to move. They get their clutches on him; they get a mortgage on him, they entangle him in their tentacles like the octopus, and finally end by exposing him at public auction according to the accepted forms of law.

When a man is sold out, "broken up," he wants to move. His financial prostration is an evidence of weakness, and is, to all intents and purposes, a defeat, and no man wishes to remain where he has exhibited his weakness—where he has suffered defeat. He seeks an outlet, and the outlet is in a new country, in a country where land is cheap, where grazing is good, where the social forms are simple, where a living is easily obtained, and where ten per cent. has not yet gained a foothold.

Of course I do not wish to be understood as saying that all men who seek a new country do so from the causes mentioned, for it would not be true. There are those who simply feel the restraints of social forms which grow as society grows older; there are those of a venturesome spirit who delight in the boundless freedom of a new country; there are those who desire to take advantage of a new country in order to improve their condition, and there are those who seek a new country because they can live in contact with wild nature without labor—the man with the rod and the gun—who wants nothing but a primitive shelter and a chance to hunt and fish. Civilization is always crowding such people and they are always running to get away from the pressure and they will continue to run so long as there is a place to run to.

Much of that part of our country which lies west of the Mississippi river was almost an unbroken forest and boundless, uncultivated prairies up to three quarters of a century ago—indeed much of it was in the same condition within the memory of the writer. It was a country that was good to look upon. It had splendid rivers—capable of bearing upon their bosoms the commerce of the continent; forests unhewn and untouched, as splendid as could be found anywhere; prairies and valleys, containing millions on millions of acres which, under cultivation, would almost supply the world with bread. Forests, mountains, valleys and plains, whose solitude except by the savage and the wild beast had never been broken.

If a person speaking only the English tongue and capable of making himself heard hundreds of miles could have taken his position where the capital of Kansas now stands and had called in his native tongue for help or for companionship, he would have received no answer; if he had gone to the present capital of Nebraska and had called in the same tongue, no one would have responded; if he had gone to Denver and sent his voice ringing and reverberating through the rocky mountains and wailing out across the sandy plains, it would have come back to him in hollow mockery, for no one speaking *his* language would have been near enough to respond. He might have gone to the present capitals of Nevada, Utah, California, Oregon, Wyoming, Washington, Idaho and Dakota and lifted up his voice and sent it up and down great rivers and over mountain, valley, hill and plain, and still his own voice would have mocked him from the depths of the solitudes and he would have received no answer except in the yell of the wild savage, the scream of the coyote and the roar of the grizzly bear.

The first settlements west of the Mississippi (excepting those under the Spanish and French) were made by the pioneers from Kentucky, Virginia, Tennessee and North Carolina with an occasional straggler from Pennsylvania or some other Eastern or Northern State.

They were a hardy set. As a rule their parents had been pioneers in Kentucky and Tennessee. They were, to some extent, inured to hardship, and they possessed faculties, both inherited and acquired, which enabled them to successfully contend with the difficulties which they daily encountered.

They were a brave, noble and unselfish people—the men being strong and courageous and the women virtuous and pure. Few had much education, so far as books were concerned; many had none. They were hospitable and generous to a fault. They literally hewed their way into the unbroken forests and formed their settlements. It was necessary for many families to settle near each other, for the Indian still possessed the land, and, notwithstanding the numerous treaties, which were intended to dispossess him and render the homes and lives of the settlers secure, yet he was a dangerous neighbor, and often made murderous incursions into these settlements, killing men, women and children and driving away stock.

Notwithstanding the dangers and difficulties which surrounded and beset them they were a happy people. There were no newspapers but they had the news. It was longer in coming but it lasted longer when they once got it. They had no theatres but they had their fun. They were an original set, and would go to more trouble and spend more time in perpetrating a joke on a neighbor than most men would spend now-a-days in organizing a mining company or starting a bank.

These people had but little. They needed but little. What one had all had. Such a thing as a neighbor wanting for anything, no matter whether he was able to pay for it or not, was unheard of. Those who had more milk, butter and eggs than they could use gave to those who were less fortunate. Even during the boyhood of the writer (and that is not so long ago) this practice prevailed. Not until the railroads penetrated the State of Missouri did our people begin to sell eggs, butter, milk and "garden truck."

The people whom these railroads brought from the crowded North and East brought these practices with them and the descendents of the pioneers adopted them in self defense.

But it is to be regretted that with the change much of the old time fellowship and hospitality has departed.

When a "new comer" came in he either camped out, or if the weather was inclement, some one would give him shelter, until a house could be built. The people would gather on a given day and would cut, haul, scalp and build a house, daub it, make the boards and cover it, put in doors and build a chimney in one or two days and the family would move in.

This was called "building a house from the stump."

If the family were poor one neighbor would furnish some bacon, another some meal, another some honey, another a pair of pigs or chickens, and, in this way the family would be "set up to house keepin'" in about as good style as their neighbors.

Every new family was scanned and their habits, talk and ways studied and discussed until the neighborhood settled down to some sort of conviction as to what kind of folks the "new comers" were. If they proved to be kind, honest and neighborly they were accepted as a part of the community, and could borrow and lend without let or hindrance; but, if anything wrong was suspected concerning them they were put under surveillance and kept at arms length until they could show themselves to be above suspicion.

Almost any kind of a character was tolerated except dishonest ones. The pioneers to the West were a rigidly honest people and they would not tolerate dishonesty or swindling in any form.

People had no locks to their doors in those days. Sometimes a man would take his family and go away into another settlement and be away for days and weeks with no other security for his household goods than a simple wooden door latch, "with the string on the outside."

Stealing was a rare thing. Occasionally there would be a dishonest man (and he was invariably a lazy one) who would steal corn or meat, and sometimes slaughter a neighbor's hog in the woods. These matters would be reported and discussed and the honest men in the settlement would almost invariably settle on the right party. Parties would be organized to watch for him and they generally caught him. When they had caught him they would guard him until daylight and then the men in the settlement would be called together and the whole party would proceed with the prisoner to the dense woods where there were fallen logs on which they could sit. The prisoner would be taken some distance away and put under guard of some of the younger men. The old men would then hear all that could be said or proven against the offender. If the case were a very aggravated one they would probably decide to "withe him" (whip him) and then make him leave the settlement. But, as a rule, they decided to simply make him leave. After the decision the offender would be brought up and notified as to what he must do. If any of his family were sick they would give him time for the sick one to recover.

If he had no team, or not enough to haul his household goods, they would furnish a team and one or two young men to go with him a day or two; but he had to go. There was no appeal from this solemn tribunal. This was the court of first and last resort, and I never heard of any man taking an appeal.

If there was a man in the neighborhood who was cruel to his family—more especially if he beat his wife—the matter would be discussed, facts obtained, and when enough had been ascertained to justify it a committee was appointed who would go in the dead of night and lay a bunch of hickory sprouts at his door. This was a warning and the offender knew what it meant and generally "improved his ways." If he did not a committee would go at night, take him out and tie him up, and one or two men would "lint him," or "welt him," or "lap the bud around him" as they called it. This was almost sure to have the desired effect. I never heard of one of these men taking revenge. A man who is cowardly enough to beat his wife rarely has courage enough to take revenge on a man.

There was very little litigation in those good old days. Property was not sufficiently valuable, as a rule, to go to law about; and then there was an innate honesty and sense of justice amongst these grand old pioneers that caused them to obey the golden rule.

If they did have differences they often arbitrated them. Each party would choose a neighbor and these two would choose a third; the committee would meet and hear both sides and then go and sit on a log and discuss it. After coming to an agreement they would call the parties to the contest and announce their award —which was generally a just one—and the parties would silently accept it. If the parties were still disposed to disagree and be unneighborly a few neighbors would often get together and call upon them and lecture them upon the unreasonableness of their differences and the bad effect it had on the "settle*ment*," and would often get the parties to agree to "make up." When they "made up" they "shuck hands" in the presence of the committee and these settlements were usually religiously observed.

Occasionally, however, men would get so incensed at each other that nothing would do but a fight. Under such circumstances they would meet at some designated point in the neighborhood, with most of the men present to see "fair play" and then fight it out. These fights were called "pitched battles." They did not fight according to the rules of the "London prize ring." nor the "Marquis of Queensberry." Knocking, kicking, biting and gouging were allowed, and they fought until one or the other said "Nuff" (enough) or "Take him off." They never used weapons. The man who attempted to do so was regarded as a coward and he was liable to get a blow from any one of the bystanders upon the mere attempt to draw a weapon. Everybody was in favor of a fair fight and if a man was getting the worst of it and his own brother attempted to interfere he would be sure to get a blow from behind that would call his attention to himself instead of his brother.

Sometimes a man would fight, when he knew, from the size, strength and reputation of his opponent, that he would get whipped; but, he would fight rather than back out. He would say to his friends "I reckon I can't whup him, but I'll keep the flies off uv him while he's a whuppin' me."

Some men were notorious for raising a row and getting others into it and then slipping out and avoiding the fight themselves. They were good "mouth fighters," but were not worth a cent when it came to the real "tug of war."

After a territorial organization was formed there

were "muster days." It was necessary to keep a trained militia, properly organized and armed, in order to be ready to meet the incursions of the Indians. There were the local musters and the general musters. The general musters were held only once each year. At these musters there were many trials of strength and personal prowess in foot racing, jumping, wrestling and fighting. Each "settlement" had its champion jumper, runner, wrestler, and fighter. These latter were called "bullies." The champions of one settlement would be pitted against the champions of another, and, when the men were not on parade, there would be a contest of some kind going on almost constantly.

As long as they kept sober the "amusements" would be confined to jumping, running and wrestling; but when they got drunk—which they often did, as these musters were generally held at some still house—the bullies would be brought out, and, after the usual amount of blowing by the friends of the "bullies," a ring would be formed and a fight would occur. The blowing would generally be in such phrases as this:

"I'll bet a hoss, saddle and bridle that Bill Johnson can whup any man that ever wore hair or walked water!"

Which would be answered by something like this:

"I've got more money than a mule can pull on a half sled, down hill with snow on the ground, an' I'll bet my pile that Butch Anderson is the best man on top of the yeth."

Some of these fights were, no doubt, terrible to

witness; but they didn't kill each other as men do now with the dirk and the deadly revolver. They may seem more cruel to the sensitive nerves of our modern casuists, but the results were not so bad.

A fight of this kind usually settled the question as to who was the "bully" of a certain "deestrict," and he rarely had to "whup" the same man a second time.

Brute force is a bad method to resort to for the settlement of difficulties, either real or imaginary, between individuals or nations; but it is the more unreasonable *when there is nothing to settle.*

Appropos of this subject an old Missouri lawyer, who has been a man of prominence in Missouri in law and politics for the last half century, related to me the following:

In the "good old days" a case was being tried before a justice of the peace. The litigants had had difficulties growing out of the close proximity of their farms to each other. Cross fences, breachy cattle and other such matters had finally brought them into court to settle their disputes. They were very bitter against each other, and, as the trial progressed, they grew hotter and hotter and finally got to firing invectives at each other right before the seat of justice. Finally they began to "talk fight" and one of them said

"If you can whip me you can have this matter your own way."

The other responded with a like statement and at it they went. They were soon down on the floor, rolling and tumbling, biting and gouging, after the fashion of those days. The jury arose to their feet and everything was excitement and confusion. Several men shouted "Don't let 'em fight!" "Part 'em!" "Part 'em!"

"LET 'EM FIGHT IT OUT."

The justice sprang into the midst of the surging crowd, and, instead of "commanding the peace," as it was his duty to do, yelled, "Let 'em alone, men; let 'em fight it out; if they can settle it that way it will save the costs."

And they "settled it."

This economical idea as to "costs" does not prevail in our justice's courts to any large extent at the present day.

While speaking of courts I am reminded that in

those times the counties were very large—one county being as large as a Congressional district is now. A circuit judge would sit in turn in three or four of these counties. Men who had business in court were often compelled to go from thirty to one hundred miles. Those who went so far would remain until the court adjourned, or until their business was disposed of. The jurors often lived from fifteen to thirty miles away. Those who only lived fifteen or twenty miles would return home at night and attend to their stock, take breakfast by candle light, and would be back at the county seat by the time court would convene at 9 o'clock, a. m.

A story illustrative of those times is told of one Gill R. He lived on the southern border of what is now Cooper county, and was on the panel of the grand jury for this particular term. The grand jury had particular instructions from the judge to be in their room at 9 o'clock, a. m.

One morning Gill R. did not report until ten o'clock. The judge called him up and said:

"Mr. R. you are an hour late. You understand the rules of this court. If you can not give a reasonable excuse for thus delaying the work of this court I shall fine you."

Gill was a great wit and also stammered. He excused himself after this fashion:

"Well, Jedge, you k-know I live t-twenty mile away, and I have to g-go home every n-night to f-feed my s-stalk. Well, I h-hain't got but one s-shirt an' I've been w-wearin' it all the week an' it got p-purty d-dirty.

Last n-night my ole 'oman t-thot she'd b-better w-wash it, so I went to b-bed an' l-let her w-wash it. This m-mornin' I had to l-lay abed 'till she ironed it, and w-when s-she w-went to iron it it w-was so r-ragged she g-got it so t-tangled t-that I'll be dad rot if *sh-she d-didn't have to r-reel it b-before s-she c-could* ontangle it!"

"AN' SHE HAD TO REEL IT."

This was greeted with a burst of laughter from the jury and spectators in which the judge joined.

"Very well, Mr. R." said the judge, "your excuse is a valid one; take your place with the grand jury."

Such an original story in those days was worth more than an eloquent appeal. Everybody appreciated it, laughed over it and told it when they went home, so that, in a few weeks as many persons would know all the details as well as if it had been published in a paper.

The attorneys in those days " rode the circuit "— that is, they would follow the court from one county to another. There were no stages, so that attorneys would ride on horse back for a hundred and fifty miles to court. They generally went four or five together, so that the trip would not be so lonesome.

They were a jolly set and often played severe practical jokes on each other.

There was a lawyer living at B—ville in those days who was an original character. He wore his hair long and plaited it in a queue and let it hang down his back. He shaved his face perfectly clean every morning, had a high, piping voice, and was a perfect terror to a witness on cross examination. He was original, witty, severe, tyrannical, terrific. Strong men grew speechless when H. opened fire on them.

On one of these long trips to court at Springfield, Mo., H. and three or four other jolly fellows were together. They were arguing, bantering and joking each other all the way. They had their regular stopping places on the way where they were well known, but there was one place where they were accustomed to remain over night where the family had moved away and a new family had moved in.

Just before they got to this place H. met some one he knew and stopped to talk. The others rode on, and, at the suggestion of one of their number, decided to play a joke on H. They stopped at the house, told the lady who they were and got permission to stay all night. Then one of them spoke to the lady in a very serious tone ; said he :

"Madam, we have something to tell you which is very disagreeable. There is a woman dressed in men's clothes who is following us. We have tried every way that we could to get rid of her, but we can not. We do not know what her designs are, but we do not think

"YOU NASTY, STINKIN' OLD HUSSY."

that they can be otherwise than bad. We are married men and we do not want this woman in our company, and we hope you will not permit her to remain here. She is very impudent and will insist that she is not a woman ; but don't you believe her. Whatever you do don't let her stay. She will soon be here for we left her only a few miles back."

He had scarcely told his story when H. rode up and alighted. As he came into the house the old lady met him on the front porch with broom in hand—

"Don't you offer to come in here, you nasty, old hussy!"

"Why, madam, what's the matter?" asked H. in his piping voice. This voice was enough to confirm the story and she made at him with the broom:

"I'll show you what's the matter, you brazen, impudent old baggage. Get out 'o here, I say! You ought to be ashamed of yourself, you nasty old thing. You'd better take them men's things off and put on your own clothes and go to your 'man' if you've got one."

H. dodged and protested and the old lady grew more vehement in her denunciations of "the old hussy," and pursued him with the broom. The other lawyers were falling all around the front porch and splitting their sides at the fun.

After they had enjoyed the matter to their heart's content they went out and captured the broom and explained to the lady that it was a joke. It took some time to convince her that he was not a woman. Even after supper as they sat around the fire and talked she would eye H. suspiciously for awhile and then look over toward the broom as if she would like to "give him a swipe" anyhow.

It was a long time before Judge H. heard the last of this story.

CHAPTER II.

EDUCATION AND PIONEER SCHOOLS.

DISADVANTAGES AS TO EDUCATION—THE PIONEER SCHOOL HOUSE—THE OLD IRISH TEACHER AND HIS TERRIBLE DISCIPLINE—TEXT BOOKS—EXAMINING THE TEACHER—TURNING THE TEACHER OUT—STIMULANTS—JOE—THE MAD TEACHER.

IT will be readily understood that, in a community so new, so far from the old civilizations, and with a new territorial organization, with large counties—as large as congressional districts now are—I say it will be readily surmised that the advantages as to education were limited.

The settlers themselves were ignorant as to books. They knew and thought little of the advantages that education confers. There was little to stimulate the young to study, because their parents knew nothing of books and of the enjoyments which they bring.

Ignorant children do not study of their own accord, as a rule. In the matter of the development of the mind there must always be *some one above the pupil* who does the *drawing out*. Hence, in a new country—where education seemed to be worth so little—and where, if one were educated, his education only served, in a measure, to isolate him from his fellows—it is no wonder that so little attention was given to the development of the mind

But, there was a start. There are always men in a community, even amongst the pioneers, who know something of the advantages that accrue to one through the education of the mind. These persons, scattered here and there through the settlements, stimulated their fellows, and, after awhile, they began to build school houses.

The first school houses were, like the dwellings of the settlers, built of logs. There would be a meeting, and noses counted, a calculation made as to the number of logs needed, and then each man assigned his proportion. After the logs were on the ground, there would be a meeting to which all would bring their dinners; the house would be raised, the logs "scalped," boards made, the roof put on and "weighted," a chimney built and, sometimes, a puncheon floor laid. "Sometimes," I say, for oftener there was no floor, except the ground. The school houses were invariably daubed with mud, a half of one log cut out at a proper height the full length of the house, in order to admit light to the writing bench. Over this opening the school girls would paste old thin muslin, or greased paper in order to admit the light and still keep out the air.

There was never more than a three months school during the year, and the teachers were almost invariably of the Irish nationality.

The political oppressions, revolutions and upheavals in their own unhappy land had driven many educated men of that nationality to this country. They seemed to seek oblivion in the far away new settlements, and many of them became teachers. The old Irish school teacher was as much a fixture in these new settlements as the log house, the rifle or the fort. Their methods were crude, their text books few and their discipline terrible. I have heard many a tale from my grandparents of the terrible whippings which these stern masters used to administer to the youth of those times.

If a young man were big enough to whip the teacher and resisted the proposed thrashing he would be given his choice of either taking the whipping or leaving the school. So eager were some of the young men to avail themselves of the slight advantages which these poor schools offered that they would often submit to the humiliation of being mounted on another boy's back with arms around his neck and tightly held while the teacher satisfied his wrath and the violated law. The discipline was a mixture of that of the British army and navy of that period, and was, no doubt, borrowed from these two institutions of old England.

Beyond the spelling book and small dictionary, and an arithmetic of these old times (in the latter " Tare and Tret " constituted a most important part) the text books were anything—The New Testament, Bunyan's Pilgrim's Progress—anything that the family might possess. Weem's Life of Washington, Franklin, Marion and other heroes of the revolution were about the only histories used. St. Charles, Boone and Howard counties (outside of St. Louis) were the first to enjoy anything like school advantages, beyond those named, for a long time. As new counties would be laid out and settled the inhabitants would go through the same stage with the log school house, with three month's schooling during the year, the indifferent text books and the sometimes still more indifferent teacher, who, if he were not a married man, generally "boarded among the scholars."

The writer went to school in the log school house, with the wooden chimney and only one-half the floor laid with plank, with the peculiar long window above described, and afterwards taught in the same kind of a house and "boarded among the scholars."

Before there was a state and county school fund and a law creating a county commissioner the Trustees would often *examine* the teacher themselves. These examinations were, no doubt, in many instances, very funny.

There is an old story told that at one of these examinations, one of the Trustees asked the applicant if the earth was round or flat. He answered that he wasn't sure, but he could teach it either way. The funniest part of it was that they decided that *he should teach that it was flat.*

There was a custom very common in those old

pioneer days, which fortunately or unfortunately, has become obsolete—that of turning the teacher out for holidays. Just a few days before Christmas the boys would begin to talk about "having Christmas"—enjoying the holidays. The teacher would almost certainly insist that he couldn't spare the time and intended teaching during all the Christmas days. As a rule the boys waited until the 24th of December, when a number of the larger ones would go before daylight, and would enter the school house, make a fire and then bar the door with benches from the inside. As the children came they would be let in, by removing the benches or by being pulled through the window. When the teacher came he would scold and threaten, would push at the door, make great feints of breaking it down with an improvised battering ram, and would often climb on the house and put his coat over the chimney in order to smoke them out. The boys would then cover the fire with ashes in order to stop its smoking. As a last resort the teacher would come to the door or window, and after giving the boys a serious lecture, would inform them that if they did not intend to let him teach he would go home. This would bring the boys out and after a long chase the teacher would be caught, and then, after a short struggle, he would be tied hand and foot.

The boys did not only demand "holidays," but they also wanted a treat—apples certainly and candy, if it could be had—and sometimes, I am sorry to say, whisky.

EDUCATION AND PIONEER SCHOOLS.

If the teacher did not yield they would take him to the nearest creek and proceed to duck him. If ice were on the creek a hole would be cut in it for that purpose. The writer has helped to "turn out" many teachers and has been often "turned out," and always enjoyed it, and when "turned out," always treated, but never but once was he carried to the creek.

This time there were three or four very rude boys

"THEY HELD ME OVER A COLD LOOKING HOLE."

who demanded whisky. I would not yield and so was carried to the creek and held over a very cold looking hole in the ice. Matters looked quite serious. I promised the treat of candy and apples, but informed the young rowdies that I would be drowned before I would buy whisky for school children, and informed them further that, if they ducked me, I would whip the crowd, one at a time, with my fists or with clubs afterwards. The large girls (who generally took part in the "turning out") here came to the rescue, and with sticks and stones beat their brothers away and unbound me. When once unbound I seized a big club and, taking a position *on high ground* (in more senses than one) I dictated terms. The terms were, candy and apples; and they were accepted.

This demand for whisky grew out of the fact that almost everybody in those days had whisky at their homes during the Christmas days. This practice prevails, to a large extent, all over the country, to-day— except that the wealthy keep wine instead. I have never been able to understand why it is that so many people desire to drink on Christmas.

It is a time which is supposed to represent the birth of Christ; therefore a man feels excused in getting drunk.

The Savior is sent to redeem the world; therefore men put themselves in the worst possible attitude for redemption.

The Son of God came upon the earth with healing in his hands; therefore a brutal man gets drunk and goes home and beats his innocent and helpless wife.

Another, while intoxicated, sends a deadly bullet crashing through the brain of his best friend, because "God so loved the world that he gave his only begotten Son," and so forth.

In short, Christmas drinking and Christmas drunkenness is the greatest contradiction, and the most inexcusable of all drinking.

The Christmas eggnog is generally a harmless affair, but it is often the first step toward the drunkard's hell, and therefore should have the condemnation of all right thinking men and women.

But I digress: As I have said the schools of those days were inferior to what they are now. Their methods were crude; the teachers often ignorant and the text books few and indifferent. And yet the children learned. Their greatest drawback consisted in the fact that they were not permitted to advance.

If the teachers were ignorant (which was often the case) then the pupil would be turned back as soon as he had mastered all that the teacher knew on any given subject. This was discouraging.

Many funny things occurred in those schools. I remember once when teaching there was a boy in the class named Joe. Joe was an oddity. He looked odd. He was as dull a boy as I ever saw in school. He was "bug eyed" and had an enormously large upper lip, which was always red. It always had the appearance of having been recently chafed by the contact of something rough and irritating. Joe had been to school many terms before he came to me, but he had not yet learned all of his a b c's. He could not tell b d p and q apart for the life of him.

As an evidence of just how stupid Joe was, there was a bright, mischievous boy who went home the same road with Joe and he used to play the same trick on Joe every afternoon. He would get his right hand full of loose dirt, then going to Joe he would say:

"Joe I'll bet that you can't hide a pin so that I can not guess where it is at three guesses."

Joe would bet, of course. The other boy would turn his back while Joe would hide the pin. Then, after facing each other, the guessing would begin:

"It's in your vest."

"No-h."

"It's in your shirt."

"No-h."

"Well then, it's in your mouth."

"No-h."

"Now, open your mouth and let me see."

Joe would innocently open his mouth and in would go the dirt out of the other boy's right hand.

Joe would strangle, sputter, cough and bellow. He would go home and tell his parents and tell me the next morning, and then suffer himself to be drawn into the same trap again in exactly the same way. I gave the other boy a slight correction once or twice, but it did no good. The boy would rather submit to correction than lose the fun.

As I said, Joe would not or could not learn. He would get over as far as "baker," in the old Webster's elementary spelling book and it would get to be such hard pulling that I would have to turn him back. He had an inordinate desire to go into the second reader with a class in which he had some playmates and intimate associates:

I had told him once or twice that he must learn to spell first. (This may not have been the best method with such a pupil, but it was the best I knew then.)

One morning as Joe came in I noticed that he had a second reader under his arm. He took his seat with the second reader class. He found the lesson by the "pictur," and seemed to be intently studying it. I paid no attention, but went on with the morning's work just as if Joe were in his proper place.

Finally I called the class in the second reader. Joe came up in the middle of the class, no doubt having a sense of being protected or backed up by having somebody on each side of him. The class read by paragraphs, and criticised each other in the pronunciation of words, the observance of punctuation, and so forth. turned my back, for I was so full that I could scarcely refrain from exploding. The very sight of Joe always had this effect on me, and the ludicrous position in which he had placed himself almost broke down my self control.

When it came Joe's time to read there was a pause.

"Read, next," I said.

There was a titter in the class and then I heard a staccattoed "Umh!"

"Read, next," said I, somewhat louder, and there was another "Umh!" and the class bursted into an uncontrollable roar.

Joe's "Umh!" came as if some one had punched him in the ribs suddenly.

I looked around, in feigned surprise.

Joe's face and attitude were a study. He had his shoulders humped up; one foot was off the floor and going through the performance of scraping an imaginary mosquito off the opposite shin; his face was awry, and he was altogether about as ludicrous an object as I ever saw.

"What are you doing here, Joe?" I asked with feigned surprise.

"I'm a readin' in the second reader," was the answer.

"You are? well, why don't you read?" I asked.

"I could if I could make out this first word," said Joe. The first word was *"the!"*

"Who told you that you might read in this class, Joe."

"Pap did."

"Your pap did? When did he tell you?"

"This mornin'."

"You are sure of that, Joe."

"Yes sir, I am; for I heard him when he said it."

"What did your father say, Joe?"

"He said fur me to bring my second reader to school an' read in this class."

"Joe, I don't believe your father said any such thing, for he knows you can not even read in the first reader. I feel sure Joe that you are telling me a falsehood. Now, are you sure that that is what he said?"

"Yes sir, (hesitating) I–I think he did."

"Now, Joe I will give you one more chance to tell the truth. Are you sure-now-that-you-heard-your-father-tell-you-to-bring-your-second reader to school and read with this class? Be careful now."

Joe was in great distress. He shifted his weight on to the opposite leg, fought an imaginary mosquito off the other shin, shrugged up his shoulders, walled up his eyes and ran his tongue away down to the point of his chin—

"IT MOUGHT A BEEN A HOSS NICKERIN'."

"What do you say Joe? Did you hear your father say that?"

Joe made a profound struggle, heaved up another "Umh," and answered:

"Well, sir, I heard somethin'; *it mought a been a hoss* nickerin'!"

This was too much. I couldn't restore order for ten minutes. Indeed I don't think that I "came to order" much before that time myself.

A few years before the war I was riding through one of the sparsely settled border counties, looking for a point for a summer school—having exhausted the appropriation and the willingness to personal sacrifice with a long winter term in another county. Along in the afternoon I came by a log school house, and before I got to it, I could hear the teacher's voice,

"Git yer lessons!"

He seemed very harsh or angry.

I got down and went in.

The teacher was a strapping big fellow in his shirt sleeves without shoes, and with a foot as big as a fiddle box. I introduced myself but didn't get much in return except a request or order to "take a seat." I had not more than sat down when he raised a great long hickory sprout, brought it down its full length on the floor and yelled,

"Git yer lessons!"

The children seemed to be very much afraid and stuck very close to their books.

I remained a half hour or more, and at least a half dozen times he brought down his sprout and yelled,

"Git yer lessons, I tell ye!"

I got tired and bade him good afternoon and went on.

I stopped in the neighborhood for the night, and, after getting acquainted with my host, I told him of having stopped at the school house, and of the seeming wrath of the teacher. The old man laughed long and loud:

"Why," said he, "that's Bob. Musick; he's madder'n a wet hen. Ha! ha! ha! ha! Jementally, I reckon he *is* mad, shore enough. You see, he went down to the crick at playtime yesterday an' went in swimmin' an' the big boys slipped aroun' an' stole his clo's. He couldn't find 'em no whar. Well, he worked his way roun' through the bresh to ole Jake Peterses, where he boards, and cum up at the back of the field a yellin' for Jake to bring him some clo's. Ole Peterses' dogs heard him and lit out atter him an' he clim a tree. Ole Miss Peters and the two big gals heard the racket and went out an' got a peep at him afore they found out what the matter was. Atter a while he got some clo's an' went in, but

"'AN HE CLIM A TREE."

they say he wouldn't eat a bite las' night and scacely anything this mornin', an' he's jest swore vengeance agin' the boys. They're hiding out an' skippin' roun' now. I'm reely afeard he'll hurt somebody, if some one don't take a gun to 'im and make 'im shet up. Oh, Peters says the feller's jest a'most ravin' deestracted. He haint found his shoes yit, an' that's why he was barfooted to-day. They aint no other shoes in the settlement that he can git them live calves o' his'n into. I feel kind o' sorry fur the big footed fool, but he'll hev to larn to take a joke if he stays in these parts."

The boys' trick and the teacher's discomfiture was regarded, all over the neighborhood, as a good joke. So it was; but it was rough.

CHAPTER III.

OLD TIME DANCES AND PARTIES.

COUNTRY DANCES AND THE DANCERS—FEMALE CRITICS—
THREE STORIES OF THREE GENERATIONS OF MEN.

HE parties in the good old pioneer days were generally held at night. One of the "settlers" would build a new house, or barn; clear a piece of new ground or have a log rolling or tobacco stripping.

On such occasions the "women folks" would have a quilt in the frames and ready to be quilted; the men would raise the house or barn, or do whatever was to be done, and at noon there would be some jumping, wrestling and foot racing. The women and girls would put in their time quilting and preparing dinner.

These dinners were something to be remembered. They had everything in general, but chicken pie and "pound cake" in particular. These two dishes constituted the rare and the good at one of these gatherings. I should add pumpkin pie also. He who has never eaten the good, old fashioned spiced pumpkin pie which was prepared at one of these old fashioned gatherings has not tasted of all the good things that are made for man.

After the "raising" was completed the young men would repair to the house in the dusk of evening. If the quilt was done it would be taken out of the frames; if not it would be wound up—that is lifted to the ceiling or "loft," and then securely tied overhead. If there was a bed in the "big room" it would be taken down and removed. The fiddlers would get ready while everybody ate a hasty supper. This evening meal was enjoyed most by the old folks, for the younger ones would be so elated with the prospect of what was to come that they could not eat. The "fiddlers" (there were no violinists in those days) would take their places in the corner and begin to "tune up." Four young men would seek partners and take their places for a cotillion. Then the fiddlers would strike up a familiar strain and the dancing would begin.

And it was dancing.

None of your gliding and sliding to and fro, a little hugging here and there, touching the tips of fingers and bowing and scraping. Oh, no. This *was* dancing. The music was such as "Fishers," "Durangs," "Rickett's" and "The Sailor's" hornpipes, "The Arkansas Traveler," "Cotton Eyed Joe," "Nancy Rowland," "Great big 'taters in sandy land," "Pouring soapsuds over the fence," "The snow bird on the ash bank," "The Route," "The Rye Straw," "Run, nigger, run," etc., Sometimes one of the fiddlers would act as "prompter," or, if he could not, then some one else would be selected.

The following constituted some of the figures:

"Manners to your pardners;" "balance all;" "promenade eight;" "swing your pardners;" "first four forward;" "first lady cross over;" "three to one;" "gentleman dance;" "swing opposite lady;" "swing your pardner;" "four hands round;" "back again;" "balance to your places;" "balance all;" "promenade eight" (all). This figure would be varied by having "second lady cross over," until they went entirely around. After this figure had been exhausted others would be called such as "ladies to the center, cross hands and swing half 'round;" "change hands and back again," "swing and ketch your pardners"—the ladies here with one hand joined to the lady opposite, would "ketch their pardners" with the other as they passed and they would go swinging around with the men on the outside, like an immense pair of winding blades, or a cross. The men being on the outside would have to "kiver more ground" in the process of swinging and many active young fellows, with pants in boots, would cut some "high didos" as they went around. The "balance all" and "promenade eight," however, gave those fellows a chance to "come out strong." In the "balance all" they would "cut the pigeon wing" and the "double shuffle," and in promenading a big fellow with a small partner would often catch her by the right hand with his left, seize her around the waist with his right, lift her to his right hip and go careering around like a wild horse in a muddy lot. The girls would generally affect to get angry at such familiarity and you would hear such expressions as this:

"Now, John, you've jest got to behave yourself, or I won't dance another bit;" but she generally continued dancing, nevertheless.

This dancing would be continued into the "wee sma' hours"—a new set taking the place of the one just finished, and scarcely any getting to dance as much as they desired, unless it would be an unusually pretty girl, who had many admirers.

Such a one was often in demand—dancing, if she would, almost every set, to the envy of the less favored ones.

"And were there pretty girls in those days?"

Yes, there were pretty ones *in that locality*. The human face is pretty only by comparison. There is always some woman, in every nook and corner of the earth, who is prettier than her neighbors. There is always a woman with a better eye, more regular features, a better shaped and more tempting mouth, a smaller foot and a better figure than the others; and she usually has better taste. She can make more out of a pink ribbon and a flower—out of the few little things in color which the winds of chance blow in her way.

With these and the flowers she bedecks herself in a simple and charming way, and she invariably catches the eyes of the men. These are the women that men fall in love with and rave about at first sight. They are not always the best but they generally have pick and

"JEST LOOK AT SALLY SLEEPER HOW SHE TWISTS AND WIGGLES HERSELF."

choice amongst the men. But as to the beauty—well they were pretty by comparison, as I said. I do not know how one of those rural beauties would look in a modern Boston, St. Louis, or Louisville setting. Not well, I fear. They were not educated. They were not cultured. They knew nothing of " society," etiquette books, etc. Few things of the human kind, male or female, that are uneducated, are pretty. Men and women like the domesticated fruits and shrubs, grow prettier as they are more and more cultivated.

" And better?"

Alas! no. Unfortunately, no. The purest women that ever lived were these same women.

The women who stood around the walls and watched the dancers would criticise those in the dance just as women criticise each other under similar circumstances now.

"Jest look at Sally Sleeper how she twists and wiggles when she's a dancin'. She's jest a puttin' on airs. Anybody knows that's onnateral." And, " Look at Cyntha Smiley, how she's a leanin' on Joe Blessin'. She's jest dead in love with him. Look how she looks up into his face and rolls her eyes like a dyin' calf. The way she's a takin' on jest makes me sick; an' I'll lay that he don't keer a cent for her;" and so on, just as it occurs now, modified only by the education and talent of the critic.

Women have done this from the foundation of the world and will continue to do so until they are called from their criticisms by the blast of Gabriel's trumpet at the " crack o' doom." I presume the wild Indians in the mountains, and the negro women in Africa criticise each other.

There has never been but one woman who was not criticised—dear, old mother Eve. How happy she must have been in having no one to make remarks on the way she wore her fig leaf and "wiggled herself when she walked!"

I met with three men on a train about ten years ago. They were all old Missourians and aged eighty, sixty and forty. They had all seen more or less of pioneer life, and, of course, the conversation turned upon the "good old days." They were talking about the old time dances when the man of eighty said:

"Yes, they put on a heap of airs at their dances in these times. They didn't use to do it when I was a young man sixty year ago.

I recollect when I was a young man about sixty year ago or more we used to wear buckskin clothes and buckskin moccasins. After awhile we got to raising sheep there in Howard county and our mothers got to making brown jeans suits for us for Sundays, weddin's and parties.

There was a new settlement up in Randolph county, and some of us boys that had new jeans clothes, concluded to go up there to a party. We put on our new clothes and rode nearly all day to get to the place in the new settlement where we heard the party was goin' to be. When we got there we found all the young fellows in the new settlement still wearin' their buckskins. We were dandies! We jest cut a swath. The gals jest tuck to us like a young kitten to a warm jam, and them fellers in their buckskin begun to git all fired mad an' we soon found that we had to let up a little or we would get a lickin'. Oh, they jest considered that we was dressed too fine for anything and that we was jest a puttin' on airs and they wasn't agoin' to stand it. I tell you we had to be powerful mute the balance of the night or we'd a cotch it shore.

About the same time I was makin' me a fine pair of buckskin moccasins to wear to a weddin' that was goin' to come off in the neighborhood. I jest got 'em finished the day the weddin was to come off and sot 'em out on the kitchen steps to dry. I'd used ruther green hide in makin' em, for I didn't have time to dress the hide as it ort to have been dressed. Well, as I said, they was purty wet an' I sot 'em out in the sun to dry, an' when I come to git 'em they wasn't thar. I didn't know what to make of it and begun to look around and inquire, when lo! and behold our ole houn' attracted my attention. We had one of those ole, lop-eared, deer houn's, that was everlasten'ly hungry. He would eat anything on top o' dirt. I've seed that ole houn' poke his nose into a pot o' grease when the grease was hot enough to burn anything an' he'd lap that grease an' howl jest like somebody was a beatin' uv him. Well, sir, I spied this ole houn' a walkin' off side ways, with his sides potted out sorter onnateral, an' I begun to suspicion where my moccasins had went. I cotch ole Drum an' tuck him to the stable and tied a rope aroun' his hind legs an' drawed it over a jiste and pulled him up 'till he didn't tetch the ground nowhere; an' I got a swingle tree and let into that dog like a house afire. I jest lambaisted him for all that was out. Atter awhile he seemed to git sick, an' begun to shrug his shoulders an' kind o' heave. I kept a fallin onto him like dead timber in new groun' on a windy day, and dad blame me if he didn't throw up them moccasins!

I tuck 'em to the house and looked 'em over and found that he'd warped 'em a leetle; but, he hadn't chawed no holes in 'em, an' I cleaned 'em up and straightened 'em out and wore 'em to the weddin'! Yes, sir, wore 'em and danced in 'em, but every time I tho't of that dod blasted ole houn' I could hardly keep from kickin' my partner!"

The man of sixty then took the stand:

"Well, sir, when I was a young man forty year ago or more we used to walk to church. The preachin' in them days was mostly in the woods, as there was no church buildin's. The gals most always went barefooted at home when the weather wasn't cold, and when they went to meetin' they'd take their shoes and stockins' under their arms 'till they'd get nearly to church, an' then they'd stop at some branch or hole o' water and wash their feet an' put their shoes and stockin's on. They done this in the first place because it hurt their feet to keep their shoes on all day, as they wasn't used to it; an' then shoes wasn't such an easy thing to get and they didn't want to wear 'em out.

Well, long about that time I tuck two neighbor gals to a dance one night. The weather was gittin cool an' they wore their shoes and stockin's all the way. It had rained the day before an' when we come to a branch that was up we didn't hardly know what to do. There wasn't any bridge nor any log, nor nothin'. But we must go to the party.

The gals proposed that we all take off our shoes an' wade. I wouldn't hear to their wadin', so I told 'em if they'd ride on my back I'd take off my shoes and

"OF ALL THE KICKIN' AND SQUEALIN' YOU EVER HEARD WE HAD IT THAR."

socks and carry 'em over, one at a time. They was as full of fun as mule colts, an' after laughin' awhile they said they'd do it jest for the fun o' the thing.

I pulled off my shoes an' socks, rolled up my britches above my knees (the water wasn't quite knee deep) an' stooped down an' the oldest one of the gals got on my back, cotch me 'roun' the neck with her arms an' 'round the sides with her knees, an' I waded over.

Of all the kickin' an' squealin' that you ever heard we had it thar. When I got into the deepest of the water I kind o' wobbled a little, as if I was about to fall, an' she'd clamp me around the sides with her knees an' squeal an' it tickled me so an' made me feel so curis that I'll be dod blasted if I could hardly keep from kickin' up right thar in the water! But we got over all safe an' sound and went on to the party. Nothin' would stop young folks in them days when thar was fun ahead.

Now, some people might think that these gals was not what they'd ought to have been; but let me tell you that they was as true blue as any young women that ever lived. They would take a rifle and help defend their homes if necessary an' the man who would use any insultin' talk to one of 'em would git a rap in the mouth he wouldn't forgit very soon."

The man of forty then told his story:

"More than twenty years ago (It is more than thirty, now:—Author.) I used to go to the dancing parties. I was a wild young imp then and loved fun, and I would ride any distance to a dance.

Some young fellows had invited me to a party out in "The Hills," as that part of the country was called; and, as girls were scarce, they insisted on my bringing my partner. Well, I made arrangements with a young girl, about eighteen, named Jennie Rayburn. She had auburn hair and was as freckled as a turkey egg, but she had more mischief in her to the square yard than any girl I ever saw. When the evening for the party came I went by after her and when her mother found out what was up she declared that Jennie shouldn't go. Jennie got her mad up and declared she would. The old lady sent one of the boys out and had all the horses turned out, and, for a time, it seemed as if the game was blocked. But it's a hard matter to keep boys and girls from having their fun if they are determined, and so it turned out in this case.

I whispered to Jennie,

"Why can't you ride behind me?"

She flushed for a moment, stepped to the door of an adjoining room and, looking at me intently, nodded her head and disappeared. In a few minutes there was a tap on the window, near which I was sitting, from the outside, and I got up and went out. Jennie was there all rigged out for the dance,

"Hurry," said she, "for, if mamma sees us she'll raise a yell."

We darted through the gate, I hastily mounted and Jennie jumped on the "stile block" and in a twinkling she was on behind. As we disappeared around a curve in the road we heard the old lady's voice,

"Never mind, Missy, you'll ketch it for this."

Jennie laughed a low, triumphant snicker and caught me around the waist with both hands. I yelled, for I couldn't stand it for a girl to touch me on the sides.

"What's the matter with you?" Jennie asked.

"You're ticklin' me; catch higher up," I answered, still yelling and almost jumping off.

"Why, do you want me to choke you?" she asked.

"Choke me, or do anything; but, for heaven's sake don't touch me on the side!"

"I COULD HEAR THE ROOTS OF OLD BESS'S TAIL BEGIN TO CRACK."

"You're a big goose," said Jennie.

And in this way, yelling and laughing, we went on —both so hilarious over our victory and the prospects before us that we could scarcely contain ourselves.

After a while we came to an immensely long, steep hill which led down to a branch, and there was another hill just like it on the other side. After we had started down, both of us began to slip forward, and, almost before I knew it, I felt as if we were going over the old mare's head. I turned the mare cross ways of the road and stopped. I was puzzled to know what to do. I was riding a large, fine mare of my father's, and she had a tail that almost touched the ground. A bright idea struck me. I told Jennie to reach back and hand me old Bess's tail. Jennie scrambled back, and reached for the tail. The old mare begun to squat, but, with a few words from me, she quieted down and, pretty soon, Jennie handed me the tail. I made her put it over her shoulder and I pulled it over mine and took the end of it in my left hand. We went on down the hill then in perfect safety and in some of the steeper places, I swear I could hear the roots of old Bess's tail begin to crack, and I was really afraid that we would pull it out! When we went up the hill on the other side we still held on to the tail and, before we got to the top, Jennie slipped back into the bow formed by the bending of the tail. When we got to the top she clambered up on to her seat again and we went on to the party in triumph. We had a royal time and, as we came back, we repeated our process of the night before at the hill. I dumped Jennie off at her home, and don't think she ever " ketched " anything worse than her mother's jaw."

"And did you kiss her?" asked the octogenarian.

"Union Depot! Kansas City," shouted the porter, and as the party broke up, I heard the man of forty say, "Oh, may be I didn't; Yum! Yum! Yum!"

CHAPTER IV.

CIVILIZATION AND PIONEER WEDDINGS.

GOOD FELLOWSHIP AND HOSPITALITY—EFFECTS OF CIVILIZATION—DANCING PARTIES—A CONSPIRACY AND WHAT CAME OF IT—TOM'S APPETITE WORKS HAVOC—WEDDINGS—THE PREACHER'S TWO STORIES.

IT is something remarkable what good fellowship existed between neighbors in those good old days. I have spoken of the clearings, the log rollings, house and barn raisings, and tobacco strippings. Every settler felt it to be his duty to go to his neighbor's assistance on all such occasions, and he very reasonably expected a return, in like assistance, from his neighbor, when he had anything to be done which required the help of others. I have known men to go fifteen or twenty miles to one of those gatherings and then ride home in the dusk of the evening, unless they remained to the dance which almost invariably followed the work of the day.

Nobody had locks on their doors and it was a most

common occurrence for a neighbor who desired to borrow meal, meat, tools or anything which he wanted, on finding the family away from home, to enter, take what he desired and inform the family of what he had done the next time he saw any of them.

Here is a most ludicrous incident illustrative of this perfect confidence which existed between neighbors. The incident is true, for the writer knows the names of both parties to it.

A pioneer was awakened one night by some one entering his house, and who seemed to be fumbling around as if in search of something.

"Hello! who is that?" he asked.

"It's me, John," answered the intruder, revealing the familiar voice of a near neighbor, "I'm out o' tobacker; ain't had a chaw sense dinner, an' I jest couldn't go to sleep without some. I tho't, mebbe, I might find your britches without waking you up."

"They are over thar on a cheer at the foot of the bed," said John who turned over and was snoring so loud in a few minutes that he didn't hear the "good night" of his neighbor as he went away with enough "tobacker" to do him a day or two.

This perfect confidence between neighbors does not now exist in the older settled or so-called more civilized parts of our country. It is civilization that makes locks and bolts necessary. It is education which makes man suspect his fellow man; in other words, it is the crowded condition of the older communities—where education, refinement and knowledge have entered—where wealth has accumulated in the hands of the few, and want and *desire* have come to the many, that the burglar, the midnight prowler, the tramp and the dangerous men generally make it necessary for us to put bolts and bars on our doors.

In the dancing parties, before described, everybody took a part—the old, the middle aged, and even the young children. It was a common thing, however, for the grown up young men and women to monopolize most of this exhilarating enjoyment.

I remember that, at about the time that I was fourteen years of age, there arose a feeling of great indignation and resentment amongst the young boys against the "grown up chaps," for occupying the floor so much at the parties, and more especially on account of the fact that they occupied the time of the grown young ladies when not dancing, so that we could not secure them for partners when we danced. This forced us to dance with the little girls which we did not like to do.

If there is anything that a big boy likes it is to gain the attentions and smiles of a grown young lady; and if there is anything which seems to bore a grown young lady more than another it is to be compelled, out of courtesy or friendship to the family, to lavish attentions and smiles on a big boy. Young ladies naturally like young men—the fellows with beards and moustaches. This has, no doubt, been observed by the reader.

We protested against this unwarranted abuse of power, by the young men; but they laughed at us, called us trundle bed militia and other harrowing nicknames, which increased our anger but did not relieve our wants. The matter grew so bad that we became satisfied that there was a combination—a sort of conspiracy or trust—against us and we cudgeled our brains to find some means by which to break the combination.

We finally settled on a plan. Our plan was the result of our knowledge of the fact that all the girls, large and small, loved candy.

Candy was a scarce article in those days and, if I remember aright, was quite costly. It was something which was not often seen, and when seen, it was grabbed and eaten with a greedy relish by the big girls.

At a large tobacco stripping, which was to be followed by the greatest dance of the season, "our set" got together at noon and formed our plans. Two of our number were to secretly slip away during the afternoon, mount their horses and ride five miles to the county seat and procure about three pounds of candy and "kisses," and—*a quart of whisky!* This latter we deemed necessary to bring our courage up to the point of making the grand assault all along the enemy's lines. For the purpose of the purchase of these articles each "trundle bed militiaman" put in his share of money. Of the two who were delegated to this important and delicate service one was the son of a widow woman and would not therefore be whipped for his absence; the other was a queer compound of humanity named Tom.

Tom was eighteen or nineteen years old, but was beardless and, not being able to reach up into the set above, had, by the laws of gravitation, fallen back into our set. You will see these fellows everywhere in all grades and conditions of society. From some cause or another they can not enter the class to which their age entitles them and they drop back and run with boys three or four years younger than themselves. They are social Ishmaelites who are abandoned, and often no one could explain why.

Tom always had his appetite with him. He was a walking allegory of hunger. I never saw Tom when he could not eat. I have seen him eat through two or three tables at a log rolling; and, after doing so, he could get up and walk around the house and "shake his dinner down," as he expressed it, and then eat a dozen apples. It was currently believed in the neighborhood that Tom's legs were hollow!

Well, these messengers slipped away and there being so many to do the work, they were not missed. After a few hours we peered anxiously through the cracks of the barn, watching for their return. There had been a solemn agreement made that we were not to give any "big girl" any candy until she had promised to dance with us. We were exulting over the fact that we would surely win a great victory and that, for once, we would not be horned off by the larger cattle.

Dusk came on and they did not return. The work of the day was drawing to a close. The old men were "bulking down" the tobacco and the small boys (our set) were carrying it to them. The young men repaired to the house, took the quilt out of the frames, or wound it up, removed the bed and other things that of-

CIVILIZATION AND PIONEER WEDDINGS. 67

fered obstructions to a full enjoyment of the evening, and prepared for the dance.

Our work finished we sent a part of our number down the road with the hope of meeting Jim and Tom. But they came not. We grew anxious. What could have happened? More than time enough had elapsed for their return. Why did they not come?

The music struck up and I left the boys in the yard, still in serious consultation, and went into the house. There was a set on the floor, the music was excellent, everybody was fresh and in a great flow of spirits and the enjoyment was great.

Music always had a peculiar and wonderful influence over me. I never hear good music without feeling that I am possessed with wings! From the great depression and heart-ache under which I had been laboring in consequence of the non-return of our messengers there had succeeded a pleasant reaction. The music had caused it. I was standing by the door, tapping one heel on the floor, keeping time to the music, and feeling that, as the candy had not come, I might as well secure a partner and go in in the next set and thereby break the compact.

A neighbor boy came and stood in the moonlight, just outside the door and beckoned me to come out. I was spell bound by the music, and the exhilarating dance and did not move. I asked,

"What do you want?"

"Come out here," said he, with a gesture by which he seemed to intend to move me.

"Well, what do you want?" I asked again, still being unable to get out of the current of the music which enthralled me.

"Come out here and I'll tell you!" he insisted, still gesticulating vehemently.

Thinking there might be news, I went out.

"What's up?" I asked, as we walked around the house toward the front gate.

"Wait and I'll tell you," said he, still leading on toward the gate.

Arriving at the front gate we found our set, grouped together, and, standing a little apart, was Jim whittling on a stick, and near him was the tall and imposing form of Tom. Tom *was* tall, a little stooped and of a very "yaller" complexion. The moon was shining brightly, and the figures were as distinctly outlined, as motionless and as silent as a grouping of statuary. There was an air of glumness which hung over the group that made one almost afraid to speak. I saw at once that something was wrong. I managed to ask,

"What's the matter boys?"

The boy who had called me out then spoke:

"Don't you think that Tom has gone and drunk up all the whisky and then eat all the candy?"

Great Scott! could this be true?

"Is that so, Tom?" I managed to inquire, after I had swallowed my heart about the third time.

I forgot to say that Tom was an inveterate stammerer and nearly always prefaced what he was going to say by saying—"b-b-by goney."

"Is that so, Tom?"

"T-t-t-hat's w-w-hat they s-say?" Tom answered.

"Well, what do *you* say?" I asked with some anger.

"I-I-I g-g-ess it's so," said Tom with humiliation.

In all my life I never saw a more dependent, humiliated and miserable looking object. He was a very monument of despair. He actually looked *hungry!* I knew why the boys had sent for me. I generally did the talking for the crowd. *They wanted me to express their sentiments*, and I did. I turned myself loose on Tom. I denounced him as a dog, a glutton, and all the mean things that my limited vocabulary could furnish. I "cussed him up one side and down the other." I was safe in doing so then; but, if Tom had had me away from that crowd he would have spiked my guns in short order. He was physically able to do it.

I then turned to Jim:

"How much candy did you buy?" I asked.

"*Three pounds*," Jim answered.

"Well, why did you let him eat it?"

"Well, Tom drank all the whisky," said Jim, "an' got drunk, an' he first ate all the candy *he* had an' then he kept ridin' up and takin' out of my overcoat pockets what I had. We was a laughin' and tearin' around and hittin' each other an' I didn't hardly think about it until it was all gone."

There was a pause. Tom still stood humped up, in his deeply humiliated position, looking as if it were a question as to whether he would drop through the earth or quietly dissolve. I broke the silence again by asking in great desperation,

"Well Tom, haven't you got *any* of the candy left?"

"I-I-I'VE G-GOT PL-PL-PLENTY OF THE R-R-READIN'S LEFT."

Tom straightened himself up and there came a gleam of partial relief over his countenance, as he answered:

"N-no, I hain't got no c-candy, b-b-but, b-b-by goney, it a-a-ain't as b-bad as you th-th-think f-for—I-I-I've g-got pl-pl-plenty of the r-r-readin's left!"

He here ran his fingers into his vest pocket and produced a handful of the verses of poetry which, in those days, were wrapped around the candy kisses. We indignantly refused to take any of the *"readin's."*

Tom promised that, if we would not abuse him any more, he would pay us our money back; and he did, though it took him nearly a year to do it.

Tom was a great hunter and a splendid shot and he could track game almost by the scent. When Tom went hunting there was sure to be fresh meat in the house. He went to California and the last time I heard of him a friend—one of " our set "—met him dragging a grizzly bear down a mountain.

"And did they get married in those old times?"

Yes, reader, more than to-day; that is the proportion of marriages to the marriageable population was greater than to-day—and the number who lived to be old bachelors and old maids was very few.

It did not take money to marry in those days. If they only *loved*, that was enough. They trusted to Providence for the rest. Young men and women married when neither had a dollar.

A piece of land would be given them by either his or her parents; or, if they had none to give, then the young man would settle on a piece of Government land, trusting to be able to enter it in time; a house raising would be had and with the scanty start in housekeeping utensils which parents and relatives would give they would "set up housekeeping."

This was the "love in a cottage" which we have all read about, and which few of those who read this could really appreciate or even tolerate. Such a life could only be appreciated by those whose manner of life had prepared them to so live.

But they loved each other, no doubt, as dearly as those do who have been more fortunate in opportunities, wealth, education and endowed in all the good things which are presumed to make life worth living.

There was more virtue amongst men and women than there is now; and such a thing as a man running off with another man's wife, or entering into his house and alienating the affections of his wife from him and destroying his domestic peace, was unheard of. The intrigues, the jealousies, the hatreds, the scorn, the lies and the scandals amongst the educated and wealthy "upper ten" in our modern society were unknown then.

"Well, then, do riches, education, society and all the goodly endowments, which wealth and opportunity bring, tend to make men and women happier and to better prepare them for a safe entrance into Heaven?"

It depends on how we use these things. The opportunities for doing good and being good, and for setting good, pure and noble examples for others, increase and multiply, as wealth and education broaden our sphere; but, alas! how few make good use of such opportunities!

I am inclined to believe that when you and I are called upon to "Come up Higher," dear reader, we shall find many who were poor and humble here, whose opportunities were few, but who humbly and honestly did the best they could, according to their light, occupying high places; and that we shall miss many who, while they always had the best places here, utterly neglected and failed to secure seats in the Everlasting Kingdom.

"Then you think it safer to remain poor than be rich and risk the consequences?"

I think it better to be rich and use it and the opportunities it brings, well. But, if you think you could not withstand the strain, then you had better remain poor with me. Contentment, in reasonable poverty, is a very happy and a reasonably safe lot.

"And were the brides in those old times pretty?"

Yes, always pretty; pretty as they are now. Did my reader ever see a woman who was not pretty on the day she was married? I never did. They all have the same matchless complexion; the same soft, sparkling eye, the same drooping lashes and modest demeanor, and always seeming to know what is the correct thing to do at any hitch in the ceremony, or at the happening of any accident or any unlooked for occurrence. Aye, a woman is always at her best on the day she gets married.

I never saw a woman get married who I thought was selling herself for money; but I imagine that she would not look pretty. It will be surmised that I have not, therefore, seen many "weddings in high life."

That is true. I have not.

The weddings in the old pioneer days were great affairs. A runner was sent on horseback, many days before, to invite the neighbors. This invitation often extended over a large area of country. When the wedding day came the neighbors came, men, women, and children. The ceremony being over the dinner was ready. The elders came first, the young men and women next, the children last—for there were often enough for four or five tables. At night the dance, and the courting and the foundation for more weddings.

These weddings were solemn affairs, for those people looked upon this great step in life as being freighted with great responsibilities. It was not often that anything ludicrous occurred. I have heard of a few. A prominent minister—a great man in the religious denomination to which he belongs, and one of the brainiest, purest and best men I ever knew, and who in his younger days was identified with the old pioneers—told me the following:

"I had just returned from college forty years ago and began to preach. Although college bred I was yet green, as a preacher, and, I think, about as bashful a young man as ever lived. In order the better to get at the principles as we expounded them, I travelled with a great revivalist—Brother H., that I might hear him preach and take a part occasionally so as to better prepare me for the life of a preacher. Brother H. was a great man amongst the people. He was a strong man naturally, and wielded great influence as an orator and an exhorter.

We had been holding a protracted meeting over in Illinois. That was also a newly settled country and its population was much like that of Missouri.

There were many additions to the church, and finally the meeting closed. Our meeting was in a small town and on the day it ceased a messenger came saying that there was a couple who wished to be married. They had intended to be married a week hence, but as they were anxious to be married by "the big preacher," they had decided to have it come off at once as Brother H. and I were to leave that morning. Brother H. took me along.

We found the family of the bride living in a house which had been built for a hotel. We were invited into the parlor which was the room that had been the office of the hotel. The mother of the bride came in. She was a large woman, with a firm set mouth and a very commanding, bossy mien. I was afraid of her the moment I saw her. She eyed me very sharply for awhile and then asked:

"Are you a married man?"

I answered that I was not.

"I thought so," said she, and added, "I want you to walk down with one of my gals."

I assented, and ordering me to follow her she went up a steep and narrow flight of stairs. When we arrived at the top we were in a long hall with rooms on either side. She led the way down this hall until she got opposite a certain room, the door of which she opened; then, motioning me to approach, she put her hand between my shoulders and literally shoved me in, saying as she did so,

"There, they are in there!" and then she shut the door and disappeared.

This was all the introduction I had. I found myself confronting the bridegroom, who was a great, big, hulk of a fellow, and three or four young girls—one of whom, from her attire, I recognized as the bride—all of whom were engaged in the very embarassing task of putting very small gloves on very large hands. They looked abashed; I certainly *felt* so. I finally stammered out that "I believe I am to walk down with one of the young ladies," whereupon the one nearest to me sidled over and I offered her my arm, which she took. Everybody stood in confusion and I finally said "I guess we might as well go down if you are ready." At this there was a sort of general move, and knowing that the young lady and I should go first, I promptly took the lead. The awkward bridegroom, with his bride on his arm, seemed to think that they ought to be in the lead and made several desperate attempts to pass me in the hall and on the stairway, but I managed, by skillful maneuvering, to keep ahead. Arriving in the parlor the young lady and I separated to the right and left and faced each other, which brought the bride and groom in the proper position in front of the preacher, who had taken a position on the opposite side of the room when he heard us scrambling down stairs.

The ceremony was soon ended, and when the short congratulations and kissing were over, the old lady rushed up to me and said in a sharp, loud tone:

"I tho't I told you to walk down with my darter, Samantha!"

"I THO'T I TOLD YOU TO WALK DOWN WITH MY DARTER, SAMANTHA."

"Well, didn't I?" I asked in confusion.

"No, you didn't. That was 'Manda Brown you walked down with! I never seed such a goose as you are!"

I do not think that I was ever so confused, before or since, in my whole life. I was as red as a beet, my head swam, things turned 'round and 'round, my mouth got dry and I was almost blind. You could have pushed me over with a straw.

I could see that Brother H. was ready to burst with merriment, and, as soon as we got away, he began to laugh and repeat what the old lady had said.

As we would ride along during the day, when the conversation would lag, he would break out.

"I tho't I told you to walk down with my darter, Samantha!" and then he would make the woods ring with laughter.

When we would stop for dinner or over night Brother H. was sure to describe the wedding scene, repeat the old lady's sharp reproof of myself and my confused and bashful response, and describe my meek and humble appearance, magnifying everything—for he was an inimitable actor—to the great delight of the jolly people whom we met, and to my utter confusion. It really got so that I was afraid to stop anywhere.

The repetitions of the story with the varied descriptions of my awkward confusion worried and plagued me beyond description. But I was destined to get even.

We finally held a protracted meeting near Rocheport, in Boone county, Missouri. I was opening the meetings by reading and prayer, and, occasionally, adding a word by way of exhortation after Brother H. would get through ; and, for a bashful young man, was getting along very well, except at night. As we would go to a new place almost every night—that country containing many of our denomination—I had to sit and hear Brother H. repeat that same old story.

Right in the midst of our meeting Brother H. had a call to marry a couple in the neighborhood—a widower and an old maid. They had decided to have the wedding with a few witnesses in the forenoon. I was almost afraid to go—fearing that Brother H. would manage to get me into trouble again; but I was Brother H.'s Sancho Panza and must go.

When we arrived we found the widower to be a man of about fifty. He was one of those little, red, "sawed off," bow legged and frisky fellows. His face was as red as a gobbler's snout; he was bald-headed —the only hair he had being a red wisp which ran around his head on a level with his ears, and it looked like corn silks fastened to a string and tied around his head.

It was evident that the widower had taken something stronger than water, in order to bolster up his courage for the second trying ordeal of his life.

When we got into the house and everybody seemed ready for the ceremony, it turned out that the old maid was parching coffee in the kitchen and couldn't be persuaded to leave it until it was browned, as she feared it would burn. Several trips were made to the kitchen by different members of the family and by the bridegroom, but no one could persuade this female Casabianca to desert her post until the coffee was browned. The pause was very awkward, but she came finally—removing a large cook apron and throwing it aside as she approached. She had not put on any unusual dress for the occasion, and, although this was the first and, perhaps, the only time she was ever married, she treated it as a sort of a matter of every day business.

They finally stood up. Brother H. had a fashion of putting his hands up before him and joining his fingers and thumbs and praying a very pretty prayer before he said the marriage ceremony proper. He did so on this occasion; and, as soon as the prayer ended, the widower, thinking the ceremony was over, made a dive at the bride to kiss her. She, probably never having been kissed before, tried to play the giddy, bashful girl, and ducked. The widower was not going to be cheated, so he went down after her face—she dodging and ducking while the widower's face grew redder and redder. Several times his lips came in contact with her hair, and once or twice he had her head under his arm, and it looked as if victory was about to perch upon his scarlet banner, but the giddy old maid would adroitly foil him. Here they had it, 'round and 'round, up and down, when finally she broke away and made for the kitchen, he after her.

All this time Brother H. had stood with his fingers and thumbs joined, in the attitude of prayer, watching the confused scramble after a kiss, being so utterly confused that he could not call a halt nor make any sort of explanation. I remember that I was so convulsed that I crammed my handkerchief in my mouth and fell face foremost on a feather bed which was in the room. As the old maid started for the kitchen with the widower in hot pursuit Brother H. recovered his speech and bawled after them:

CIVILIZATION AND PIONEER WEDDINGS. 81

"Ah-h-h-h! Come back; you are not married!"

In a short time the widower returned, leading the old maid captive, and Brother H. finished the ceremony. As soon as he had done so the widower made another dive, the blushing bride ducked, there was another con-

"AH-H-H! COME BACK; YOU ARE NOT MARRIED!"

fused scramble, twisting, diving, ducking, dodging, and they went out at the door toward the kitchen again in a winding, whirling, confused mass, the old widower's head bobbing up and down like a toy balloon in a shifting wind. When they reached the kitchen we could hear the rattling and ringing of tongs, shovels, pots, pans and kettles, as they were being turned over or knocked down in the scramble. Finally the noise ceased, and there came a low, sobbing sound, oft repeated, like the wash of a wave against a muddy shore, interspersed with an occasional sharp sound, like ripping a yard of heavy muslin. The old maid had yielded and the widower was just drinking kisses.

Brother H. and I took our departure. As soon as we were out of ear shot of the house I looked at him and, putting my hands together before me, I exclaimed:

"Ah-h-h! Come back; you are not married!"

Brother H. reddened visibly, and, after laughing heartily, he said:

"Look here, Brother P. I guess I have worried you enough about the old lady's rebuke over in Illinois. Now, I will tell you what I will do; if you will agree not to tell this I will not tell that story on you again." I was glad to make the agreement, for I couldn't tell a story as well as Brother H., and so we kept our word.

CHAPTER V.

PECULIARITIES OF PIONEER PEOPLE.

INFLUENCE OF EDUCATION ON THE CONFORMATION OF THE BODY; SOME SPECIMENS—STORY OF THE OLD LINEN COAT AND THE MASONIC MARCH—COL. JACK'S STORY OF HIS ONLY LOVE.

THE peculiarities of an uneducated people in a new country are shown in the size of their feet and hands, the expression of their faces, the fit of their clothing, and their general awkwardness.

There is no doubt that the contact of people in large cities, the growth of wealth, the advantages of education and all the helpful things which come of a higher civilization tend to make the shapes of their bodies more symmetrical and beautiful, their hands and feet smaller, to improve their taste as to the combination of colors, and the fit of their clothing, and also to make their heads larger.

Does it make them happier?

Perhaps it does. It improves taste and gives a keener appreciation of the beautiful and the enjoyable in music, books, the theater, the sermon—in everything.

Does it make them better?

Positively, *no*. I could mention a great many of the sins and evil practices which are committed and in vogue in our larger cities which are unknown amongst the uneducated classes in our rural districts; and which, if told to them, would either not be believed or would be a most shocking revelation.

What more awkward picture could we have than that of a great big, twenty years old country boy, on circus day, with his big hands and feet, his pants too short and the third dorsal vertebra definitely located by the back buttons on his coat; with his long, carrotty hair and the frosty, gosling fuzz on the angles of his jaws and the corners of his chin, the scarlet cheeks and the white around his mouth, indicating the necessity of an *anthelmintic*; holding by the hand a little hump shouldered girl, with dress too short, large feet, high cheek bones, sweaty hands, broad hips, full bust, last year's hat, and awkward as a young cow; both eating gingerbread and gazing, with their poor hearts in their throats, at the picture of the *wallapus* on the top of the center pole, with pale, expressionless, gravy eyes—both stopping occasionally to dig the impacted gingerbread out of the vaults of their mouths with their index fingers and then sucking the fingers; and squeezing hands and working their toes, and throbbing and pulsating—two great big "hunks" of solid, unmixed bliss.

Who says that they are not enjoying themselves?

When they get inside that big fellow will laugh at the stale jokes of the clown (vintage of 1840) and open that immense mouth so wide that one will instinctively move away from him, for fear of falling in.

Contrast them with a couple at the opera in one of our large cities: The symmetrical forms, the small hands and feet, the educated and easy airs, his silk hat, elegant cane, polished boots, well fitting clothes and curled moustache; her elegant dress and costly trimmings, her fashionable hat and splendid "patent outside" complexion; note the ease with which they use the opera glasses and ogle and dissect their neighbors; hear their intelligent comments on the opera, and their criticisms of the singing and the acting. These people are educated. At the close she takes his arm and not his hand; he hands her into the carriage with perfect grace and then gets in himself. Let's not look in! Why? Because it might not be good manners.

"Are all educated people bad?" No.

"Are all uneducated people good?" No.

"Which of these couples enjoy themselves the more?"

I don't know, but I think I do.

"Which are the best, morally?"

I don't know, but I think I do.

"Which of the two couples would you rather be?"

Don't ask me!

Reference to the matter of ill fitting clothing reminds me that, in the "good old days," there was always one boy in the family who always wore the worst fitting clothes of anybody in the house. He was, generally, a second or third son. He had a brother or brothers older than himself, who would get the best of all that was new, and he would have to take their's and his father's old clothes, made over. This was especially the case with summer clothing. The linen woven by the good old mothers of those days never wore out. It got whiter each summer, but not older.

Imagine a boy fourteen years old who has an older brother. This older brother is now getting to that age when he begins to cast "sheep's eyes" at the girls and must go into society. The parents go to town in the spring of the year to market the woven fabrics—the linen, linsey and jeans—that can be spared, and to buy such things as they can purchase with it. These consist of bleached domestics, "store" shoes, a little fine linen for shirt bosoms, hats, women's straw bonnets, untrimmed; and some ribbons of different colors. They come home and lay out all the "store things" that have been bought. The children crowd around and the mother lays out the articles, one by one, and says, "this is linen for your father's and Henry's shirt bosoms; these are Henry's shoes and this is his hat; this ribbon is to trim Polly's and Mahala's hats, and this is for this one and that is for that; and poor William (Bill, they call him) stands by eating his heart and wonders when they will come to the new things for him.

When the things are about all laid out he manages to swallow his heart and find his voice and, at last, asks in desperation,

"Mamma, didn't you buy me nothin'?"

"Yes, my son, I bought you this hat for summer"

(It is a "chip" and cost twelve and a half cents!) "I can make over Henry's last summer's linen coat for you —the one your father wore summer before last, and— you will have to go barefoot this summer, as we couldn't buy any more things. Henry is older than you and must have some things that you can't have yet."

Her speech is consoling and her manner kind and regretful, but that don't do Bill any good. He almost bursts. He goes out behind the house and cries and bores his dirty knuckles into his eyes and secretly "cusses," and above all, wishes he could get a chance to plaster mud all over his brother Henry "the first time that he puts all of them store things on." He also registers an oath that he will not wear that old, long linen coat.

But the time comes when he is compelled to violate that oath. Parental authority is supreme, and the first time he goes anywhere on Sunday, or to a public gathering, his mother gets out that coat and makes him put it on. It is a little loose and entirely too long and makes him look something like a revised edition of Huckleberry Finn, and his mother says:

"You've growed so, William, since last summer that I didn't see any use in making it over. You'll soon grow to it!"

That's a fact. Give him time and he will "grow to it." The coat will surely wait, for one of those coats never was worn out.

Bill is mad and protests that he would rather go in his shirt sleeves. No, he must wear that coat, and fur thermore, his mother tells him, "if you go to cuttin' up about it, you shant go nary step." This settles it. The Masons are going to march and Bill sees fun ahead. He would wear his father's jeans overcoat rather than miss going. It is the first Masonic march and he would not miss it for anything.

He has to ride behind his brother Henry on an old mare with a mule colt following. Here is another humiliation. And that mule colt! Did you ever have one follow you, reader? No? Well, you have some chance for heaven. Every time they meet anybody that perverse mule turns around and follows them.

"OH, FOR A DOUBLE SHOTTED CANNON."

There is a frantic effort to get around it with the old mare and get it to follow. No, sir; it will not look at its mother; acts as if it never saw her before. Bill must then get down and go around it while Henry sits on the old mare in the road and whistles for the colt. When Bill thinks he has it headed off, it makes a break by him and runs off sidewise, looking back and jerking the hide with a tremulous motion from its ear clear back to its tail and brays that most aggravating mule colt bray. Oh, for a double shotted cannon! Bill gets around it and hits it with rocks, and grits his teeth and "cusses" and grunts, and does his very best to kill it; but rocks glide off the form of that devilish mule like rubber balls off the side of an iron clad. You can't hurt him. I do really believe that mules begin, when colts, to rehearse for the miserable meanness which they intend to act out in after life.

But Bill finally heads it off and they go on to town. Bill has never seen the Mason's march—in fact they have never marched in that county before. But he has heard a great deal about them. He has heard people say that they "believe the Masons ain't up to no good, else they would tell it." He has heard too that they are supposed to steal horses and pass counterfeit money. Bill thinks that, if this is true, he may join them when he gets older, for he is in a general state of insurrection about that coat, and he don't care much what he does just so it is something bad.

As soon as Bill reaches town he finds a lot of boys and begins to play marbles. He has brought along his "white alley," which is his "taw," some "pee wees," a few "pottery's" and a "glassy" or two. He knows how to play marbles. He is an expert. He has practiced alone at noons and evenings when his father and brother were resting. They play "keeps," and with his unerring precision and splendid nerve Bill wins from the start. About noon music is heard and men, women and children are seen rushing toward a certain point. The boys seize their marbles and rush off with the crowd.

The Masons are marching!

They have formed in their hall and come into the street double file, with their aprons on, with one man carrying a mace and an old, grey bearded man carrying a bible on a plush covered rest which is suspended from his shoulders by straps. They are headed by two noted fiddlers who are capable of furnishing the best music that can be made inside the limits of the county. They are playing "Bonaparte's Retreat" and everything seems very solemn. They pass around a block and Bill goes with the crowd and heads the procession off. The fiddlers have changed the tune and are now playing "The Lost Boy." This is very solemn and touching; Bill is so worked upon by the music that he could almost forgive the mule, if the mule would ask him and promise not to do so any more. The procession goes all over the little town, up one street and down another, the crowd, in the meantime, heading it off here and there, and finally they march to their hall and disappear to the touching strains of "Poor Mary Blaine."

Bill goes back to the game of "keeps;" and, after the town boys have bought some more marbles, the game is resumed and the Masons, for the time, are forgotten. Bill's aim improves as the day wears away, and his one pocket (he has but one that will hold shucks) begins to get uncomfortably full and sags heavily Bill has to walk sidewise in order to get around. He finally wins all the marbles and the game stops. The town boys go off and consult and Bill sits down in the dirt with two marbles, shooting one at the other, as a sort of challenge to all comers. He sees furtive glances in his direction from the crowd of boys, and begins to grow uneasy. They evidently intend mischief; this mischief being nothing short of throwing him down and taking his marbles away from him. He gets up and sidles over to the fence, where the long linen coat hangs, and takes it down and puts it on. For the first time he feels a sort of protection in this coat. It is a sort of armor and makes him look larger. The crowd begins to move toward him and he starts off down the street which leads toward his home, walking slowly and whistling, as though he didn't understand the meaning of their maneuvers and has no idea that mischief is contemplated. He hears one of the boys say, "go on, Jack," and a big boy steps out of the crowd and walks toward him. Bill walks a little faster. The big boy walks faster than he does. He then quickens his pace and walks much faster. The pursuer quickens *his* pace also and walks very much faster. Bill then strikes a trot. The big boy trots also; then Bill runs, and the big boy runs, too. By this time they have reached the outer edge of the little town and are going down a long hill. It now becomes a race for—marbles.

Bill is sadly handicapped in two ways; he is smaller than his pursuer and he is carrying immense weight in the great number of marbles he has in his pocket and the weight is badly distributed—all the marbles being in one pocket. But Bill lays himself out for all those marbles are worth. As they get near the bottom of the hill he hears the quick drawn breath of the other boy and the flutter of his pants. He feels that nothing but a *coup d'etat* will save those marbles.

"BILL BROKE THE RECORD IN TROTTING THE NEXT MILE."

He slackens his gait, and, as the big boy passes at full run, he catches one side of the tail of that long coat, and, carrying it over Bill's head, rips it up to the collar. This brings the big boy to an about face, and before he can recover his equilibrium, Bill, still running, delivers a powerful blow with his fist in the pit of his pursuer's stomach.

This unexpected stroke doubles the big boy up like a jack knife. He grabs his stomach with both hands, walks 'round and 'round in a kind of swing and gets awfully pale. After a while he begins to get his breath at intervals, with a loud whooping sound. Bill does not wait to see the outcome. He sees the crowd coming and he strikes out in a dog trot with those coat tails standing out on either side like the wings of an ostrich. When he reaches the top of the hill he looks back and sees the big boy lying down and the crowd around him, some of whom are shaking their fists at him; but they do not make further pursuit. Bill breaks the record in trotting the next mile, and then, feeling that he is safe, lies down in the shade and counts his marbles. He has about a hundred.

"Jee Whillikins! what will the boys say when they see me with all these marbles?"

There are two things which Bill is glad of: He has won lots of marbles, and that hateful coat is ruined beyond repair. He feels sure of it. He takes it off and carries it over his shoulder until he is near home. He then puts it on for a purpose. He wants his mother to see it in its condition of utter and irreparable ruin.

When he goes in his mother asks,

"Why, William, what brought you home so soon?"

"Oh, I dunno; I jest got tired!"

"Why, my son," (turning him around) "just look at your coat! How in the world did you do that?"

"I come acrost Turner's paster, and as I jumped off the fence it cotch on a knot an' jest *tore itself!*"

"Lawsey! Lawsey massey, William, you are jest the wust imp I ever seen! Turn around here and let me see. I do believe you've ruined that coat—no you ain't nuther; I tho't it was tore, *but it ain't; it's jest ripped; I can sew it up and make it as good as ever!*"

Merciful heavens! Bill thought that coat was ruined! and it is only ripped! His heart goes clear down to his heels. But there is some consolation—he has got more marbles than all the other boys in that neighborhood.

The above is not overdrawn and everything therein related actually occurred.

Another one of those unfortunate second sons relates his experience.

Colonel Jack and some choice spirits are sitting around the camp fire in the Confederate army. He is six feet two, forty-five and single. One of the boys asks: "Colonel, why is it that you have never married?"

"For good and sufficient reasons," the Colonel answers, "I was never in love, as you call it, but once, and as it brought me more troubles and disasters in one year than I have had, otherwise, in all my life, I concluded that I had better give the fair sex a wide berth and let them severely alone."

"Tell us about it, Colonel," exclaimed a dozen voices.

"Well," begun the Colonel, "you all know that I was reared in Missouri. My father had a few old, ashy, scrofulous niggers—enough to give the family an air of respectability—but they didn't amount to much.

They didn't keep us in the shade, I know. My father was an industrious man and he made his boys work, and my mother took the lead of the negro women and the girls in the manufacture of all the clothing for white and black.

"I was an unfortunate boy in some respects. I was a second son, in the first place. My older brother, Bob, got all the new things, all the 'store clothes,' that were bought and I had to take his and father's old clothes, made over. When the family went anywhere, to a wedding, a party or to church, Bob, being the oldest, must go and I generally had to remain at home, either to watch the house, or because my clothes were not good enough.

"Well, as a consequence, I grew up to be a great big, awkward, shy boy. I was afraid of the girls in the society in which our family moved. I was utterly mouthbound and speechless in the presence of one of them.

"When I was about sixteen or seventeen, one of those old migratory fellows came along and my father permitted him and his family to occupy an old shanty that was on the place and let him cultivate a piece of ground 'on shares.' Contrary to the rule with such people this old man and his wife had only one child—a daughter. The old man was one of those old, sawed off, pot-bellied and short legged fellows, that didn't like to move around and work much, and so took life after a sort of 'hand to mouth' fashion. The girl was about my age or a little younger, was fat—a regular squab— and her skin was as white as bleached muslin

"I soon began to slip over to this old man's home at night, or when our family was gone, and was soon on the very best of terms with the family—including the girl. It wasn't long until the girl and I were heels over head in love. It was that agonizing kind of love that just submerges and overwhelms you and gives you the backache.

"The girl and I never talked love. Oh, no, we were too deeply and sadly and madly in love for that. We just took it out in squeezing hands and looking unutterable things at each other.

"I guess we were about as sick a looking pair of young geese as anybody ever saw. I got to be very little account on the farm. I would forget to eat my meals if I wasn't called two or three times. The girl's father and mother were delighted, for they felt it to be a great compliment to have one of Judge ———'s sons as a suitor for Matilda's hand. Her name was Matilda, but they called her 'Tilda.

"There was a spring of good water near the house occupied by this old doughnut, and I would sometimes take our jug and go down to the spring after water when we would be working in the field near there. I would always manage to let 'Tilda know that I was coming, by whistling or singing, and then she would seize a bucket and come down. We used to sit on the low bank below the spring and squeeze hands and paddle our feet in the water, and I would look into 'Tilda's great blue eyes and almost die.

"This thing went on one whole summer and the following fall and winter.

"About the first of March the next year a great calamity befell 'Tilda and me. I don't know how it could have happened without my hearing of it; but from some cause, I hadn't been over to see 'Tilda for a week or so; and all at once her father, with the instinct of his class, took a notion to move. He and father had met and fixed up all their business. Father had bought what little feed stuff he had left and the old man was preparing to seek another place. I heard of it the morning they were to move. Father was over there attending to some small unsettled details with the old man. I don't remember what excuse I made for going over, but I went. I do not remember to have ever felt worse than I did that morning. I have seen relatives die; I have seen comrades whom I dearly loved shot down in battle; in short I have witnessed many calamities that are calculated to pull on a fellow's heartstrings pretty hard; but this day was the worst. I didn't know what to do. I felt like rushing into the midst of them with some drawn weapon and uttering a manly protest against the outrage. But I didn't. I didn't know how; and besides I wasn't that kind of a lover. My love made me cowardly, tremulous, weak and sick. The old man had all his household goods in an old wagon to which was hitched a yoke of oxen with an old mare in the lead of the steers—a 'spike team.' There was a chicken coop containing the chickens on behind the wagon, and some old, bottomless chairs tied on to the coop. 'Tilda was on the other old mare and had gathered the two cows and a couple of yearlings which she was to drive behind the wagon. She was riding around, keeping this stock in place for the start, while her 'dad' and mine finished business matters. I didn't get to speak to her. I just looked at her—looked that wistful, longing, painful look, such as only a lover of my age and condition can look.

"Finally the old man took up the line that was to guide the old mare in the lead, and the whip which was to govern the oxen.

"'Well, good bye, Judge,' said he; 'good bye; Jackie' (that was me) and then—'get up, Lize! Wo, Buck; come here, Broad.'

"There was a 'ronching' and squeaking sound from the old wagon, the girl got around the cows and yearlings and they dropped in behind the wagon. She looked at me as she turned into the road and with those big, blue eyes swimming in tears, said, 'good bye, Jack;' 'good bye, 'Tilda,' I answered, in choking tones, and then turning saw my father as he was turning to go home. I did not dare to risk myself in his company, for I felt that I would 'boo-hoo' in spite of all that I could do. I turned and ran for about a quarter of a mile, at right angles to the road home, in a path that led around a forty acre field. When I got around in the timber out of sight of my father I sat down on a log, and then, with nobody present but the Lord and me, I opened up the flood gates. It was the only thing to do. I had to let off the pressure or burst.

After that I was silent, moody and melancholy, devising a thousand ways by which I was to get that girl and abandoning them all because I had no courage.

"Finally one Sunday in April the family went away to church, and, as usual, left me at home. After they had gone a sense of loneliness came over me. I wanted to see 'Tilda, and, in five minutes I decided that I *would* see her, if she was to be seen.

"I put on the best clothes I had, which were mostly second hand. I caught an old blind mare which was kept up to keep her from falling over banks and killing herself, or getting lost. All the other horses that the family were not using had been turned out. I put an old blind bridle on her and an old saddle that the niggers used, and mounted and started—where? I didn't know. It had never occurred to me to ask where 'Tilda's father had moved to. He might be within five miles; he might be in Arkansas or Texas. But I determined to make an effort, and so I started in the same direction and on the same road that they had taken on the morning they went away. I must have been a sight; I was then seventeen, was six feet tall and as slender as a rail. I had on an alpaca coat which was too short; the stirrup leathers were too short, and when I got on, my knees almost met over the old mare's withers. It was nearly noon when I started and I rode five or six miles before I began to make inquiries. I couldn't hear a word of them anywhere. But I rode on in perfect desperation. I rode through two or three different neighborhoods until, when the sun began to wane, I felt that

I must be many miles away from home, and, still to all inquiries the same answer came—'don't know any such person; he don't live in this neighborhood.'

"Finally I met a man, who, after the usual inquiry, said,

"'Oh, yes, I think I know him—little, old, short, fat man, ain't he?'

"'Yes.'

"'Got a wife and one darter—fat, fair complected gal?'

"'Yes.'

"'Well, he lives over here about three mile, on Mr. Ashley's place.'

"He then gave me directions how to get there and I started off, feeling jubilant. I had found my love. I felt that I could almost fly. I urged the old blind mare on to her best speed, and that was not much, for she was about worn out. Just as the sun was setting I rode up to the place. It was a little doubled log house, with a good deal of the 'chinking' and 'daubing' out of it. I got a glimpse of 'Tilda and things began to revolve and for a moment I was stone blind. Oh, bliss! bliss! bushels and buckets of bliss! The family all came out to meet me. The old man called me 'Jackie' and was glad to see me. 'Tilda called me 'Jack,' in her most mellifluous tones, and as soon as we were alone, said,

"'You great, big feller, you! why didn't ye come sooner?'

"The old lady and 'Tilda got supper at the old fashioned fireplace, for there were no stoves in those days, and the evening being, cool the old man and I sat on either side of the fireplace and talked.

"Just before supper was ready the old lady, after having fried the meat, set the frying pan against the jamb of the fireplace near me. It was one of the old fashioned frying pans, with a long flat handle with a hole in the end. I took hold of the handle of the pan and was fumbling with it, and intuitively stuck my finger through the hole. It was a neat fit and when I attempted to get my finger out I found that it wouldn't come. Just then supper was announced. Here was a fix. I couldn't go to the table with that frying pan on my finger, and I was too bashful to announce my predicament, so I said in answer to the invitation to 'set up to supper,'

"'No, thank you, I'm not hungry!'

"This was an awful lie, for I had had no dinner, had ridden hard all the afternoon and was as hungry as a wolf. But, try all I would, I *couldn't* get my finger out of that hole in the frying pan handle!

"They insisted on my 'sitting up and trying to eat a bite,' and I persisted that I was not hungry—all the time with the frying pan handle between my knees and tugging away, trying to release my finger, but it wouldn't come, nor did they notice my predicament. After exhausting all efforts to get me to 'set up,' without avail, they sat down.

"Left to myself, and taking things quietly, I soon got my finger out of the hole. I would have given the blind mare for them to ask me to supper again; but they didn't. They had done all that good people could do and I would not eat. After supper the old man went out about his feeding and I went out and 'minded off the calves,' while 'Tilda milked. When we came in she set the bucket of milk on the table and went into the other room in search of the strainer. It occurred to me that this was a good chance to get a swig of milk and I grabbed up the bucket and drank the warm milk like a very calf. The bail of the bucket fell over my head and as 'Tilda opened the door I attempted to set the bucket down right quick and the bail caught on the back of my neck and I spilt about a pint of milk in my bosom.

"'Tilda was astonished. I then told her why I had not eaten supper. As the old folks had temporarily surrendered this room to us, 'Tilda went to work at once to prepare something for me to eat. She desired to treat me to some plum preserves, and, as they were in a jar on a high shelf, in the cupboard, she asked me to take them down. In doing so I tilted them over and spilled a lot of them in my hair. 'Tilda washed me off the second time and I finally sat down and ate a hearty supper. It wasn't long, however, until 'Tilda and I were seated 'cheek by jowl,' in the good old way, throbbing and pulsating against each other. She had a breath like a young cow just after the first appearance of wild onions. But all the blissful pleasures in this life must end, sometime. The old lady called out to us from the other room that it was bed time. They had a bed in each room, so that there was no other way to arrange things except for the old lady and 'Tilda to occupy the bed in one room and the old man and I the other.

"The old man came in and 'Tilda went into the other room with her mother. I was terribly bashful about going to bed with the old man, but finally managed to get in behind. During the night one of those terribly cold April storms came up, and, as I was sleeping near a big crack where the chinking and daubing were out, I woke up almost frozen. It was just unbearably cold. I slid out over the foot of the bed and got my pants and, crawling back, stuffed them into the crack. After this I got along very well. When I awoke the next morning the old man was gone. He had arisen and was out feeding. Pretty soon the old lady knocked on the door and called,

"'Come, Jackie, breakfast is ready.' I bounced out, and, not seeing my pants remembered that I had stuffed them in the crack; but what was my surprise upon looking there to find that they were not there. I looked all over the room, turned the covers about and got on the bed and peeped out through the crack, but nowhere could those pants be found.

"The old lady knocked on the door again—

"'Are you up, Jackie?'

"I jumped in bed and covered up and answered,

"'No'm.'

"'Well, get up,' said she, 'breakfast is ready.'

"I got up and took another look for the pants. But, it was no use. I couldn't find them. The old man finally came in.

"'Come, Jackie,' said he, in a hearty, kind way, 'get up young feller; they're waitin' breakfast fur ye.'

"I had to tell the old man that I couldn't find my pants. He then made search, and, finally the old lady was called in, and, while I covered up, she 'raked the house with a fine tooth comb,' and 'Tilda was drafted into service and sent around the house on the outside. It all ended in not finding my pants. At last they brought me a pair of the old man's pants and I got up and put them on. I was a sight to behold. The pants struck me about half way between the knees and ankles and went around me almost twice. I think I was as ridiculous a looking creature as any one ever looked upon. Even 'Tilda could not repress a smile. After

"EVEN 'TILDA COULD NOT REPRESS A SMILE."

breakfast I went out with the old man to catch the old blind mare, and there, near the stable, stood a calf—one of the yearlings—with one of my suspenders hangin' out of its mouth. The infernal thing had eaten my pants and had, I firmly believe, swallowed my pocket knife. I was a perfect sight riding home with the old man's pants on.

'I dreaded the ordeal of meeting the folks. Unfortunately I arrived there at noon, when the family were at the house, and I had to run the gauntlet of my father and mother, my big brother and the other children, and even the blamed niggers laughed at me. I had to tell the whole story in order to account for my change of pants. I didn't hear the last of the matter for years.

"I just concluded, then and there, that if a little love scrape like that would cost me so much trouble, I wouldn't have anything more to do with love matters, and I never have."

CHAPTER VI.

THEN AND NOW.

HARDSHIPS OF THE PIONEER—THE WAY THEY LIVED—MUSCLE AND ITS ENVIRONMENT—THE RESULT OF EDUCATION AND WEALTH—C. AUGUSTUS AND ARABELLA—A CONTRAST—WHY?

FEW people, who live in large cities or in old and well populated communities, are able to realize the difficulties to be overcome, the hardships to be undergone, and the discomforts to be endured by the pioneer in a new country.

If we could conceive of such a thing as an uninhabited land, rich in all natural resources, blessed with fertile soil, pure water and good seasons, and then drop a family down from some other planet, what could they do?

Everything looks well. The soil is rich, but where is the seed? The seasons are favorable, but where is the plow? The water is clear and pure, but man can not live on water alone any more than he can on bread alone. This was very much the condition of the early pioneers in the West. They had nothing except what they could bring with them in wagons.

Tiring of the restraints of older communities, or desiring to reach some goodly land where the soil was cheap and fertile, in which they could rear their families and give their sons and daughters an equal start in life with the best of those around them, these grand pioneers broke loose from all ties of home and kindred and plunged into the unexplored wilderness.

There is a sort of instinctive feeling in the heart of every brave and proud man which rebels at the idea of being second to anybody in the community. We all feel at times that "It is better to be the first man in a small town than the second man in a large one." This is the feeling that moves many a man from the older communities, where competition is strong, and drives him to the new where he may be, if not the best, at least as good as the best. But for such a man there is nothing but hardships and bitter trial at the start. He goes into the virgin forest, with untamed nature all around him, and grapples with this rough environment for his living.

He must cut down the trees and build a house, or an excuse for one, which will protect him and his from the inclement weather and from the wild beasts around him. He must plow up the new soil with an indifferent plow; he must build fences and barns, and make bridges, go perhaps a hundred miles to mill, and, in fact, do everything at a sacrifice of time and muscle which would be appalling to the man in the so-called civilized communities. And, after all his toil, if he should raise more than he can use, unless enough new comers come in to help him eat it, it is a burden on his hands.

He must raise his own sheep, and his wife and daughters must spin, dye, warp and weave and make the winter's clothing. He raises flax and from this the women spin, warp and weave and make the summer clothing for all the family.

The wild animals and birds, the squirrel, the coon and the bear, the crow, the blackbird and the jay, make incursions on his growing crops and he is kept busy, when not at the plow, in driving away and killing those pests of the pioneer.

If the streams are swollen with spring or autumn rains, there being no bridges, and the bread runs short, the family must resort to " gritting " their bread. Does the reader know what "gritting" is? If not, I must explain.

The " gritter " is made by taking a piece of old tin (usually an old coffee pot, flattened out) and perforating it all over with a nail—all the perforations being made from one side. The nail thus pushes the tin through to the opposite side and makes it rough. This is bent to a concavo-convex and nailed to a board with the convex and rough surface outward.

If the new corn is just " passed the milk " it is all right for being gritted. If not, hard corn must be taken and boiled until it is sufficiently soft for that purpose. In either case, the person who does the " gritting " sits down and puts one end of the " gritter " in a big tray and the other between his knees, and then, grasping the corn by the two ends, he passes it rapidly up and down over this rough surface, and the grains of the corn are thus cut into fine particles and fall into the tray. This is sifted and then made into corn bread in the usual way. If the family happened to have company, when in such straitened circumstances, they would want something finer than the coarser parts of the "gritted" meal for the purpose of making a pudding. That was obtained in this way:

Having a large tray of "gritted" meal, one of the women of the house would sit down with a piece of fine, home woven linen and, drawing it through the heap, catching the finer particles on it (the coarser particles falling off from their weight) she would then shake this over another tray. This was repeated until enough of the finer particles of the gritted meal was obtained to make the required pudding. This was called "sarchin' for flour."

Upon this and lye hominy the family subsisted for bread until the streams were fordable again.

This was only one of the many privations to which the pioneer was subjected.

It was almost impossible to obtain such an article as nails except to a very limited extent, and, hence the boards that covered the house and other building were laid on in the usual way and then "weighted" on with poles—the poles being held in position by wooden pins. The man who owned an auger, a drawing knife, a hand saw and a chisel was considered to be almost a bloated aristocrat, and had many opportunities to lend them.

Under those severe conditions the pioneer struggled on.

After a while plenty and comfort came. The "wild nature" was taken out of the soil by cultivation. By building and rebuilding he finally obtained a home which was comfortable. Stock grew and multiplied, children came and grew up as helpers in the family, and here great happiness reigned and the strongest virtue that, perhaps, the world has ever known was developed. In time the mills came nearer, bridges were built and other comforts of a slowly advancing civilization found their way into these far away settlements.

What a contrast between then and now!

Then such things as paralysis, insanity, and suicide were unknown. I am often asked, (as I suppose every doctor is) "Why is it that there are so many more cases of paralysis, insanity, and suicide now than in the early days?" The answer is easy when one thinks a moment. When the pioneer grappled with his environment with his muscle, it was purely a battle between muscle and courage on the one hand and the virgin forest on the other.

There was very little need for cultivated brains, for the pioneer could not use such a brain if he had it.

The pioneer's brain was rarely excited by anything. By his constant toil his excess of blood was daily drawn into his muscles in order to supply the waste occasioned by the wielding of the ax, the maul and other necessary implements of his warfare with the unhewn forests. When he lay down at night his brain was at rest. He lived (unless cut off by accident or some acute disease) until his worn-out muscular system fell to pieces like an old wagon.

But how is it now? Men do not grapple with their surroundings with their muscles, but with their brains. Every man is trying to make his head save his hands.

The Exchange, the Board of Trade and the Stock Market absorb his attention all day and sometimes all night. Those in the immediate vicinity of these modern brain destroying engines are not the only ones affected by them. There are men in every city, town and village in the country who are constantly worrying, day and night, as to the best way to overcome their fellow man. The part of the system most used and most excited is the part that gives way first. If the brain is the organ it is apt to be the first to suffer. From this constantly maintained hyper-physiological state it, after a while, becomes a pathological state. The arteries become diseased, break down under sudden excitement or strain, and the man is paralyzed.

If the blood vessels do not break the congestion continues and the man is insane; or perhaps, under the excitement of the delusions and fears brought on by these conditions, he commits suicide. This explains it all.

This is not the only contrast that one might draw between then and now.

The old man and the old woman—the pioneers—must die after a while and then their sons and daughters take their places. In their time comes more comforts and more of the arts of civilized life. The school house is built and the teacher comes to "teach the young idea how to shoot." After a while the big steamboats come plowing their way up the big rivers and commerce is established with the outside world. The enterprising ones get rid of their surplus products; men begin to buy and sell, and some grow rich. Riches thus acquired are handed down from generation to generation. With this wealth men begin to buy ease, comfort and idleness. Young men able to live without it do not labor as a rule. The head of the household in the second or third generation from the old pioneer takes it into his head that his children are too good to work. His education is better than that of his father or his grandfather; his sensibilities are keener and he feels that it is hard to make Charlie work when there is no use of it. Charles Augustus, with his sister Arabella, is therefore sent to school in the neighborhood eight or ten months out of the year. During the long and hot summer days, when the hired hands are harvesting the crop, Charles Augustus lies on his back in the shade of the trees and reads—what? He reads blood and thunder novels; that kind of literature which makes heroes of burglars, and great men of horse thieves. "Pitiless Pete, the Pirate," "Slippery Sam, the Slaughterer," and "One-eyed Ike, the Red-handed Ranger of the Roaring Rockies," and "The Red Right Hand of De Benjamin McGinnis." He knows all about prize fights and all sorts of sports, but not a thing about his father's farm which is being run by others right under his nose. His sister is very much like him. They both rise in the morning at nine, ten or eleven o'clock. Arabella gives her attention to the styles in the magazines while C. Augustus pursues his hero. After a while they are both sent away to a college and female seminary in the same town. C. Augustus here begins to show the effects of his home training. He finds himself behind poor boys who are working their way through college. But he don't care—

"It is so deuced hard, you know."

He compromises by dressing in the latest style, parts his hair in the middle and stands upon the front of the college building or upon the streets of mornings and evenings and "mashes" the girls as they pass and tugs unremittingly at a young and struggling mustache.

But C. Augustus swims. If he can not study he can dress, and his father's money freely spent gives him an entree into "our best society"—whatever that is.

Let's compare C. Augustus with the "founder of the family"—his grand or great grandfather, as the case may be. Let them stand up side by side and we will note the change wrought by education and civilization.

The old man is six feet two inches in his stocking feet, parts his hair on the side, wears "stable door," brown jeans pants (the kind that have a flap that lets down in front like the hind gate of an express wagon) has a hand like a Cincinnati ham, No. 10 feet, and weighs one hundred and ninety. C. Augustus is five feet five, parts his hair in the meridian, wears dude clothes from head to foot, has hands like a lady and feet after the same pattern. C. Augustus may know more about the world than the old man, but his great ancestor could take him by the collar with one hand and throw him over a ten rail fence without even grunting.

C. AUGUSTUS AND HIS GRANDFATHER.

But these are not the only differences in these two people. This contrast is great enough but there is a still greater contrast in their habits, tastes, manners, and feelings. C. Augustus would not be seen walking on the street with a poor person, ("common people," he calls them) nor help a poor woman out of the mud for any consideration. The old man will do anything that he believes to be right, just and good and is not ashamed. C. Augustus would rather violate the laws of his country than the laws of etiquette, so-called, which govern society. The old man would not violate the laws of the land under any circumstances, but he cares not a fig for etiquette. He does not know what it means and he does not care.

C. Augustus has been taught in his book on etiquette that none but the most horribly brutal natures ever put their knives in their mouths when eating; and the danger to which he exposes himself of cutting his cheek clear back to his ear has been fully impressed upon him. He will therefore struggle with a piece of pie, with a soggy, tough, sole-leather bottom, with his fork for an hour before he will dare to cut or lift it with his knife. He puts his fork in his mouth with impunity because etiquette has never warned him against the danger of prodding and perforating his pharynx. The old man eats in a way that suits himself. When he comes to pie, instead of wallowing it around with a dull fork he picks it up with his hand by that part which represents the arc of a circle, and, advancing the acute angle into his capacious mouth, he closes on it, and when he lays it down it looks like a three years old mule had trod on it.

"AND WHEN HE LAYS IT DOWN IT LOOKS LIKE A THREE YEARS OLD MULE HAD TROD ON IT."

While at college there comes all at once the most

dreadful news to C. Augustus and Arabella from home. Their father has been speculating, is caught on the wrong side, is "pinched," "squeezed" and finally "crushed," and has made an assignment for the benefit of his creditors. He writes that he "hasn't got a dollar in the world." C. Augustus and Arabella may flatter themselves that "our set" in society will take care of them; but poor, dear things, how mistaken they are, and how little they know about a society to which they have been so much devoted. Society would have done anything for them so long as Col. Johnson (their Pa) was rich; but now it will do nothing. C. Augustus will try to get a place in the store where he can still keep his hands white and soft, part his hair at the noonday point and talk soft nonsense across the counter to the girls; but the merchant does not want a young man who has learned nothing, knows nothing and can do nothing. C. Augustus then begins a tiresome job for Street, Walker and Dolittle. He becomes a "brick presser" hunting for a soft place. There is a plenty of work at good wages amongst the farmers, but, oh, no; he wouldn't do that for the world:

"What would 'our set' think of such conduct, you know."

He borrows from old friends until they get tired and refuse; his credit for clothing and board is no longer good, and finally, in his desperation he goes to his room, writes his parents and his girl a pathetic note on the "trials of life," of which he, poor fool, knows nothing, and then takes a pistol and blows his poor little brains into batter.

Arabella visits (at her own invitation) some of her girl acquaintances until she plainly sees that she has worn out her welcome; then she decides to teach music. This will give her a living and still keep her in "good society;" but she soon finds out that she knows little or nothing about music. She has learned to "bang" the piano as she learned to "bang" her hair; but "banging" the piano and giving other people the toothache will not do. She tries and tries again and fails. Then she retires to her room and writes a pathetic note to Pa and Ma and dear George (who is already courting another girl) takes a dose of strychnia and turns up her delicate, tapering toes to the nodding daisies.

This is a sad, sad ending of the once prosperous Johnson family, is it not, reader?

Now, really and candidly, what was the matter here? Why should two young people who have had the very best advantages in life, turn around at the first little trouble and commit self destruction? What would the old pioneer, the hardy, founder of the family have done under like circumstances? He would have taken the proper implements of war and would have plunged into the forest and would there have grappled with the trees, the streams and the wild beasts and would have wrested from them the right to continue his existence until his allotted time came. The great maternal ancestor would have done something but she would never have thought of strichnia as a remedy for her ills. Why didn't Arabella and C. Augustus do as their great ancestors would have done under like circumstances? Education, dear reader, education. They had been taught différently. They had been taught that people in their "station" should not labor under any circumstances. They think it degrading and dishonorable.

I know of nothing more degrading than an education like that and nothing more dishonorable than that which results from such an education. There may be circumstances in which the best and most sensible thing a man can do is to take his own life. But to take one's life under the circumstances herein detailed is dishonorable and cowardly in the highest degree. I have known an able bodied man with a wife and two or three children to take his own life in a most cowardly way, because he could not get an easy job, and leave the poor wife and helpless children to battle alone with an unfeeling and unfriendly world. This is a most cowardly way of shirking responsibilities and a most dishonorable refusal to "face the music."

CHAPTER VII.

SUPERSTITIONS, TRADITIONS AND FOOLISH IDEAS.

ANTIQUITY OF SUPERSTITION—MAN A SUPERSTITIOUS ANIMAL—"SIGNS"—CROWING HENS, BELLOWING COWS, ETC.—LOSING HER "CUD"—M'GEE'S DIAGNOSIS—BIBLE WITCHERY—RAISING HER PALATE—THE SILVER PLATE, ETC.—PASSING THE HANDKERCHIEF—NEGRO SUPERSTITIONS.

SUPERSTITION is of great antiquity. The young world was very ignorant and ignorance is the foundation of superstition. Unlearned men in the earlier ages of the world, witnessing natural phenomena and not being able to give a rational explanation, attributed their occurrence to supernatural causes. The history of the world and the greatest achievements of the greatest men that have ever lived, are blotted and blurred all over with acts grounded in the darkest superstition. The histories of the Greeks, the Romans and the early German races show them to have been so full of superstition that we are made to wonder how they could have been great. The man, in our day, who would decide upon going to war or upon bringing on a battle, or any other important matter, by the turn of a blaze of fire or something else as foolish, would not be tolerated and would not be allowed at the head of affairs in any position, civil or military, any longer than it would take to appoint his successor.

The most enlightened people of the present day have descended from an ancestry, either near or remote, who were ignorant, and therefore superstitious. The superstitious ideas of those ancestors have come down as a part of the inheritance, and many persons of education *will* suffer themselves to be impressed and influenced by them almost in spite of themselves.

The gamblers, who, as a rule, are a shrewd and smart set, are blindly superstitious concerning many trivial things in connection with their vocation.

If people are superstitious concerning anything they are sure to be so concerning medicine, sickness and remedies. In my early recollection there were some very strange superstitions—some in connection with sickness and medicine, some that were not. Many of those things are believed by many people yet—not only in the West, but in the East—everywhere.

A belief in ghosts and witches was not dead in the second quarter of the present century and it is not dead yet—everywhere. In the backwoods, forty years ago, a belief in such things was quite common, and there were "signs" innumerable—a "sign" for this and a "sign" for that—bad signs in particular. It was a bad sign to see the new, full moon through a tree top or through anything that obscured it; but if you could see it for the first time full and fair over the right shoulder it brought good luck. It was a bad sign for any one of the household to take up a chair and twirl it around on one of its legs. It was a bad sign for a male person to come into the house with an axe or hoe or any sharp implement on his shoulder. He must either go straight through, if there were an opposite door, or back out the way he came; but, in the name of all the Deities, he must not take the implement from his shoulder until he was outside again.

There was a superstition in regard to crowing hens and bellowing cows. It is a fact that, from some cause or other—the breaking up of her nest or the loss of her chickens or some such calamity that befalls her—a hen will take it into her head to crow and will go about crowing in a wild, boisterous and insane way, for days; and that a cow will also try to assume the functions of a male by going about and bellowing. We see the same things sometimes in certain women, who seem to desire to assume the functions of the stronger sex, and they generally succeed about as well as the hen and the cow —for I never heard a hen crow nor a cow bellow that could deceive me for a moment.

These crowing hens and bellowing cows were a great terror to the superstitious. Something was going to happen; somebody was going to die; the hen must be killed, and the cow (being too valuable to kill) must be beaten away from the place with sticks and stones. If a bird flew into the house it was a sign that some one was going to die. If a person were sick and one of these messengers (taking refuge in its terrorized flight from a pursuing hawk) flew into the house, it was a very bad sign. It did no good to cite the fact that nobody got sick, or that the sick person got well, after one of these strange visitations. It was still a *bad sign*.

There were "faith doctors" in those days. They cured everything—especially the maladies that are incurable. Cancer was their great forte. They did nothing but simply look at the patient and, perhaps lay a hand on him. If one person in a thousand who visited these reputed faith doctors recovered, it was sufficient to forever establish the reputation of the "doctor." There are "faith doctors" now, but there are not so many, I hope, who believe in them.

The people had a peculiar idea about a cow "losing her cud." If a cow got sick from any cause there were the knowing ones who were ready to declare that she had "lost her cud." They knew the symptoms. They did not know that a cow has three stomachs, and that the first and largest is only a great receptacle into which she hurriedly passes her food when feeding, and that she afterwards, when quietly standing or lying, belches up a mass and chews it and then, by swallowing it in proper condition passes it into the second stomach, and that, in case she should drop her cud from any cause, all she would have to do would be to simply belch to get another; or in case the first stomach were empty, to go and eat something.

There were people who professed to be able to give a cow her lost cud. These were generally old women and negroes. If the old woman were quite old, lean and skinny, so much the better. I have seen those cuds. They were made, generally, of fat meat, horse hair and some other things which a cow never eats when she is well, and which, one would think, would be calculated to make a cow sick if given her when she was well. It is pitiful to think how the poor brutes suffered while those ignorant people were ramming this nasty mass down their poor throats.

A few years ago I wrote a series of papers under the heading of "Popular Fallacies," for a local paper, and in one of them exposed this very subject. The next morning I met a friend, a very intelligent gentleman, who was at that time the General Passenger Agent of a great railroad. He said to me, "Doctor, I read your article and I am glad you wrote it; for I have a sick cow and there was a negro man at my house making her a new cud while I was reading it. I instantly went out and stopped him. The negro thinks you are wrong, but your explanation satisfied me."

In a neighborhood where I once lived there was an Irishman who professed to be a veterinary surgeon. They did not call them veterinary surgeons in those days; they were horse farriers. The Irishman did not know anything about the diseases of animals, but he was full of the superstitious nonsense of those days. Among other things he knew how to "give a cow her cud." But Mac. was destined to come to grief.

He was sent for in the case of a sick cow. After a most critical examination of the cow he exclaimed, "Phy, yez ought to know phat's the matter wid the cow;

she's loisth her cood." He at once prepared the abominable bolus which was to supply the "loisth cood." He thrust it down her throat as well as he could with his hand and arm and then took the butt end of a black snake whip and used it as a ram rod. He either made his substitute too large or he got it into the windpipe—

"EF YEZ NEVER SEEN A COW PHAT'S DIED FROM THE LOSIN' AV HER COOD YEZ SEE IT NOW."

the cow, after a short struggle, straightened out and died.

Some one remarked, "She's dead." After contemplating her very seriously for a few moments McGee said, "Yes, she's dead; an' ef yez never seen a cow phat's died from the losin' av her cood yez see it now," and he departed.

But the cause of the death was too plain.

At another time there was a public sale in the neighborhood. There was a great crowd. Somebody's horse took sick with colic, or something more serious. The horse was lying down and there was a great crowd around him, each man suggesting a different remedy, and each clinching the argument in favor of his abomination by the statement that he "never knowed it to fail."

Mac. was walking around on the outside of the crowd with a sort of assumed professional air, expecting to be called, but everybody knew about the cow "that died from losin' av her cood," and the owner was afraid of Mac's heroic remedies.

Finally the horse died. The crowd broke up and separated. As I walked away alongside of Mac. I said, "Well, Mac, the horse died."

"Phy, av coorse the harse died," said Mac. indignantly, "Av coorse he died, an' there wasn't a d—— wan o' yez that knowed phat was the matther wid um."

"What do you think was the matter with him, Mac?" I innocently asked.

"Phat do I *think?*" exclaimed Mac, still more indignant, "Phat do I *think?* I don't *think*, I *know*; but not a d—n wan o' yez knowed phat wus the matter wid um; not a d—— wan o' yez. No wundther the harse died!"

"Well," I asked, "what *was* the matter with him, Mac?"

"Phat was the matther wid um?" asked Mac. "Phy it was plain enough to anny man that's got his two eyes in his head; the throuble was the hairt lay too near the midriff, an' fin the hairt bate, the ligament jumped aff the spine and the hairt quit batin' an' the harse died. Anny d—— fool ought to know that."

I must beg pardon for indicating Mac's profanity here, but his statement of the etiology and pathology of the case would be incomplete without it.

There are some things which people believe in regard to medicine which might be viewed in the light of ignorant tradition merely, and yet they are so absurd that one must be superstitious in order to believe them.

There are thousands of people in the world who have an unfaltering faith in certain barks—sometimes I find it one kind of bark, sometimes another; but the virtues attributed to it are that, if peeled upward and a tea made of it, it will act as an emetic, and if peeled downward it will act as a cathartic.

There was one superstition with which I became acquainted when a boy, and I have met it everywhere. It is the process of stopping hemorrhage by a kind of ceremony, the operator, or the person who is doing the *hæmostatic act*, not being necessarily present with the bleeding person. In my boyhood there was a woman in almost every neighborhood who pretended to be blessed with this very desirable accomplishment.

The operation consisted in repeating a certain verse, or verses, in a certain chapter in some part of the Bible. The power to do this could be communicated to another; but could not be given by a woman to a woman, nor to a man by a man. The secret was given me by a woman once but, I am sorry to say, that, since I have been ligating arteries and veins with silk and cat-gut, I have forgotten the magic verse.

These people often succeed—in their minds—because most small hemorrhages cease without interference.

Only a few years ago a reputable medical friend of mine was attending a man for an extensive *cellulitis* of the leg and thigh. When the case was at its worst and he expected to use the lancet at the next visit a boy came into his office and said:

"Dr. J. you needn't come up to Mr. L's this morning."

"Why," asked the doctor, "is L. dead?"

"No," answered the boy, "but Mrs. M. is a doctorin' him."

"Who is Mrs. M.?" the doctor inquired.

"Oh, she's a woman that lives acrost the street."

"What does she know about it?" the doctor asked.

"Oh, she knows lots. She's cured more'n a hundred cases like it. She's got somethin' that never fails."

"What is she doing for it?" was asked.

"Why, she tied a silk string around his leg and read some verses over it out of the Bible."

Now, my intelligent reader may be ready to exclaim that this sort of blind and ignorant superstition could not occur anywhere except in the uncultured West.

For the benefit of such person I will truthfully state that Mrs. M., the sorceress in this case, was from the *cultured East*.

There is also a false and very foolish belief among the laity about "the palate coming down." In some forms of posterior nasal and throat inflammations there is a very serious choking sensation. In such cases many think that the "palate has come down," and many and ludicrous are the methods resorted to to "raise the palate up."

I have not the space to record all of them, but will give one:

I was called once in my early practice to see a boy, who, the messenger said, "had got his palate down and couldn't get it up." When I arrived at the house I found the whole family assembled in one room and all very much excited. In one corner of the room, near an open window, sat the unhappy victim of this curious accident, and an old lady (of course such a delicate operation could not be entrusted to any one except the old lady "who had nussed more sick folks than anybody else in the neighborhood") standing over him, with a stick, twice as large as a pencil and six inches long, twisted into a wisp of hair on the crown of his head.

SUPERSTITIONS, TRADITIONS AND FOOLISH IDEAS. 129

"I got it up jest so fur an' couldn't git it any furder; so I jest hilt it where I had it an' waited fur you to come."

The boy's face was flushed, his eyes protruding and his mouth wide open. There was an expression of fear and apprehension on his face, as if he expected "to hear somethin' pop" when the palate went back.

"I GOT IT UP JEST SO FUR AN' COULDN'T GIT IT ANY FURDER."

The old lady gave an extra hitch on her stick and the boy's eyes bulged out a little more and he raised up about two inches off the chair. I untwisted the stick and swabbed his throat with a solution of nitrate of silver and the "palate went back" in a very short time.

Certain persons also have unbounded faith in dog oil, snake oil and fish worms, as ingredients for liniments for rheumatism and for swellings about joints. If I remember aright these same things and others still more ridiculous were extolled as remedies by Aristotle centuries ago.

In my early practice I was called to see a sick man at a saw mill. He was a strapping big fellow, and had been down with articular rheumatism for some time. As I was the second physician in the case, the other having failed to do him any good, I was doubly anxious to relieve him. I think I saw the case three times and then gave orders for the family to report to me. I heard nothing of the case for several months and so concluded that my last prescription had done the work. One day, three months afterward, this big fellow walked into my office with an air of bravado and a swaggering gait which I took to be natural with him. I did not recognize him until he gave his name.

"Oh, yes, Williamson," I said, "you are the man who had rheumatism so bad. The last medicine did the work did it? I thought it would."

"Naw, sir," said Williamson, leaning back in his chair and unbuttoning his vest. "Naw, sir, it didn't do me no good at all. Ef I'd a depended on you doctors I'd a been dead, long ago. But I've found somethin' that will knock it as cold as a wedge; an' what's more it'll knock it every time. Look at that," said he as he triumphantly went down to his waist and untied and brought forth a rattlesnake skin which he had been wearing under his clothing as a belt.

There was no use in arguing the case. The facts

were against me. The most that I could do was to present Williamson with his bill, which he paid under protest.

Many people have a tradition about a silver plate being put in the skull in place of bone lost in injuries to the head. In every neighborhood that I have lived in there has been some person who either believed or affected to believe that he was wearing a silver plate. I knew two or three of those silver plated fellows in my boyhood, and so I grew up a strong convert to the silver plate theory, which I strenuously held until it was lectured out of me by an eminent surgeon. So strong is this belief with most people that many a country doctor loses his popularity in cases where he must remove large portions of fractured and detached skull in recent injuries. The bystanders will insist that he ought to do it, and, if the patient dies afterward, they are apt to attribute the death to the fact that the silver plate was omitted. The local papers in my town a few years ago, in giving accounts of accidents to different persons in whom the skull was fractured, repeated the statement that "the doctor skillfully inserted a silver plate to replace the lost bone."

They finally stated that I had performed this wonderful operation on one of my patients who had suffered from a fracture of the skull with the loss of a large amount of bone. I had my fears that, perhaps, the profession had lent itself to this fraud by not denying it. Many doctors are willing to take the credit of having done brilliant things—whether they have done them or not. I presume that I am as willing as any one to take credit to myself for what I actually do. I think that is both laudable and defensible, but I never saw the day when I desired to profit by a falsehood and by the propagation of an unreasonable and lying theory. Feeling that the truth about this thing, as about all things, ought to be known I wrote an article for the paper denying that I had done such an operation, and stating positively that no such operation had ever been successfully performed—giving scientific reasons as to why it could not succeed, and concluded by offering one thousand dollars for the production of a single case where the fact of the successful performance of such an operation could be demonstrated.

My office was besieged for a week with people of all grades of society—learned and unlearned—claiming the reward. They all knew people with silver bearing *crania*, but they neglected to bring them along.

An intelligent minister—with a collegiate education—knew three persons who had silver in their heads. They all wanted the reward, but no one could bring a patient with a quarter in his skull. Of course, I sat back and read my terms from the paper and said, "bring on your man, demonstrate the fact and get your money."

Nobody could do it.

A most ridiculous circumstance happened to me about a year after this.

Coming out of my office one afternoon I met one of those self conceited and trifling sort of fellows who hang about the street corners on pretense of awaiting employment and run at the first approach of an employer ; who hang about saloons and salute all respectable looking men who approach the bar with friendly recognition and effusive compliments, with the expectation of a treat, while their poor slab sided wives take in washing. This fellow had the deeply imprinted lines about the corners of his mouth of an egotistical ass, and natural born liar written in an indelible hand all over his face. He introduced me to a fellow lounger, much like himself, but not quite so talkative.

"Ef ye ever want a doctor," said he to his friend, "here's the man that can raise ye from the dead. He can come as near to it as the next 'un. Jest as soon cut yer leg off as to look at ye. I've seed the Doc. in blood up to his eyes and, you bet, he never flinches. I seed him take out a hull lot of a feller's skull onst, an' put in a big silver plate in its place. The Doc. tho't I wusn't lookin', but I seed 'im when he done it. You bet he's sly, ef he ain't afeard."

This compliment was too much; I didn't deny it and went away feeling like a sneak.

I think popular prejudice in favor of this standing falsehood springs from this fact: In injuries to the skull where a part of the outer table is lost it is frequently the case that the *periostium* (the covering of the bone) is not destroyed; and from this, and also from the bone itself, new bone is formed. The friends and neighbors stand by during the operation and see a large portion of the outer table removed and may, perhaps, keep the bone. When the person recovers, with the lost substance replaced by a growth of new bone, and they find that there is no depression where they think there ought to be, they can not account for this unexpected condition of things on any other hypothesis than that "the doctor slipped a piece of silver in when we wusn't lookin'." They know nothing of the reformation of bone, and they would as soon expect to see his great toe grow out again, after being amputated, as to see bone reform. The neighborhood liar, who is always present at an accident, a circus or a dog fight, takes advantage of the occasion and says he "saw the Doc. when he put the silver in the hole. He tho't I wusn't lookin', but I seen him when he done it." This lie is accepted as evidence, as it seems to explain what they do not otherwise understand, and hence the delusion. The man with the injured skull hears the story, feels of his head, and says, "Yes, I guess it's so," and soon begins to exhibit himself as a man with a silver plate in his skull and ever after he is a living lie.

Some people have a strong prejudice in favor of blowing a silk handkerchief through the chest in case of gun shot wound of that part of the body. In the first case of gunshot wound that I ever treated I met this difficulty and got badly worsted. I believe this barberous practice used to be resorted to, but it took its exit along with the practice of immersing amputated stumps in boiling tar and searing them with white hot irons.

I was called to see a young man who had been shot under the following circumstances:

He went out "turkey calling" just at daylight.

Hunters and frontiersmen hunt the turkey in this way when he is strutting in the spring of the year. They make what they call a "cowker," or "caller" out of a bone from some part of the body of the turkey, and, with this in the mouth they imitate the turkey so cleverly that they deceive the very elect—the turkey himself. There happened to be two young men out on this particular morning (both ex-members of the 3d Wisconsin Regiment) who got to calling each other—each taking the other for a turkey. One had on a blue army blouse and was hidden behind a bunch of sprouts, and the other was coming up behind him. The latter saw him in the uncertain grey mist of the morning and blazed away. A bullet from a large Indian rifle passed through the right lung from behind and emerged near the nipple. When I reached his home, to which he had been carried, I found a large crowd of curious neighbors there.

Amongst them was a fellow who had been a fellow-comrade in the same regiment. He had about his face the unmistakable lines indicating the common liar and the egotistical donkey. He put numerous questions to me while I bandaged the young man's chest and gave him an opiate. He asked me, among other things, if I was going to "blow a silk handkercher through his chest."

I answered that I was not and went on with my work.

When I started home I found him in the yard entertaining a crowd of interested spectators. He was standing with his legs far apart, his chin thrust forward and I could see the index finger of his right hand come down into the palm of his left occasionally as he emphasized his remarks. He was laying for me and, on seeing me, motioned me to approach. When I entered the circle of his auditors he asked:

'Doc., ain't you a goin' to blow a handkercher through his chest?"

"DOC., AIN'T YOU A GOIN' TO BLOW A HANDKERCHER THROUGH HIS CHEST?"

I answered that I was not.

"Well," said he, "they always done it after a battle in the army. I have helped old Doctor Mott, of New York, do it a hundred times."

"What good does it do?" I asked.

I have always found it a good plan to put these

smart people on the witness stand and let them throw themselves; but I got caught here.

"What good will it do?" he repeated after me, affecting great astonishment. "I should think you ought to know," he continued, "*that it will keep the corpuscum from diagolatin' on the diaphragm!*"

I still maintained my ground and asked,

"What does that mean?"

He looked at me with eyes wide open, and seemingly paralyzed with astonishment and exclaimed:

"Well, young man, ef you are a doctor an' don't know what that means you'd better quit!"

In the language of Micawber, I was "floored." There was no answer to that outburst of learned indignation, except with a club, but in keeping with my usually mild and gentle nature I didn't kill him. The scoundrel may be living yet. If so he owes his life to the fact that the writer is a lineal descendent in a direct line from a party by the name of Job, who used to live at Uz.

There is a practice among the midwives and old "grannies" of the West (and everywhere else, I presume) of shaking new born infants for an imaginary disease which they call "liver grown." If the new born infant does not do well they assume that "it's liver has growed to its side." They essay to remedy this imagined difficulty by turning the poor tender thing upside down; then, holding it by the heels they give it a slow, downward movement, as if they would drop it, and then suddenly jerk it upward. This they repeat several times. If the child gets well they "broke it loose;" but if it dies "it was growed so tight that it couldn't be broke." A great number of times I have prevented this cruel performance; many times, I believe it has been done, in my absence, with my own little patients, in spite of me, and so no doubt, with all other physicians.

But I can not dismiss this subject without referring, briefly, to the superstitions of the negroes. They have some superstitious ideas which their ancestors evidently brought from Africa, and which have been handed down from generation to generation. The one thing which worries the negro more than any other is, perhaps, the fear of being "conjured." They have a belief that certain persons (generally of their own race) have the power to "conjure" them, or "put a spell" on them, and they are so impressed with this belief sometimes, and it takes such complete possession of them that, I am credibly informed, they actually dwindle away and die. The person feared is generally a "red eyed nigger." We see negroes occasionally who (like some white people) have large hemorrhagic points in the "whites" of their eyes. The more ignorant negroes are in perfect terror of these "red eyed niggers." The conjuring is generally done, as they think, by the conjurer placing certain articles—sometimes one thing, sometimes another; sometimes wrapped in a package, sometimes placed in a phial or bottle, and placed in a path where the victim is known to travel and permitting him to unconsciously step over it.

The negroes sometimes carry very queer things about their persons to prevent the operation of the conjurer's spell. The rabbit's foot is deemed to be the best among the counter charms, though the mole's foot stands high with many.

I held an inquest a few years ago on the body of a stalwart negro man, who had died suddenly. He was a man of more than ordinary intelligence for one of his race and was a leader in colored church circles. In one of his pockets I found a small wad securely wrapped and tied with a string. Cutting the string and removing the outer wrap I came to a piece of buckskin; and under this was a wrap of red flannel, and inside the flannel was a lodestone or magnet with a great number of iron or steel filings adhering to it. This was, no doubt, a highly prized charm, and was intended to keep off the spell of the conjurer.

While traveling on a Missouri Pacific Railway train a few years ago I noticed a negro woman get off at a way station. Soon after she had done so the porter found a small pocket book in the seat which she had occupied. He brought it to the conductor who asked me to witness its contents, as there might be a claim that something was missing. When it was opened the contents were found to be a quarter of a dollar and— *a rabbit's foot!* She was, no doubt, in great distress until she recovered that rabbit's foot.

Some negroes who are sharper than the rest of their race and who are utterly unscrupulous, make money by preparing these charms, which resist the power of the conjurer's spell and bring good luck to the possessor.

The negro has a mortal fear of the cat under certain circumstances. If one of the more superstitious sees a cat cross the road or street ahead of him he will traverse an unreasonable distance in the country, or go any number of blocks in town, in order to head the cat off so as not to cross its path.

They impress many of their superstitious ideas upon the white children with whom they come in contact, for childhood is a rich field in which to sow the seeds of superstition—and it takes hard work in after years to educate it out of them.

If a negro baby is having trouble in cutting its teeth, the mothers procure the brain of a rabbit and rub it on the gums so as "to make de teef come froo easy."

I have had any number of white mothers consult me about this matter, desiring to use it on their babies if I thought it would do good. In every instance I found that they got the idea from a colored nurse, or a colored washer-woman or servant. There is something about "Brer Rabbit" which the negro thinks brings good luck.

A few years ago I had a patient for whose baby I desired to procure a wet nurse. I knew a young colored woman whose baby had died only a few days before. In order to be sure of getting her I sent for the old negro woman with whom she was staying in order to procure her influence. The old woman came promptly to my office.

"Auntie, I wish to get the young woman who lost her baby at your house to nurse a white baby. Do you think I can get her?"

"I dunno, sah, wheddah yo kin o' not; but it won' do no good, ef you do. She ain't got no milk no mo'."

"She hasn't?" I asked; "why, I should think she ought to have. She is young and healthy."

"Yes, sah, she is, an' she had plenty ob it, but it's all done gone and dried up long ago."

"That's strange," I said, "it has only been a few days since her baby died."

"Ain't nuffin strange 'bout it ef ye knowed how it's done. I'se found out somfin dat'll dry it up ebery time, an' it'll do it quick, too."

"Ah, indeed. Well, I'd like to learn how you do it."

"Why, yo' jest put some camp fire (camphor) on a piece ob cotton, an' put it in de coffin wid de baby an' it jest keeps a drawin' an' a drawin' till it draws all de milk away!"

I didn't argue the point with her. There is no use in doing so with one who is capable of believing a thing so ridiculous. The only thing to do to rid the race of such superstitions is to educate their children.

CHAPTER VIII.

PREACHER DOCTORS, MIDWIVES AND NURSES.

REASONS WHY THE PROFESSION DO NOT LIKE PREACHER DOCTORS—THE NURSE AND THE "NUSS"—STORIES ABOUT "NUSSES."

THERE is an abiding prejudice among medical men against preachers practicing medicine, and against midwives and certain self-styled nurses. This, as a rule, is well founded and there are good reasons in the minds of those entertaining such prejudice—reasons that are born of experiences in their lines as practitioners of the healing art.

It is a fact that, in the western country, and in the more sparsely settled districts, especially, there are many men following both the professions of medicine and the ministry.

They either started out in life as preachers and then studied medicine, or pretended to, or began as practitioners of medicine and then tacked on to that the vocation of a minister. The prejudice against them arises mainly from the fact that every well informed physician knows that no man can follow both professions and do justice to either. He will be either a very poor preacher or a very poor physician, or both—probably both. Either profession, well followed and well filled, is sufficient to tax the intellect and the energy of the best man to the utmost.

It is then a sort of presumption, in the outset, for any man to assume to fill *two* places which, under the ordinary rule, only *one* man is expected to fill. He arrogates to himself a degree of ability and a power of intellect which we know that no one man possesses. He, therefore, puts himself in the position of a pretender and no good man likes or approves of a pretender.

In the second place such a person is almost sure to attach more importance to a little prayer, added to his medication, than he does to his medication. Whether this be sincere or pretense, to the ordinary physician it looks like pretense. It savors of cant to such an extent that, in some cases, it becomes contemptible. Then again, the preacher physician is apt to get a hold upon the members of his flock, through his preaching and his church associations, by which he obtains their practice, whether his abilities as a physician, entitle him to it or not. He does not only obtain their practice, but their influence upon those who are not members of the flock, and thereby gets *their* practice.

This, to the ordinary physician, looks unfair. He has met this man in consultation, perhaps, and he knows that he is shallow, and yet this man goes to the country church, or to the school house on Sunday, and preaches; he puts on a sanctimonious air, and talks about being good; talks about dead children and rakes up death scenes which touch people's hearts and make them cry, and himself joins in the crying. They say he is "such a good man!" People naturally like a man who can make them cry—and laugh. It is singular, but it is true

I do not wish to be understood as including here men who have quit the ministry and become physicians, or who have quit the field of medicine and become preachers. That is legitimate and proper. I only speak of those who attempt to do both. I have known several of the latter, and must say that I have invariably found them to be poor preachers and poorer doctors.

I was once attending a wealthy gentleman for a pneumonia of the right lung. He was a bad subject, being a slight, weakly man, and when the second stage ensued, the symptoms were somewhat alarming. While I did not despair I honestly informed the family, as is my habit, that his condition was critical. They at once desired to send for a man who was once their family physician in another state, and, who was now a preacher; but still practiced some, they said, "among the brethren."

I protested and desired one of my colleagues called. But nothing would satisfy them but to have this man. He lived one hundred and fifty miles away and was telegraphed for.

He came, but, fortunately for me, the crisis was over and my patient was better. In a very short conversation with him I ascertained that, if he had ever known anything about medicine he had forgotten it. The first thing he did upon entering the sick room, after greeting the patient, was to get down and pray. I didn't protest but I thought it out of place. He then proceeded to make the examination. I handed him my Camann's binaural stethoscope. *He put it to his ears backward*—in a position in which, every competent physician knows, he could hear nothing.

After a very patient and painstaking examination (he had come one hundred and fifty miles, remember, and must pretend to be doing something) he turned to me and said, "pneumonia of the left lung!"

"Of the *right* lung, doctor," I quickly explained.

"Yes-yes," said he, correcting himself, "the right lung; that is true—the right lung."

I could afford to let him make a mistake with the manner in which he had used the stethoscope, but I had been poulticing that right lung, and I could not afford to let him change the locality of the disease.

Now, he appeared to be a good fellow, but I could not suppress a feeling of contempt for him. A man knows when he does *not* know a thing, although he may not be right sure when he does know a thing. Otherwise a man may be in doubt about the accuracy of his knowledge, but he can not be in doubt about his absolute lack of it.

I have never called one of those persons in a serious case, nor been called with them, that an extemporized prayer meeting didn't result. I object to this. I object on account of the fact that it does many sick ones more harm than good—the weeping and wailing of relatives and friends, and the fact that the patient, if still in his or her right mind, is apt to be seriously shaken up. The death bed is not a good place for reformation. This is a matter which should be attended to when we are not sick. I do not believe that people ought to be scared into Heaven, even if they could be.

The prejudice against midwives is based on grounds as strong as, or stronger, than that against the preacher physicians. The principal objection against them is on account of their ignorance. No good physician will object to any woman going to the assistance of another in a time of serious trial, when a physician can not be had, and doing all that she can in such ways and to such an extent as any woman, making no pretensions to knowledge may reasonably go. But when a woman, without possessing any more knowledge than the rest of her sex, sets herself up as a practitioner in this particular line to be sent for, even in opposition to a physician, then the latter has a right to object. The people have a still better right to do so. I have known many women who would not go except when a physician could not be had, and, who, upon the very slightest suspicion that all was not right, would inform the family and friends and insist on a physician being called at all hazards. Such women deserve commendation and praise. I have known others on the other hand who would set up their limited knowledge against that of a competent physician, and who, when called to a serious case, demanding instrumental interference, or the manipulation of a skilled hand, would sit and wait day and night, while the patient became exhausted and the foundations for *septicemia* and death were laid, and who would object to the calling of a physician, insisting that "all will be right in a few minutes." I have even known them to resort to the most horrible methods to remedy existing difficulties. Such women deserve criminal prosecution. Many, very many beautiful lives have been sacrificed by the wilful stubbornness, selfishness and greed of these old hags.

The first one of these self appointed doctors that I ever met was in my early practice. She was as large as most men and decidedly masculine in appearance. She had a big nose, high cheek bones, a strong under jaw and firm set mouth. She smoked strong tobacco in a cob pipe and was decidedly fond of whisky. In speaking of her professional work I asked, "what books have you read on obstetrics, Mrs. G.?"

"Well, I hain't read none, because I cain't read, but I've had a heap read to me!"

"I suppose that you have done a good deal of practice in your special line," I suggested.

"Yes, I used to do a heap; but I don't do so much now. But, when I was young and strong I used to go and nuss and take care of the sick; and I'd *super* and I'd *tend*, but I cain't do it no more like I could then."

The old lady had divided the word superintend into "super and tend," which was new to me.

This woman had lived in the county twenty years,

and she was so wofully ignorant that she invariably called the name of the county seat wrong. It was Nevada and she called it Sevada! Yet this woman had the assurance and effrontery of "Old Nick," and would not hesitate to take into her hands the issues of life and death, in cases in which she knew no more than a wild hog in the woods!

This woman is only one of more than a score whom I have known and while her ignorance, about things in general, is rather more dense than the average, yet she knew as much about the special work to which she had appointed herself as the rest. The truth is none of them know any thing about the serious work which they pre-

"AN' I'D SUPER AN' I'D TEND."

tend to do. If all is right anybody can attend to it. If there are serious complications they are as ignorant of their duties as the unborn child, and must either stand by, and see the poor mother wear herself out in helpless, hopeless agony, or by their ignorant interferance do things which are almost as bad as murder. All that the act needs to be murder is the intent.

While discussing this subject a few years ago with a friend, eminent in the profession of medicine, he remarked:

"If an ignorant woman lives to be fifty or sixty years of age and finds herself a failure at everything else, and then wants to be a doctor, if she does not, providentially, die, some one ought to take her out and kill her!"

This seems to be a harsh sentence, and one that the speaker himself, in his broad humanity, could not see carried out; and yet, in strict truth, there would be a great saving of life if these women were penned up in some asylum, as soon as they began to manifest symptoms of wanting to "doctor" people, and kept there until cured of their monomania.

Many of them will not hesitate to come in in the absence of the physician and change the treatment in cases of childbed fever, or in the serious ailments of small children.

They always end what they have to say in praise of a certain remedy, or a certain measure,

"I never knowed it to fail, and then, what's more, ef it don't do no good it won't do no harm."

This is what the family have been looking for—

an unfailing remedy—one which, if it does no good will do no harm.

It is astounding what influence those women often acquire over families, and more especially over young mothers. They say "she is an old lady an' knows more about babies than the doctors; what does a *man* know about a baby, or about a woman either?"

The habit of those women of dosing new born babes with saffron tea (a mean, unwashable sort of vegetable yellow dye) and cat nip (good for cats, no doubt) and giving them fat meat and "sugar teats" to suck deserves the deepest condemnation. I am sorry to say that many weak kneed and careless physicians permit these atrocities against the weak and helpless, new born thing. I never do. So long as midwife or nurse obeys my orders and does as I direct, she is my friend, and will meet with nothing but gentleness and kindness from me; but, whenever she invades the domain of what strictly belongs to me, and "takes the bits in her teeth" and proposes to do as she pleases she will find me as relentless as a Comanche Indian. Human life is a precious thing, whether it be the life of the babe, the belle or the octogenarian, and the physician who permits the life which has been placed in his special care and keeping, to be lightly dealt with by others, has not learned all that he ought to know.

There are nurses and "nusses." A good nurse who knows her duties and who implicitly obeys the directions of the physician is a "pearl of great price." The self appointed " nuss " who thinks she knows more than the doctor, who tells lies about the number of years she has been in the business, and who secretly gives compound cathartic pills to your typhoid patients because she thinks that "the only thing that ails her is that her liver ain't actin', an' the doctor hain't give her a single thing to make it act and clean it off," deserves nothing but a decent burial at Christian hands and a small attendance at the obsequies.

The trained nurses that are now coming into use in the larger cities are a great help to the physician, but it will be a long time, I fear, before they can be utilized in the small towns and in the country. On the other hand the miserable old gin guzzlers (who kill our patients with their doleful stories and portentious prognostications) with whom the physician in the country and country towns has been compelled to forbear, in order that he may not be numbered with the murderers, will still hold the fort.

There are many good nurses in families who do not set themselves up as such, and I would much rather have one of these nurse a sick patient of mine than to have many who set themselves up as professionals. The worst feature of the professional who has had no training for her vocation is that many of them take up the business in order to keep from taking in washing or going out to service.

They are ignorant and have no natural qualifications for the business, and besides, when once employed they forget that they are employed as nurses only, and want to assume the functions of a doctor. It is most annoying to the physician to be confronted by the ignorant nurse at each visit, as if she desired a consultation. No physician, who is a kindly gentleman (and all physicians ought to be both kind and gentlemanly) feels like thrusting a woman aside with a rude rebuff.

"Well, doctor, what do you think of her this mornin'?"

Now, it may be that you do not care to have her know just what you think. If you think the patient is not doing well, or is in great danger, and tell her so, she may go and repeat what you have said to the patient, or, if not to her, to the family and neighbors and will crowd the house with interested relatives and friends and thereby injure the sick one.

If your opinion is favorable she may disagree with you and argue the point in the patient's presence after you have gone.

Another bad feature about some of the nurses is that they seem to be afraid that they will either not earn their salary, or that, by not being busy may get a reputation for idleness and therefore they want to be doing something *all* the time. The one needful thing, for seriously sick patients, is that they be kept quiet. After all is done that should be done then let them alone.

I had a lady patient who was seriously sick complain to me once that she thought she would do well enough "if the nurse didn't pick at me all the time."

I asked her what she meant by the nurse "picking at her."

She requested me to remain awhile and see. As

the nurse was not present during this conversation I consented to do so.

When the nurse came in she began "picking at her," and this is about the way in which she did it:

She would smooth the patient's hair with her hands; then she would get a wet rag and apply it to the patient's lips; then a larger rag and wash her hands; then, after the lapse of a minute or two, she would bathe her feet with a wet rag, and then dry them off with a dry towel; then she would tuck the cover around the feet and, while she had her hand in in the tucking business, she would go up to the head of the bed and tuck the sheet around the patient's shoulders. After carefully surveying the patient for a minute or so she would ask her if she didn't want a drink of water. If the patient didn't then she would begin on the hair again or something else just as annoying.

I invited her to the parlor before I went away and gave her a lecture and concluded by asking her "in the name of heaven and all the angels" to let the woman rest. I frankly told her that, well as I was then, if I were to lie down on the bed and permit her to worry me one day as she worried that poor, sick woman, it would make me sick.

"Well, but what must I do; it looks like I ought to be doin' somethin'."

"Do nothing except what common sense dictates; give the medicines according to directions, bathe when and as I tell you; above all get the patient quiet and keep her quiet. Do not disturb her unnecessarily and do not permit others to do so."

The lecture was salutary and bore good results. The nurse was not altogether bad. She was new at the business and desired to earn her wages and establish herself in the opinion of the community as being a person who was not idle, and therefore thought she "must be doin' somethin'," in order to ingratiate herself into public favor.

In a somewhat tedious and prolonged case of parturition I once had one of those old gin-drinking smokers who was ignorant, self assertive, and full of remedies and suggestions. I knew my case and was patiently waiting for the time when I could safely interfere with instruments and end matters with satisfaction to myself and perfect safety to the patient. This old self conceited creature had retired and consulted the gin or whisky bottle and her pipe for about the tenth time, each time coming back with a suggestion as to what might be done to bring matters to a sudden termination.

Each time I had kindly and firmly blown her suggestions to the winds and waved her away by saying, "But that will not do in this case."

She finally came in with the suggestion that I give the patient a tablespoonful of gunpowder. She had been in a similar condition once—"was worked jest like she is, an' I tuck a tablespoonful o' gunpowder an' it was all over in ten minits."

I looked at her with a quizzical expression and spoke in the hesitating manner of Mark Twain and The

Doctor, when tormenting the guide about the bust and hand writing of Christopher Columbus, and said,

'Well, Mrs. J., but how can we touch the powder off?"

Her face was almost ablaze with astonishment;

"Why, you don't have to touch it off! You jest give it to her like any other medicine an' let it work that way."

"WELL, MRS. J., BUT HOW CAN WE TOUCH THE POWDER OFF."

I answered that gunpowder was made of saltpetre, sulphur and charcoal, and when combined was not good for anything on earth except as an explosive; and, unless she could devise some way by which we could set fire to it, I couldn't see what good it was going to do. The old lady seemed utterly astounded at my ignorance and, no doubt, considered me to be almost criminally so.

I was once called in a case where there was a young

baby and the young mother was suffering from *septic peritonitis*—childbed fever. I had not been the attending physician before, but learned that the nurse in the case was an old maid friend of the patient. She desired to quit the occupation of seamstress, which she had followed before, and become a nurse, and this young married friend in her kindness and friendship had decided to "let her begin on her," as she expressed it.

The young mother was so sick that I gave little attention to the baby, and as the "nuss" seemed rather shy and kept out of my way—leaving the care of the patient to her mother—I saw but little of her and paid little attention to her. They told me that she was taking care of the baby.

After the lapse of several days I was told that there was something the matter with the baby and they desired me to see it.

On questioning the "nuss" I brought out the astounding fact that she had been feeding it on milk and —*crackers!* When informed that a child of that age could not digest crackers she was so disgusted with herself that she went back to her dressmaking and the world lost an honest "nuss."

CHAPTER IX.

THE BRANCH-WATER MAN.

HIS GENERAL CHARACTER AND HABITS—HIS DOG, TEAM AND WIFE—STORIES OF KEESECKER AND OLD DARLING.

THE Branch-Water Man is a peculiar product of the frontier and the West. While you will find others much like him in the loungers, the dead beat and the shiftless in our larger cities, yet the opportunity to become the man that he becomes and to live the life that he lives, is not offered to any but him.

The Branch-Water Man is, usually, descended from a long line of Branch-Water ancestry. He inherits nothing but flabby muscles, a flabby intellect and constitution and a disposition to roam all the days of his life; for this man has no place that he can call his home. He does not want it, and he would not keep it if he had it. He does not want a home, for if he had one which he could not sell, it would prevent him from moving.

He is the American gypsy without the ability to barter and trade and care for one's self that other gypsies possess.

He generally lives at the back of another man's

farm and drinks branch water in preference to digging a well—because to dig the well would cost him some exertion and, if there is one thing which this man dislikes above all others it is exertion. He is the only living example of the law of inertia—that is one part of it; that part which teaches that, when a body is at rest it can not move until put in motion. The Branch-Water Man is happiest when not exerting himself.

You can tell this man from other bipeds by his dog, by his wagon, and his team, and his dress. I know a Branch-Water man's dog, even when his master is not with him. He is not like any other dog. A blooded dog—the pointer, the setter, the spaniel and others of the more intelligent and useful of the canine species, will not remain with this man any longer than it takes them to get away. Intelligent and fine dogs like intelligent and fine masters. So, if you ever see a dog of the better kind with the Branch-Water Man you may know that that dog has either done something mean and fallen from grace, or some great calamity has befallen him. Something has occurred to this dog which has compelled him to accept a position which he knows is a disgrace to him every day that he lives and he feels it and is ashamed of it in his very bones.

This man's dog is a mongrel. He is a mixture of nearly all the dogs of the meaner kind that you ever saw. He is generally a yellow dog, and has a long body, short legs and a bushy tail. As said before he is a mixture of many breeds of dogs; but, he is most all Branch-Water man's dog.

When you see that kind of a dog on the streets of a country town you can find his master by going around to the wood yard and picking out the man with the smallest, trashiest and meanest load of stove wood in the lot.

You will here not only have the opportunity to inspect the man himself, but you will also get a chance to see his wagon and his team. His team is small, old and boney—perhaps a big horse and a small mule, or a small horse and a large mule with a crooked knee. One or the other is almost sure to be half or altogether blind.

This man gets this kind of a team because it comes cheap, for he can not own a team unless he can get it for almost nothing. They are the cast off and used up stock that other and more thrifty people do not want and will not have.

His team is poor and looks like hair covered, animated hat racks, and they have to lean against each other to think. When the Branch-Water Man wants to move he has to wake them up, for these poor, miserable and solemn stacks of bones stand and sleep in the sun and rarely move except to occasionally threaten a tormenting fly; but they rarely do more than threaten. It would take an expenditure of force and a wear and tear of tissue to knock the fly off which the horse can ill afford.

This man never thinks of moving into any other kind of a house than an old outhouse on some one's farm—a house where the door and floor and a part of the chimney are gone. This one-gallused Arab will move into a house like this and do a little work around the neighborhood occasionally and will take his pay in hog's jowls and corn meal and be just as happy as a prince. He sometimes puts in a crop on the farm of some one else and half way 'tends it until the crop is partly raised and he will then sell it for what he can get, and, suddenly hears of some "good place to move to" and gets up and moves.

He can move on a fifteen minute's notice. All he has to do is to hitch the old scarecrow team to the old rattle trap wagon, put the old woman and children and a few other rags into the wagon, pour a bucket of water on the fire and call the dogs and be off.

He is happy now. He will drag along all day and go into camp near a small stream at night, where his wife will bake some corn pone, fry some fat bacon and make a horrible decoction which they think is coffee. He will turn the team out to graze and he and his family will sit around a smoky log fire and fill up on this stuff and speculate about the good things they are going to have when they get to their destination and get as much enjoyment out of it as other people have in other ways.

The Branch-Water Man is a hopeful creature. He is always looking forward to something which he never reaches; he is always expecting something to happen which never happens, and he is too lazy, ignorant and shiftless to make anything happen.

He just waits and hopes. I never knew one of those fellows to raise a crop of anything and save enough of it to have seed for another crop. They always beg or buy seed in the spring. If he can not sell the crop before it matures, and nature is so bountiful and the season so good that he raises more than he can use, he will either let it go to waste, or he will keep his fences so poorly that the neighbor's stock will get in and eat it up.

WAITING TO "GIT IN TO HAUL."

The next spring or the next autumn is too far away for this man to consider anything in relation to that time. What he wants, he wants right now; what does he care for next week or next month or next year?

His mind can not grasp things so far away in the dim, uncertain future.

These people will often flock to the small towns in the West with a view to "gittin' in to haul" and will live in the little shanties in the suburbs or along the railroad tracks and will haul lumber, dirt, rock, sand, wood and such things when they can get this kind of work to do. But they will not work, until pushed to the last extremity, unless they can use the pious and solemn old crow-bait team also.

They will sit around on dry goods boxes on the corners and in front of the stores, in their shirt sleeves and old flop brim hats and with green baize patches on the rear of their pants, and seriously discuss matters of great national concern about which they know no more than the old horses that they drive, and they will almost run from a man, if they think he wants to hire them to work and does not want to hire the insane old team also.

The Branch-Water Man will follow a hand organ with a monkey attachment all day. He is always at a dog fight. He does not *go* to the dog fight, but just seems to *turn up* where one is going on; and he will stand for hours and listen to the jokes of the patent nostrum vender and will guffaw inordinately at his silly talk. He never misses a circus. A circus is, perhaps, the only thing that ever tempts this man to think of parting with his team and rickety old wagon. He will resort to all sorts of shifts to get hold of a little money in order to take the "ole 'oman an' the brats" to the show.

I knew one of those fellows who actually came to town on circus day and brought his wife and children, and brought in and sold their old cooking stove to a second hand dealer for two dollars and fifty cents in order to get money with which to attend the circus.

I knew another case where another just such a man came seventy miles in the same kind of an old wagon and the typical Branch-Water Man's team, and brought his wife and two children (they had only two; these kind of people usually have eleven) and hauled a young calf (the only one he had) in the back end of the wagon, in order to attend "Barnum's Greatest Show on Earth."

The calf was to be sold in order to get money with which to buy tickets.

He had calculated on getting four dollars for the calf, but the first butcher he met offered him six dollars for it It astonished him so that he could scarcely get his breath.

After making the sale he went down to a jewelry store and made a statement of his good fortune to the jeweller, and added that, as he had more money than he thought he would have he had concluded to buy something for the children. The jeweller asked:

"Well, little man, what do you want?"

The boy wiped his nose on his sleeve, looked around a little, and answered:

"I want one o' them French harps."

The price was forty cents and the boy and girl each got one. Both of them were barefoot.

No doubt, this happy man even yet dates everything back to the time "when we went to the circus." It was the one great event in the ordinarily uneventful life of this poor fellow.

The Branch-Water Man's wife is much like him. She is a piece off the same stuff. She is prematurely old, is slab-sided, tanned and wrinkled, wears an old cotton handkerchief of bright colors around her head and tied under her chin, and, almost invariably smokes a cob pipe with a short stem.

She will light this strong old pipe and sit down with her knees somewhat apart and will rest an elbow on each knee, put one hand under her chin and hold the old pipe with the other, and, in this leaning attitude, will sit and smoke and gaze intently on one spot in front of her in sort of day dream and will scarcely move or speak for an hour unless spoken to.

I have often wondered what she thinks about while she is being soothed by the strong tobacco. She dreams, no doubt, somewhat like other and more favored people. She dreams of moving into some goodly land where her husband can "git in to haul" without trouble; where the days are clear and the running streams are full of fish that bite readily; where bacon and corn are cheap and the papaws and the black haws ripen early, and where strong, dog leg tobacco may be had for the asking.

This is the kind of country that the Branch-Water

Man longs for, and it is, no doubt, the place of which his wife dreams, where her tooth ache is soothed and her digestion is improved by the stimulus of the old cob pipe and the strong tobacco.

The poets are not the only dreamers, for the Branch-Water Man's wife dreams and, I do verily believe that his old horse dreams sometimes.

What does he dream of?

Of a goodly land, where the weather and the roads are good, where the loads are light and the green grass is plentiful; for, even the Branch-Water Man's horse gets tired of eating fence rails, stumps, sprouts, the wagon bed and the neighbor's front gate.

Reader, did you ever notice that a man's horse and his dog are much like the man?

A spirited man will own a spirited team and when they are brought out and hitched up it takes a strong, spirited man to hold them in check and keep them from running away. But the Branch-Water Man's team never runs away. They are too solemn and religious to ever think of such a thing.

When I was a boy I knew a man of this type who owned a serious and grave looking old horse, and, one hard winter, after a bad crop year, the Branch-Water Man was not able to procure food for both the family and the old horse; so he would go out and cut down slippery elm saplings and the old horse would eat the tops and small limbs and gnaw the bark off the body and large limbs, and, in this way, managed to get through the winter. But he was very poor and bony when the spring came. He would stand and sleep and dream, with that grave, religious look on his countenance, and occasionally, he would put one ear forward and his face would suddenly light up with a sort of ecstatic smile, as if he had just discovered an oasis of green grass. There can be no doubt about what that poor old horse dreamed. Then the red birds came. When the red bird comes in the early spring he will sit on a limb for hours and whistle the peculiar notes that a farmer whistles when he is calling his horses to their feed. When the old horse would hear this whistle he would wake up suddenly, a heavenly gleam would overspread his countenance and he would hoist his head and his old " chawed off " tail and would go careering and whickering through the woods like he was crazy. About the time he would get well under way another bird would whistle in some other direction and he would stop and listen; and, on hearing it again, he would turn and charge in that direction. He was so weak and emaciated by his slippery elm diet that he would run against trees and fall over logs, and the man had to tie him up to keep him from breaking his neck.

The Branch-Water Man's wagon is in keeping with his team and with all his other personal property. It is old, gnawed, rickety and shabby, has no paint on it and he rarely ever greases it; so that, when he is on one of his semi-annual tours you can hear the old wagon howling for grease further than you can see it. This wagon looks as if it would catch chickens if you would turn it loose in a horse lot. You can always tell where one of these wagons has gone along the road by the track in the dust. Either one or both hind wheels wabble and continually crosses back and forth over the track of the front wheel, making a sort of plaited track.

The Branch-Water Man don't care as a rule where he goes when he moves, except that he almost invariably heads for the south in the autumn and for the north in the spring. The extremes of heat and cold oppress him and he uses all of his surplus nervous energy in trying to live where the extremes never come.

This man is the *bete noir* of the doctor's life. His family is often sick and he never pays. He scarcely ever goes after the doctor in good weather and rarely ever in the day time; and, one peculiarity about his calls is he is always in a hurry—wants you " jest as quick as you can git thar "—and he never knows what the symptoms are.

This is a shrewd way he has to keep from being sent away with a prescription. Press him all you may he will insist that he does not know of what his wife is complaining; and he will invent the most ingenious lies to get out of telling you the symptoms. He " jest cum in from work and found her almost dead," and he started right off for you and he wants you to come " right away; fur, if ye don't, Doc., I'm afeard she'll die."

When I was young, innocent and tender hearted these fellows used to really alarm me. Laboring under the fear that I might let some poor mortal die by neglecting her I have trudged through the mud on a dark night for nearly a mile, and when I arrived at the shanty, found the woman sitting up in bed with a hot stove lid or plate to her epigastrium—the case being a plain, old fashioned cramp colic from eating too much cabbage, and the scoundrel knew where the pain was, for he placed the hot stove lid to her stomach before he started after me.

When upbraided on occount of his deception he would get out of it by saying:

"Well, Doc., I was so scared that I didn't sca'cely know *what* the matter wuz; an' I was afeard ef ye didn't come she'd die."

This man always tells you that he has "heard that you are the best doctor in town an' wants you and nobody else." He informs you that he always pays his doctor's bills and will pay you as soon as he gets through hauling sand. But he will not do it. You couldn't squeeze a dollar out of him if you put him in a hay press.

After I had been practicing three or four years I received an urgent call one Sunday morning to go about ten miles from the little town where I then lived to see a man who was reported to be very sick. Could he pay me for my visit?

"Oh, yes," the messenger answered; "he is perfectly good—always pays his bills."

He lived in the hilliest and poorest part of the county, in a neighborhood which had received the name of the "greasy nation," for the reason that it was inhabited principally by Branch-Water people.

As I had but little to do and the weather was pleasant I decided to go. I took with me a young doctor who had just graduated, but had, as yet, done no practice.

I learned that this man was a son-in-law of an old fellow named Phillip Jackson. Jackson was noted in that part of the country as an inveterate stammerer. He was one of those stammerers who halts on a word and chews his ear for a minute or two before he can "get her off the center." It was reported of him that he went into a drug store once after a bottle of turpentine, and the drug clerk put up two prescriptions for another man before old Jackson could say "turpentine."

Before arriving at the place we passed two or three small fields with poor fences around them and then came to a log house, built of very crooked, unhewn logs and daubed with mud. The place was surrounded by a low, straggling fence, and the wood pile was in front of the house. We encountered a half dozen Branch-Water men, who were sitting on the wood pile and whittling and chewing bad tobacco, as we went in. Just before we got to the door five or six girls—ranging from fourteen to seventeen years of age—ran out at the only door with their hands over their mouths and went giggling and snickering around the house.

Inside were a half dozen or more women, all wearing dresses too short in front and too long behind, and each holding a baby.

The sick man's name was Keesecker and he was badly "salivated." That is, he had taken calomel and was suffering from the constitutional effects of that drug. His mouth was very sore—so sore, in fact, that, when talking, he did not move either jaw, tongue or lips. He talked entirely with his throat.

Now, reader, open your mouth until your front teeth are a half inch apart, place the tip of your tongue against your lower teeth and, thus holding your jaw, tongue and lips perfectly immovable, do Keesecker's part of this conversation:—

"How do you do, sir?" I began.

"How do you do, sir?" he answered.

It sounded as if he had said, "'ow uh 'ou uh, her?"

"How long have you been sick?"

"About two weeks." ("a'out oo ceks.")

"How was you first taken?"

"Well, I first got bilious, and I took some calomel and it salivated me; and then I got this pain in my side."

His salivation was of the "wet" variety and he was drooling a great deal; and, at this juncture, he turned over and spat on my foot. His wife got a dirty rag and made it worse by trying to wipe it off. I looked at my young friend, and he was swelled up and almost ready to roar with laughter.

"Anything else," I asked.

"Well, I got a little better once and went up to Nevada; an', as I came home I got awful hungry; an' I stopped at a house an' asked for somethin' to eat, an' a lady gave me a piece of bread, an' I think it h-e-l-ped—me."

"What is your name?" I asked.

"Keesecker," said he.

"I don't understand you," said I.

"Let me spell it for you. K-double e, Kee, s-e-c-k, Keeseck, e-r, er, Keesecker," said he, pronouncing it, in his mouth-bound condition, like "Heehecker."

I looked at my young friend, and, from his appearance, felt satisfied that his safety valve would not last much longer. An explosion was inevitable.

Just then Keesecker raised up and spat on my other foot. His wife got the same rag and spoiled the shine on that shoe, also, by trying to wipe it off.

After examining and prescribing for the patient I arose to go; and, as I did so I encountered all the women in the house, standing in a semi-circle, with their babies astraddle of their hips and each desiring me to look at her baby for some fancied or real ailment.

May be the reader does not know what a "straddling" baby means. These mothers, not being able to procure baby carriages, all teach their children to "straddle," as they can carry them much easier in that way. They take the baby astride of the waist above the hip, when it is quite young, and teach it, by their manner of holding it, to cling to the mother's waist with its little legs.

They will go to town to the circus and walk all day with the child in this position. Sometimes a child will get refractory in the presence of strange people and under the excitement of the crowd, and will refuse to straddle. I once heard one of these women speak of this perverse action in her child. She was talking to another woman.

"Miss Williams," (these women almost invariably say "Miss" for "Mistress" or "Misses") "Miss Williams, does your baby straddle?"

"Straddle!" answered Mrs. Williams, "well, I reckon he does. He's been straddlin' real good for more'n three months."

"Well," continued the other, "my Johnny's been straddlin' for longer'n that; but, I tuck him to the show the other day, an' he jest wouldn't straddle nary bit; an' I tried every way I could to make him, but he jest wouldn't. I threatened to spank 'im, an' I did shake 'im right hard once, but whenever I'd put 'im on an' try to make 'im straddle he'd cry an' git jest as limber as a rag an' act jest like he was possessed. Oh, ef I hadn't been in that big crowd I'd a spanked him 'till he was sore," and so on.

As I said, these women were in a semi-circle, each with her baby astraddle, and each with her hip elevated giving her the appearance of having a lateral curvature of the spine, and each wanting her baby looked at and prescribed for. I went along the line. One had an eczema on the face, another sore eyes, another an eruption on the scalp. Each wanted to give a history of her child since it was born; but I cut them short and compelled them to confine themselves to the necessary record.

I noticed that my young friend was still swelled up, red in the face, and holding one hand over his mouth.

When I came to the last, who was a little, dumpy

woman, with a dress too short in front and too long behind, I asked:

"Well, madam, what ails your baby?"

She answered in a very high keyed voice, and talking very rapidly,

"Well, Doc., I don't know jest what is the matter with him. He always has been a little h-i vey," stretching out the word "hivey" to about three times its proper length. I heard the young doctor start to explode, but he pressed down the valve and held on.

AND SHE WENT OVER BACKWARDS, CARRYING THE BABY WITH HER.

As they turned around and took seats one large, fat woman sat down in a rickety chair, one hind leg of which went through a crack in the floor, and she went over backwards, carrying the baby with her. My young friend broke down and laughed aloud and incontinently bolted for the door. He went around the house with his hand over his mouth and his head down, and, before he knew it, ran right into the crowd of big girls which we had seen on entering the house, and flushed the whole covey. They went yelling and laughing in all directions.

The other women formed a line with the regularity and alertness of trained soldiers and covered the person of the fat woman until she scrambled to her feet.

I bade them "good day," and called my confused young friend. As I went out one of the women was talking somewhat angrily, and I heard another one say,

"Hush, Manda, he'll hear you."

"I don't care ef he does," the other answered, "I don't see no use in nobody laughin', if somebody did fall over."

This was meant for the young doctor, for I had maintained my equilibrium throughout.

After we had gotten away from the house the young doctor asked:"

"Doctor, is this just an ordinary day with you?"

"No," I answered, "fortunately, no. This is the spice. We get our pie, good, bad and indifferent; but this is the spice that goes into it. This kind of thing shakes the doctor up, and brings the rich butter to the top."

"Well," said he, "I will take my mince pie without any spice."

But, really, such things do a doctor no harm, unless he is weak enough to lose his temper. I didn't get any pay out of my visit to Keesecker; but I got what is better, many a jolly laugh, and, at last, a good part of this chapter.

Does the Branch-Water Man tell lies? Yes, almost necessarily. His life and actions will not bear the truth. His conduct and habits as a man, husband, father and citizen are so contrary to what they should be, that he is compelled to lie in order to bolster himself up. His lies usually take the form of reasons and explanations, as to why he did this thing, or did not do that.

He is always explaining the condition in which he is found—his abject poverty and his utter lack of all that goes to make life not only comfortable, but even bearable.

When he goes to a new place he will tell most wonderful lies of this kind. He will tell how well fixed he was, "back yonder where I came from;" and what a streak of bad luck struck him; how his stock died; how all the members of his family were sick, and the immense sums of money he paid out for doctor's bills. If one half of the story were true it ought to make him a hero.

Old Darling was a typical Branch-Water Man and he was one of the worst liars I ever knew. His lies were so abrupt, far-fetched, unexpected and startling that, while you were compelled to admire his genius (the Branch-Water Man is not a man of genius, as a rule) yet you were left with a feeling of having been outdone and overmastered, and that, too, by a man who was, in the commonest acceptation of the word, "or'nary."

I have known liars whose lies had a soothing effect upon me; whose lies fell like a benediction on a pained and wounded heart; but not so with Darling. He literally overcame you with his lies and nothing that you could do or say would in the least way compete with or offset them.

I was attending the child of an industrious mechanic when Darling came in. My first view of him told me plainly that he was no ordinary man of his kind. He was tall—full six feet three; was stoop shouldered, and he had a neck which was long in front and short behind —giving the back of his head the appearance of lying almost between his shoulders. He had the largest "Adam's apple" that I ever saw, and when he would swallow, it would make excursions up and down like a small elevator; and he had the worst bow legs that I ever saw. Now, as the reader knows, tall men are not bow legged as a rule; but Darling was an exception. If his legs had been straight I do verily believe that he would have been over seven feet high. His legs looked like exagerated parentheses. I have heard of men being so bow legged that they could not head off a pig. Darling could not of headed a yearling calf; and his legs were so very long in proportion to his height! Why, he looked like he had been split up almost to the neck. There was just a little space left, just above his hips, for lungs. Well, he came in, and, after making a profound bow, asked:

"Are you the doctor?"

"I am *a doctor*," I replied, "but not *the* doctor."

"Well," continued Darling, "ef you have no objections I'd like to ask you a few questions."

I authorized him to go ahead.

"Well, now," said he, "in the first place, does a woman ever go crazy from hysterics?"

"Yes," I answered, "we have a form of insanity which we call *hysterical mania.*"

"Well, now, another question: does a woman ever go crazy from epilepsy?"

"Yes, we have a form of insanity called *epileptic mania,*" I replied.

"Well, now, can you *cuore* it?"

I evaded and explained and then asked Darling for the history and symptoms. He gave them—the case being none other than that of his young wife. He wound up his statement of the case by informing me that "no longer than this mornin' she throwed the skillet at my head and run a young man that is stayin' at my house off the place with the ax." He continued,

"She's ben sick, sir, more'n four year, an' in that time I've paid out twenty four thousand dollars in doctor's bills."

I suggested, in a quiet way, that I presumed that the doctor to whom he paid this large amount of money had retired from practice.

"They was more'n twenty of 'em sir. Yes, sir, more'n twenty, an' they hain't none of them done her no good."

Would I see her?

I evaded and explained some more and the matter ended with an understanding between Darling and myself that he would see the mayor and have him direct me to see the case on behalf of the city.

I found the woman to be really insane. She was the young wife of an old man, had a young baby, and with, practically, no home, with poor nourishment, added to a natural tendency, what little intellect she had had left its seat and taken a walk.

With city drugs, city groceries and city doctor the woman soon recovered.

At my last visit Darling asked if he could ride down town with me.

This was a thing that I did not often permit men of his class to do; but, as I had some sharp talk for Darling, I told him to get in. When he sat down in the buggy his knees came almost up to his chin.

I began:

"How is it, Darling, that you find yourself here, at the age of fifty, in such a condition as you are—with the city furnishing you with a doctor, drugs and victuals? It seems to me that, with the advantages that such a country as this has afforded you, and, with nobody to care for but your wife and baby, you ought to do better than you have done and not half try."

"Well, sir," said Darling, "it's jest as I told you, I've spent twenty-four thousand dollars in doctor's bills on that woman in the last four year."

"How was it when you came here? Didn't you have a team or something?"

"Yes, sir, I had as fine a pair of hosses as ever sot foot on Mesoora soil."

Just at this juncture we came in sight of a livery stable, in front of which a beautiful span of black horses stood hitched to a nice rig. I saw Darling look at them and then he continued:

"AN' IT FELL ACROST, ER–AH, ACROST THE WETHERS OF ONE AN' THE LINES OF THE OTHER."

"They was a par of, er-ah, of-er-blacks. I brought them from Eelinoy, an' I paid three hundred dollars for 'em before I started for Mesoora."

"What did you do with them, Mr. Darling? Did you sell them and eat up the proceeds?"

"No, sir. I tuck 'em out to my father-in-law's in the country an', er-ah-er-rum, I er-turned 'em out in his paster, an' they was, a-er-ah-er-rum, a big storm come up one day, an', er-ah, they was a standin' about as them hosses is a standin' thar " (pointing to the blacks) "under a tree—a-er-ah-a big oak tree, an' the storm blowed the tree down, an' it fell acrost er-ah acrost the wethers of one an' the lines of the other one, an' er-ah an' killed both of them, an' er-ah, an' er-rum, an' killed twenty-three hogs for my father-in-law!

There was a painful pause and then I asked:

"Darling, were there any cattle in that lot?"

"Well, er-ah, no; why?" answered Darling with some astonishment.

"I didn't know," I said, "but what such a terrible storm as that might have killed some cattle, also!"

"No," said Darling, "no, sir, they wasn't no cattle killed—nothing killed but jest them hosses an' them hogs."

But, he evidently saw the point in my question. He grew uneasy. He shifted and twisted around in his seat and tried to cross his legs, which he failed to do; and, finally, looking somewhat embarrassed, he reached out his right hand and laid it on the lines; and, in a dazed sort of way, said,

"Who-o-o-o."

I stopped the horse.

"I guess I'll get out here," said Darling, as he untangled his parenthetic legs. He climbed slowly out of the buggy and walked straight away—not looking back and not saying good bye.

A few days afterward I came up behind Darling on the street. He had on a short coat and I could look between his legs and see the people on the street beyond, like looking through an arch or a tunnel. I walked past him and he saw me; but he did not recognize me, nor speak to me. I had mortally offended him by doubting one of his best lies.

CHAPTER X.

THE UPS AND DOWNS IN EARLY PRACTICE.

THE COUNTRY DOCTOR—THE YOUNG DOCTOR'S DREAM—OBSTACLES—MY FIRST CASE—LAUGHING DOWN HER THROAT—THE WIDOW B. AND THE NIGHT I SLEPT WITH THE CAT—A BLOOD CURDLING INCIDENT.

THERE are few callings in life which bring so much of toil and hardship without recompense, and so tax a man in his mental and physical powers without adequate return as that of the practice of medicine. This is especially true of the country practitioner, and more especially true of the young country practitioner.

I know what the dream of the young doctor is before he starts out in practice. He imagines himself settled in a prosperous and growing city. He occupies two or three magnificently furnished rooms in one of the best business blocks for an office. In imagination he sees himself sitting in this splendid palace, and the "Judge," the "General," and the "Colonel," the first citizens of the town, coming to him to have their ailments attended to, and calling him to their residences in cases of serious illness, "and all goes merry as a marriage bell." He is cruel enough in his vain-glorious imagination to get up a case of serious sickness, with the Judge's only daughter as the patient. She is sick almost unto death, and he gets up some private theatricals when he announces that the crisis is passed and the fair one is safe; when the mother in her joy weeps out her thanks upon his scientific neck, while the Judge, in a gruff and dignified way, hands him a check big enough to buy a small town, and says:

"Take her, my dear doctor, take her; you have fairly won her and she is yours."

This is the way it happens before we begin, but it is far from the reality. We find at last that it is in our profession, as it is in every thing else, that which is worth having must be procured at the sacrifice of great labor.

The young doctor, in order to do any practice at all, is often compelled to begin his professional career in a very small town, or, it may be, at a country cross-roads. His first calls are generally to such cases among the poor as have exhausted the patience and skill of the "old doctor." He has a chance to begin the practical part of his business where poverty dwells, where rags and squalor greet the eye. True charity and the young doctor make their visits to the same places—the abodes of the humble and the poor. He soon finds that the life of the true physician is one full of hardship and toil, of heart aches and disappointments, and brings, perchance, as much weariness of body and mind as any other business or profession he might have chosen.

Our business would be relieved of half the toil necessary to its successful prosecution, if there was a more intelligent understanding of it and less superstition concerning it than there is.

The young student or the layman who reads this may fail to see how these things affect the doctor, but the student will find out after he enters upon the practice. He will find that he is practicing a mysterious art, amongst a people whose ancestors hung persons suspected of the power of witchcraft, and who abused and ostracised the unfortunate insane and their families. These people *will* have it that there is a great mystery hanging about our profession. They have inherited many of the queer ideas and superstitious notions of their ancestors. We find them still carrying potatoes in their pockets for the cure of rheumatism and buckeyes for another complaint; and, notwithstanding, the so-called enlightenment of this century, they insist on putting their faith in such things as burnt feathers and laying on of hands. Almost any man we meet (no matter how intelligent he may be concerning other things) will attach more importance to a remedy if there is an air of mystery about it than he will if it is something so simple that its value can be practically demonstrated to him. We find that these people insist that a man must die in the third congestive chill, and that, if he falls into the water and sinks the third time, the " Ready method of Marshall Hall" will be of no avail, though he may not have been in the water but one minute.

It is a great damper upon the feelings of the young practitioner to leave his patient one day doing well, and return the next to find his or her nerves knocked into "pi" and half the neighborhood holding a prayer meeting in the supposed chamber of death, because some one has discovered that a bird (seeking refuge from a hawk) has flown into the room, or an innocent dove, bereft of its mate, has cooed in the vicinity, or an aspiring hen, imitating her liege lord, has crowed aloud in the barn yard.

The intelligent and worthy young doctor who is struggling to earn his bread can not feel otherwise than chagrined when he sees people, whose practice he thinks he ought to do, patronizing the most blatant quacks and quack institutions and sending away large sums of money for advertised quack nostrums.

I saw, several years ago, in one of our large western cities, the following sign:

"Lee Chung,
Washing, Ironing
and
Headache Doctor.
Buttons sewed on and old clothes repaired.
Patients attended at all hours day or night."

There are respectable and so-called intelligent people in that city, who would be ashamed to be seen entering the Celestial "Washee house" as a patient in the day time, but who will climb his back stairs in the "wee sma' hours" and sit awed and dumb in the presence of Chinese herbs, dried toads and pulverized lizards.

The reader will, perhaps, recognize a familiar fact, when I state that there are not three ladies out of five in his state (it makes no difference which state) who will dare to have a dress cut and fitted on Friday, and very few men or women who will change their places of abode or start on a journey on the same awful day.

If any young man who enters the profession should start out and travel from town to town dressed in the fantastic costume of an Arab, perched upon the back of a camel, and should proclaim by hand-bills and posters that his remedies are all "purely vegetable," and were brought from Central Africa by the Stanley Expedition, he would, no doubt, do much better than he would by doing an honest and legitimate business. If obtaining money were the only consideration we might all adopt the motto: "Mankind is a goose and I was made to pick him," and succeed much better than we do by being honest, truthful, conscientious and wise.

If any man disputes this I will simply point him to the magnificent palaces occupied by ignorant and blatant quacks in all of our large cities, and then to the humble houses of the many, many hard working and deserving physicians everywhere.

The many disappointments and heartaches of the young doctor are sometimes relieved or varied by the queer and ludicrous things that he hears or that happen in his daily rounds. If he has a keen appreciation of the ridiculous he may be saved from suicide at least.

Does my professional reader remember his first case? I shall never forget mine. When on the way to see my first patient, I felt like I was preparing to go up in a balloon. On entering the sick room I had a sensation as if I were walking on sand which was giving way under my feet; and when I felt his pulse (about which I am afraid I knew very little) and tried to look dignified and wise, the objects in the room grew double and danced around like puppets on a hand organ. But I prescribed. I got a half-pint bottle, partly filled it with water and put in something for each symptom I had noticed and some other things "just for luck." The mixture heaved and swelled a few times like the tide, turned all the colors of the rainbow in succession, and then settled down to the consistency of soap suds with a heavy sediment at the bottom; and the poor fellow lay there and took a teaspoonful of that stuff every three hours and actually got well. He believes yet that I cured him, but I know better.

I came very near losing the practice of a good family once by an inconsiderate and untimely laugh. It was in my early professional life, and I did not have that control over my emotions that older persons possess. I was called to see a lady who was suffering with a sore throat. She was a good woman but had an unearthly mouth. It was simply cavernous. When I took her to the light to examine her throat she opened her mouth so wide, rolled up her eyes so peculiarly, and put on such a doleful expression of countenance that I broke down and laughed right down her throat. That laugh echoed and reverberated through the deep and mysterious labyrinths of that awful chasm. She closed her mouth with an ominous snap and asked me what I was laughing at. I don't remember what answer I made, but this I do remember: I told a little " white fib " and came out of the difficulty covered all over with mortification.

I shall never forget the first case in which I was beaten and routed by the manifestation of the superstitious ideas of which I have spoken.

There was a family of three men and two women recently from Canada, who had been penned up all winter in a little log cabin with two rooms and living upon bread, coffee and over-salted meat.

They were all more or less affected with a peculiar blood condition, popularly called scurvy. One of the women was in a deplorable condition. Her gums were bleeding and her limbs were purple and swollen. I prescribed lemons and vegetables and went home and read everything I could find bearing on the subject. I called two days afterward to see how my patient was getting along and found that they had bought, killed and skinned a sheep, and had wrapped her limbs in the hide and had applied small bits of raw mutton across her forehead, under her eyes, and on her lips, chin, and neck. *They knew the remedy as soon as I told them what the disease was.* I admitted to them that fresh mutton was a good thing but told them that they had *applied it to the wrong side!* The woman got well when turnip greens got ripe.

I came home one night after having been lost in the dark, timbered bottoms of the river. I had floundered around in the darkness for two hours during which time I had dismounted several times in order to find the road, and got myself covered with mud. It was a warm, cloudy summer night, dark as pitch and threatening rain. I had taken off my muddy clothing and was preparing for the rest which I so much needed, when the familiar "hello!" came from the front gate. I let the fellow repeat it several times and then went to the door and asked what was wanted. He said he wanted me to go out into the state of Kansas about seven miles to see the widow B.

I asked him to give me the symptoms and I would send her some medicine and come out the next morning. He didn't know the symptoms; couldn't give me the least idea of what her ailment was; knew nothing in fact except that she was very sick and he feared she would die if she was not relieved that night. Fearing that the woman might be in danger and hoping also to receive the influence of a, perhaps, rich widow, in a new neighborhood I decided to go. By the time we started the rain began to pour down in torrents. The thunders pealed and boomed and the lightnings flashed and blazed in our immediate vicinity every second.

The very earth shook and trembled with the shock of the storm. It was a grand, an awful and a terrible night.

> "Sic a night I tak the road in,
> As ne'er poor sinner was abroad in;
> That night a child might understand,
> The de'il had business on his hand."

We rode on through this war of the elements—this pitched battle of Heaven's artillery—with nothing to guide us but the lightning's flash and the instinct of the scrub horse which my messenger rode. We finally emerged from the timber and, being informed that I was near my journey's end, I strained my eyes and peered through the darkness to catch a glimpse of the stately mansion of the supposed rich widow. Upon ascending a gentle slope in the edge of the prairie there came a vivid flash of lightning, and by its light I saw, clearly outlined against the western sky—*a single log cabin with no fence around it!*

We dismounted and my messenger directed me to go in while he tied the horses. I went in and groped around in the darkness until I found an excuse for a chair. My messenger came in and struck a light, and this is the way he struck it:

He uncovered some coals in an old fashioned fire place; turned an oven lid on its back on these coals; got a chunk of bacon from a sack in the corner, from which he cut some slices which he threw on the oven lid. While the grease was frying out of the bacon he got a bucket top in which he placed a cotton rag twisted like a whip lash; he then poured the grease into the bucket top, and then got down in the attitude of a Japanese making a *grand salaam* before a Tycoon with ten tails, and blew until the rag ignited.

It sputtered and fried and sizzled, and cast shadows which were constantly changing from the walls to the floor. By this light I was enabled to make out two beds, in one of which were four boys. On the edge of the other sat a woman about forty-five years of age, with dark hair, combed down close upon the sides of a low forehead. Her eyes were small, black and penetrating; her nose long and sharp, and her mouth gave her the appearance of having been struck across the face with a corn knife, the angles of the gash turned down and the wound healed "by the first intention."

She was busy folding some article of wearing apparel into as small a compass as she could get it, and then just as deliberately unfolding it again.

After viewing her awhile I said,

"How do you do, madam?"

"How do you do?" she said.

"Are you the sick lady?"

"Yes, sir," she answered in a whining voice.

"How long have you been sick?"

"About thirteen years."

"Well, but you are worse than usual to-night, are you not?"

"No, I am always about the same."

"Great Heavens!" I thought; "here is a woman who has been sick for thirteen years and has waited for one of the worst nights of her whole life to send for me."

I felt and thought unutterable things, but I did nothing rash. I had a family and couldn't afford to be a murderer. I think now I ought have thrashed the fellow who came after me for his participation in the outrage. I continued:—

"What do you complain of?"

"I have a pain over my left eye. Dr. Morse says it is a sun pain."

The truth of the whole matter was, as I afterwards learned, that she had got mad at her

THEY HAD A REGULAR ALL HANDS AROUND FIGHT.

oldest son and sent him after the "new doctor" for a punishment. She was part Indian, but had enough white blood in her to make her mean.

I gave her a quieting powder and prepared to remain all night, as I could not think of going out into the storm again.

The messenger prepared me a bed and this is the way he gave himself to this task:

He dragged one of the four boys from the bed, and while he was dragging number two out number one climbed back again, and number two got in while he was pulling number three out.

I sat and watched the circus. They had a regular "all hands around" fight, in which all took a part, but he finally "put down the rebellion," and triumphantly pulled a feather bed off and threw it on the floor, without sheet, blanket or pillow, and said,

"Doc., you kin sleep thar."

I was utterly tired out and so lay down with my pants on. He threw over me for cover, an old Federal army overcoat.

This was just after the war and I held a blue overcoat in perfect horror.

The bed was dirty and greasy—so greasy that my face actually stuck to it—and the overcoat was worse. So, from shrinking downward from the coat and upward from the bed I was somewhat in the condition of the old negro's fish—"awfully swunk up."

Pretty soon a cat came and got in bed with me. he did not say so much as "by your leave, sir," but got in with an air of confidence which indicated that he was in the habit of sleeping in the "spare bed" with company.

Under the influence of his gentle and soothing purr I soon fell asleep. As I had my wet clothing on I soon got hot on the under side which necessitated my turning over. I did so, and, of course, turned over on the cat. That cat "humped himself" and clawed for the free air and liberty. He uttered an exclamation, *in cat*, which I translated to mean that he wanted me to move

He did not have to repeat it. I moved. The cat seemed to be ruffled in his feelings and so concluded to sit up a while. I went to sleep. I do not know how long it was before he came back to bed, but I know that when I turned over again, he was there and received me with *eclat*.

This time I grabbed the cat and wildly threw him from me. He went into the fire. Then the ashes and spit did fly! He sat before the fire, looked into it pensively and licked his feet.

If it had been the widow I wouldn't have cared, but I was sorry for the cat. I turned over on him about a dozen times

I WILDLY THREW HIM FROM ME.

that night—the cat becoming more demonstrative and obstreperous each time. Taking it altogether he succeeded in setting up a lively counter irritation along the course of my spine. My wife said my back looked like a railroad map of the state of Illinois, or the ledger of a Chinese laundry.

When I awoke the next morning the sun was pouring his gentle beams on a refreshed earth, and the adjacent forest was vocal with the music of the song birds.

I think the flies of Kansas were holding a state convention in that cabin, with a full delegation from each township and ward in the state. When I attempted to make out some quinine powders they sent a committee of one from each township to see what it was. It was a "smelling committee" and it went vigorously to work. They sat on my powders and when I would "shoo" them away, with the flapping of their wings and the kicking of their legs they sent my quinine flying in all directions.

I tried it over and over again until I wasted about fifty cents worth of quinine. I then adjourned to an oak tree some twenty rods away and finished making out the powders.

Reader, I went through all of this without getting mad or swearing (though I confess the cat wounded my feelings) and, as I rode home that beautiful summer morning I thought that if old Uncle Job (I think I had a right to call him uncle, then) could have made his appearance on earth and had met me, he would have taken me by the hand and said,

"My son, I am glad to meet you; I am really proud to meet you. There are so few of our family left down here that when I do meet one of them I feel like embracing him. Shake!"

I remember another incident about this time which I think worth recording.

A messenger came one summer Sunday afternoon

for me to go eighteen miles to see a sick family. I knew the messenger. He was a well-to-do farmer, a bachelor, and an occasional drunkard. He delivered the message, received my promise to come, and rode away.

I prepared myself for the journey, got into my buggy and started on my lonesome drive. Twelve miles of my route was over a prairie, without a tree or a house to break the monotony. It was late in the afternoon when I got away and by the time I had traversed the first six miles—where I had timber, the river and farms—darkness had set in. It was dark, not pitch dark, but that uncertain light mixed with the darkness which made it as bad as if there had been no light at all. There was a shimmering lightning playing low down upon the horizon in the south and south-west.

After I entered on the prairie it seemed to me that I was either just about to plunge into a deep chasm or run into an impassable bank all the time. I drove a moon-eyed horse—which was a born idiot. When I entered on the prairie I struck a mere path in the high grass which lead diagonally across the country, from south-east to north-west; and this was all the road I had to my destination. My horse soon began to puff and snort, and would occasionally sidle out and leave the path entirely. He seemed to feel that the air was full of spooks and ghosts and all manner of supernatural things. His apparent fright put me to thinking of robbers, murderers and other beasts of prey. I soon found that I was scared. I am not ordinarily, and never have been, afraid of nights; but on this particular night I felt the cold chills run up and down my spine, and my hair would rise up in spite of me.

When I had gotten about midway of the prairie and was driving at a lively trot my horse suddenly shied, and there loomed up just to my right a great black something—I could not tell what. I knew there was no tree or bush or habitation of living thing within six miles either way. With the instinct of self preservation and defence I struck out at this object with my whip, and there came, of all the sounds I ever heard the one least expected—*that of a leather saddleskirt!*

Anybody who ever struck a saddleskirt with a stick or whip knows that it does not give forth a sound like anything else, and what was more, the saddle was on a horse, and the horse jumped and snorted. My own horse rose, plunged forward, and went some ten paces before I could stop him. I listened. The horse would snort and then chew. Then I thought I heard men talking in front of me. Then the sound of conversation, which was low and indistinct—seemed to get around to my left; then it would shift in some other direction. Then the horse would snort and chew again. I finally located what I had taken for the low conversation in the neighborhood of the horse. I determined to ferret the matter out and see what it was.

I dismounted from my buggy, tied my lines securely and went slowly and cautiously back toward the horse. I found the animal quite gentle, patted him and felt about his head, and then felt for the bridle. I found the reins and discovered that they led toward the ground and were fast. I followed the reins toward the ground and here found them—*in a man's hand!* The man was prostrate and apparently asleep. I got down on my knees, made out his outlines and then shook him and called. He came to a sitting posture in a jiffy and reached for his pistol. I knew he was reaching for his pistol because I had him by the arms. I threw him on his back

I THREW HIM ON HIS BACK AND PINNED HIM TO THE GROUND.

and pinned him to the ground with my right knee on his chest. He struggled but I held fast—telling him to "be quiet and don't shoot." He raved and swore, and finally, discovering that I was the better man, asked:

"Who are you, and what do you want?"

"I am Dr. King," I answered.

"Why, how are you, doctor?" said he, in a natural voice which I at once recognized as the voice of my messenger.

He had got into a saloon, "by that little side door," and bought a pint of whiskey, which he told me he drank in the first six miles. By the time he reached this place he was so drunk that he felt that he would soon fall off; so he dismounted and lay down to sleep off his drunk and give his excretory organs time to throw off the alcohol.

The voices I seemed to hear was nothing more than the occasional snoring of this drunken man.

But it was the worst scare I ever had in my life. From that hour until now my hair has been a light chestnut sorrel—*the same color it was before.* *

---

* This notion about a person's hair turning grey in an instant, or in a single night, is a myth. No such thing ever occurred. It is a physiological and physical impossibility. Even if the hair follicle should die at once the hair would remain its original color until it grew out. It is always safe to doubt anything which can not be explained or accounted for on reasonable or scientific grounds.

CHAPTER XI.

UPS AND DOWNS, CONTINUED.

A CONTRAST—HOW TO TELL WHEN YOUR PATIENT IS DEAD—CUPPING THE OLD LADY—SMART PEOPLE—THE SICK HORSE—FIGHTING FIRE—THE PRAIRIE MIRAGE—HOME AGAIN

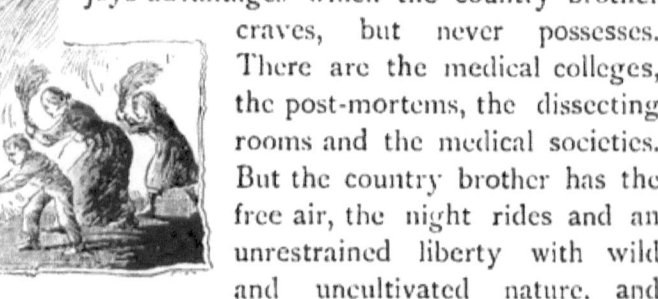

THE city physician has opportunities which his less favored country brother has not, and enjoys advantages which the country brother craves, but never possesses. There are the medical colleges, the post-mortems, the dissecting rooms and the medical societies. But the country brother has the free air, the night rides and an unrestrained liberty with wild and uncultivated nature, and above all, he has for his clientele the great middle classes—the farmers—the noblest and best of God's creation in any country. Of course he has his poor, who are ignorant and don't pay. So do all, everywhere; but the best of all is that the best of those who patronize the country doctor are a noble and free people—a people so free indeed that they will not suffer themselves to be hampered by foolish social customs.

There are many things which the country doctor learns by experience besides how to give medicines.

He learns how to tell when his patient is dead before he reaches the house. Now, the city doctor would look for crepe on the door; but not so with the country brother. You do not find crepe there. Now my æsthetic reader raises his, her or *its* hands in holy horror and says:

I APPROACH THE HOUSE SLOWLY AND LOOK FOR THE BED.

"What awfully hawid customs! How can they die without cwape on the door?"

"Well, they just die. People have died, my dear æsthetic noodle, where there was no crepe—they died even before crepe was made, you poor silly thing. It requires a great deal to help us to live, but it requires nothing to help us to die. Of all the things that we do dying requires the least assistance. A man will die sometimes, if you will go off and leave him alone and don't help him any.

But how can the country doctor tell before he reaches the house whether or not his patient has "stepped across the way," since his last visit?

By the bed on the fence!

The people (at least, many of them) have a habit, when one of the family dies, of taking the bed upon which the dead one lay and the clothes which covered him and putting them on the yard fence. As a rule the more ignorant, uncultivated and thoughtless they are, the nearer they will get it to the front gate.

Oh, how I have strained my eyes and looked for that bed. I left my patient the day before with a high fever, a rapid and weak pulse, and all the evidences of coming disorganization and death, and went home to think and wait. My opinion is that I will never see him alive again. I approach the house slowly and look for the bed. I think that, perhaps, they have made a mistake and put it on the back fence. I therefore pull my horse over a little toward the horse lot in order to get a view of the back yard; and if I see no bed how my heart leaps. I have one more chance to stimulate and bolster up the vital powers and perchance to save his life.

But the country doctor makes his mistakes as well as his city brother.

I remember well my first mistake, and it annoyed me not a little.

In my first practice I soon met the smart old woman "who loved to nurse sick folks." She wore a bandana handkerchief around her head and a mole on her nose, and was good at making mustard draughts, mush poultices and suggestions. The old lady and I soon became fast friends, and would have remained so, I suppose, if she had not fallen sick. She sent for me. She had a terrible pain in the region of the umbilicus and I decided to cup her. Having no cupping glasses, I had to resort to something of domestic use, and, after some thought, decided upon a glass tumbler. They brought me a very large one. Having exposed the parts to be cupped I put a burning paper into the bottom of the glass and when the air was expelled I quickly inverted it over the abdomen. The abdominal parieties were lax and unresisting and so, the whole abdomen just walked right into the glass. It went in with a whiz, in fact. The old lady howled and the glass kept pulling in more abdomen. " Nature abhors a vacuum," but I don't think I ever saw nature where she was so abhorrent as in this case. She seemed disgusted with it in fact, and determined to fill it if it took the whole abdomen and the old woman with it to complete the job. The glass pulled in about a quarter of an acre and then stopped and shook itself, but didn't let go. By this time the old woman began to yell vociferously and declared that I was killing her. The vacuum had pulled the symphisis pubis up to one side of the glass and the scrobiculis cordis to the other, and she was doubled up so that her back began to crack, and I really began to have fears for the integrity of her spine. She yelled louder and I attempted to pull the glass loose. Did you ever try to part two fighting bull dogs? Well, that was nothing to the glass. When I tried to insert my finger so as to let the air in some more abdomen crawled in, and the old woman's shoulders hung forward and looked suspiciously like a sub-caraoid dislocation of both humeri and her knees flew up. I am not easily disconcerted but this upset me. I felt like a fool, and for the time I thought I was but I know better now. I was just mistaken a little in the matter of how to cup. But I was the Alexander who had to untie this Gordian knot and I did it in much the same manner as Alexander. I got a hatchet and broke the glass. When I drew back to strike the blow, the old lady threw up both hands, shut her eyes, raised her voice from "A minor," to "high G," a key she had not struck before. But I struck the blow. The glass flew

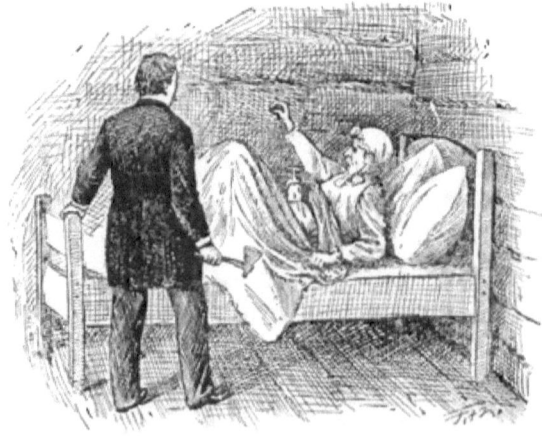

I GOT A HATCHET AND BROKE THE GLASS.

all over the house and the mountains went back to the valleys again.

She called me a fool and I didn't dispute it for I was so confused that I didn't know whether I was or not.

We never spoke again.

The country doctor has the same trouble with smart people who wish to prescribe, or teach him how to do so, that his city brother has.

You may find a man occasionally who is willing to admit that he does not know how to treat a sick horse, but you do not find many who do not think they know how to prescribe for a sick neighbor. It requires adroit diplomacy, in city or country, to get these people out of the way without the aid of the coroner.

Speaking of prescribing for sick horses reminds me of an incident which happened only a few years ago. Passing down the street one day in company with a prominent minister of the gospel in my town, we discovered a horse lying on the other side of the street and a man standing by and holding the bridle. The horse was lying flat on his side with his head and legs extended. I said to the minister:

"There is a sick horse. Let's go over and see what proportion of the passers-by will prescribe for him."

"What makes you think they will prescribe?" he asked.

"Never mind," said I, "come along and we will see."

We stood near the horse and waited. A man came along, stopped and looked a moment and said:

"Hello! what's the matter with your horse?"

"Got the colic," answered the owner.

"Why don't you give him fresh lye off of ashes? That'll stop it in a jiffy; always cures mine."

Then another came.

"Hello! what ails your horse?"

"Got the colic," was the answer again.

"Why don't you give him butter-milk and molasses? That'll knock it every pop."

Then another:

"Hello! what ails your horse?"

Same answer:

"Give him ginger and pepper, and he'll be all right in fifteen minutes."

Another:

"Why don't you bleed him in the mouth?"

"I have," said the dejected owner, "don't you see the blood?"

"Oh, yes, sure enough. Well, just let him alone; that'll fetch him out all right."

We stood there about thirty minutes, during which time seventeen men came along and fourteen of them prescribed—scarcely any two having the same prescription—which goes to show the unreliability of veterinary therapeutics as it comes from the crowd.

"Well," said the minister, "that beats all."

He came to my office the next morning, laughing as if he would split his sides, and said;

"I went home last night and told my wife of our funny experience with the sick horse, and before she had time to see the point she asked: 'Why didn't they give him water off of green coffee? That's the way pa always cured his.'"

This only shows the proneness of mankind to prescribe for anything that is sick. The disposition often comes from an inordinate self conceit, but I am led to believe that it comes oftener from a desire to do good.

I think I have had some patients killed and I know I have had many seriously injured by this unwarranted interferance of ignorant outsiders. I have no doubt that this is the experience of every physician. The younger, the newer to the community, or the more timid you are, the more trouble you will have from this source.

As the doctor grows older and especially if he develops a little bull dog courage as he goes along and gets a reputation for mercilessly handling those who change his treatment, the less trouble he will have.

My first practice had many hardships. The country was new, and what settlements there were had been broken up during the war, the people driven out and the houses and farms burned. Immigrants were coming in in great numbers. I waited on them in wagons, tents, under sheds and in stables. I would occasionally find three or four in one bed all sick, and when they were stirred up there was generally an odor strongly suggestive of a saddle blanket full of wet cats.

I had an unlimited range of territory. Sometimes in going or coming on my long journeys at night I would get lost on the prairie. This is easily done on a dark night, more especially if you have a young, green horse which does not know the way home. Horses are like men—some have large brains and good judgment; others have small brains and no judgment at all. It is important to the doctor that his horse shall know every thing excepting how to prescribe. He should be such a horse that—no matter how far you may be from home—you can drop the reins, shut your eyes, and let him go. Ah, how many a sweet mile I have slept when returning home at night, sleepy, tired and travel worn, on the back of my dear old " Tom." I used to say that " Tom," could "cipher to the single rule of three." He could come as near to it as any horse I ever knew. But if your horse be young and ignorant you may get lost in spite of yourself.

When the prairie fires come and the atmosphere gets murky it is very hard sometimes to make out ground with which you are ordinarily perfectly familiar. These fires were a terror to the new comer. With prairie, unlimited prairie, all around for miles, with high grass, dead and dry as tinder, the farms, crops and houses unprotected, well may the frontiersman be afraid. Men and women all learned to be exceedingly shrewd in regard to fires, as well as to many other things ; for upon their knowledge of their situation, their surroundings. and all things that threatened them, often depended their safety. Here is no uncommon case in those days:

The father is away from home. The family is sitting, perhaps, at dinner. A little boy comes in and says:

"Mamma, I see smoke over yonder."

"Over where?" asks the mother.

"Why, over torge the creek."

The mother rises and goes to the door, puts the thumb side of her hand over her brow, and strains her eyes "torge the creek." She goes back, uneasily finishes the meal, and then looks again. The smoke hangs along the edges of the timber and the atmosphere looks hazy. Glancing up at the sun she notices that it is red and the outline is sharp and clear cut. Gazing toward the creek again she sees a deer loping gently toward the farm. He stops at the corner of the field, looks back over his shoulder in the direction of the smoke, then passes on across the prairie. Then the mother hears a bell.

"Why," says she, "that's our cow bell and there comes all the cattle, old "pink" with the bell on in the lead. Yes, there must be a fire comin'."

Then cautioning the younger children to stay at the house, and taking the larger girls and boys with her, she seizes a burning stick from the old fashioned fireplace and starts for the back of the field. When she ascends the ridge at the back of the field she sees more smoke, and an occasional red tongue leaping up in the river bottom a mile or two away. Now she knows there is fire, and she begins the task of "back firing" so as to save the farm. She takes the little path that leads around the field as her line of defence and begins. With the children gathered around her she gives instructions. She is the captain who is to conduct this battle.

and her orders must be obeyed. The children are armed with bushes or with old sacks tied on sticks and dipped in a bucket of water which has been brought. She sets the first fire and orders the children to whip out the fire on the side next the farm and not let it cross the path. When one place is made secure she passes to another, her faithful lieutenants following closely so as to be ready to execute her orders. In this way she passes from spot to spot, always securing one point before beginning another. The air becomes rarified from the heat and the wind rushes in to fill the vacuum.

"I wonder what makes the wind all'ys rise when you're fightin' fire?" says one of the boys, who knows nothing of rarified air and a vacuum, and who, therefore, looks upon the conduct of the wind in such a case as being purely a piece of reprehensible perversity, for which there is no excuse.

"You keep at work and never mind the wind," says the captain mother, who is growing anxious, for another boy who has been sent up on the hill to note the progress of fire has reported that "it's risin' the ridge, Mamma, you'd better hurry."

The smoke thickens, the air grows more murky and the sun is now almost hidden. Occasionally a blade of burning grass jumps the path and sets the grass afire on the side next the field. Then all the children leave their places and fly to that one spot until this nucleus is extinguished. Once in a while a youngster falls back from his work and with flushed face and protruding eyes breathes hard for a few seconds. He has swallowed smoke and become strangled.

Now comes a sound as of cracking whips, and the red tongues of the destroyer are seen "risin' the hill." Below this cracking sound, there is a low, dull roar as of rushing water, or low, distant thunder. The captain mother now directs each child to take a piece of fire and run along the path and fire at regular intervals and fight it for him or herself. She moves rapidly from one to another and helps where she is most needed. Some fire jumps the path and quickly takes hold upon the dry fence which is near at one point. All hands rush to the spot, a panel is thrown down and the fire quickly extinguished. They now reach the corner of the field and the danger is almost passed. The main body of the fire which has passed the summit of the ridge, gathering force from the rising wind, comes thundering down on them like an army with banners. It shrieks and roars and leaps in the air, like a million devouring demons, and sometimes jumps twenty or thirty feet and takes hold in a new place. The "back firing" was all done when the corner of the field was reached, but they must now "side fire" down the other side of the field. This is not so hard, for the destroyer does not come at them directly in front. He is passing and they "take him by the flank" as he goes by. The captain with her tired little band well in hand now pass rapidly down the last side and fires and whips as before. The main body of the enemy comes sweeping down and picks up their little "side fire," appropriates and makes it a part of itself, and then rushes madly on to the timber along the little branch below the field. Here its headway is so great that it rushes into the woods, licking up the dry leaves and all inflammable things, even climbing the dead trees to their very tops and sopping the lichen from their aged trunks. These old trees will burn far into the night and light up the heavens all around—standing as a monument to the heroic captain mother and her gallant little band.

The mother now gathers her forces and goes back over the ground and carefully inspects every doubtful point. Then going home, with flushed face, and bare, red arms, she gets supper, while the tired children fall asleep here and there on the floor. They are awakened to eat and then to go to bed, while this splendid mother takes to her breast and suckles one of the future heroes of the Great Republic.

Oh, such a woman as that is worthy to be called mother. At the breasts of such as these have been nursed the greatest men that this or any other country has ever known.

When the father returns he hears the story, and then looking around at his wife with pride in his eye, says:

"Well, old woman, I guess I'll have to buy you a new calico dress."

This was high praise, indeed; for a calico dress cost a whole dollar.

If a modern belle were to do such a heroic deed

there is no telling the reward she would receive and the newspapers would be filled with her praise.

By the way, when I have seen the modern belle go up the street clothed in modern toggery, walking with wrist drop, high heeled shoes and the " Kangaroo dip " and leading a little dog by a long ribbon, I have often contrasted her with the heroic border mother whose heroism I have so feebly described. I have wondered at such times what the modern belle is good for. I can think of but one thing. She is certainly intended for the mother of the dude.

Chesterfield said,

"It takes three generations to make a gentleman."

I don't know how many it takes to make a dude, but, judging from his general unfitness for all things useful I am forced to the conclusion that the generations have about run out when the dude is made.

But I digress. I started out to tell about getting lost on the prairie. If you travel through the timber you have your points which will prevent your losing yourself. But not so of the prairie. Here is a great, wide waste of prairie, covered with grass, and you have traveled over it during the summer time and have educated your sense of sight to a certain perspective from certain positions. There is a house in the distance which, when seen with a different coloring of the grass of the low and high lands, looks to be two miles away. When this grass is burned you have nothing but a continuous, black foreground between you and the house which jerks the house up apparently to within a half mile. If you strike this point just at dark you will be deceived. So are the changes everywhere. But to come upon these changes when they are taking place—when a part of the prairie is burned and a part unburned, with a wall of fire between and smoke over-head and the uncertain light that comes with sunset and a glowing western sky, it will deceive almost anyone, excepting the man who is an experienced woodsman, hunter or trapper.

I have met these fires in coming home after a long journey, and I must say that, notwithstanding the seeming peril to which one is exposed and the annoyance consequent upon being lost, it was worth while to see the pictures I have seen. I have seen the line of fire extending for miles. The grass was damp and burning slowly. The atmosphere was damp and the smoke hung low. The sun was just setting and the whole western sky was aflame with crimson. Between the fire and the red sky was the timber and the smoke hung in dark grey wreaths and festoons over all. Here I have seen the mirage. The fire seemed to be in the midst of a great sea of water—the trees looked like mountains and palaces on the further shore; men and living things moved about upon the face of the water. I have seen the outlines of the most beautiful palaces on this other shore and great ships move from point to point in the sea, and small boats dart here and there, and men would get up and walk and dance on the crest of the fiery billows.

As the sun would sink a little further and the sky change a little in coloring the whole scene would change and I would get an entirely new view with an infinite variety and beauty of coloring. The fire is in my front, but I can not pass it, so I am forced to the necessity of heading it off—going around it, in fact. This I undertake to do. With the changes constantly taking place in the picture before me I soon lose my bearings. I went out in the morning over a country with which my eyes were perfectly familiar and return at night with a fairy land in front of me and not a single object in any direction which I recognize as ever having seen before.

I SAW MEN GET UP AND WALK ON THE FIERY BILLOWS.

I move on, keeping my eyes fixed on the mirage to watch the wonderful transformations taking place under the changing chiaroscuro of lights and shadows. I finally head the fire off and put it at my back, but I am a stranger in a strange land. Darkness has set in and I am utterly and hopelessly lost. I desire to go in a certain direction, but my faithful horse, when given his head, presses in another. While I have more faith in him than I have in myself, I *will* press him in the direction that I think my home is. I look at the stars. There is the north star directly in the south, with the unerring great dipper pointing directly to it. The seven stars and all the prominent celestial land marks are turned entirely around. I feel dizzy, confused and foolish. While I am under the pressure of a sense of having been picked up bodily and transferred to another planet, something jumps up and goes away with a rushing sound just in front of me. It is a deer or some other wild animal. Just here my horse comes to a dead halt and refuses to move. I see something in front which looks like a great mountain, which suddenly loses its shape and there is a gulf. I dismount and feel around in the darkness to see why my faithful horse has stopped. I find a deep gully in front of me—a "wash out" with sides so steep and bottom so deep that it is impassable. I stand beside my horse and think I will yell and see if I can get an answer from some one—from some other person who is lost, perhaps. A sound from any human being would be welcome now. I hear a scream which sounds something like a boy hallooing. I am about to answer, when I am saved the trouble, for there comes another yell very much like the first but from a different direction. I know now that it is wolves.

  I mount again and give my dear old "Tom" his head and say "go home Tom." The faithful horse turns square around and starts off at a lively pace just in the opposite direction from home, I think. But I am lost and I must now trust to the *instinct* of my horse. We move on. The old horse stretches out his neck and groans and snorts and quickens his pace. He goes as if he knows where he is going. We soon come into a a road; then we strike timber and then come to the creek. This looks a little like a creek that runs close to my home, but I approach and cross it from the wrong side. Coming out on the prairie on the other side I see a light which indicates a human habitation. I will turn off and go to that light and inquire the way. My horse turns toward the light without suggestion or motion from me. I ride up to the fence and note that this man has a house, barn and surroundings much like my own. In fact I would think they were mine, if it were not for the fact that the house and barn face north and mine faces south. I approach it from the wrong direction and I know it is not my house. I "hello" once or twice, a woman opens the door and asks what is wanted.

There is a strange familiarity about that voice. I have heard it before but to save my life I can not tell whose it is. (When you are lost you do not even recognize the voices of your nearest friends). I ask who lives there. The voice says:

"Get down and come in. I should think you would be too tired to be playing tricks after such a long ride."

The voice is strangely like that of my wife's and yet she can not be here occupying the house of some one else.

I begin to protest when she says:

"Oh, get down and come in, you goose; don't you know your own house?"

I alight, hitch "Tom" and go to the door. Yes, here is my wife and here are my babies! "There's pa!" they all say in one breath, and rush for the door. I look back toward the gate and find that the earth has swung around just one hundred and eighty degrees since I got to the door.

The faithful animal is stabled and fed. The coffee pot is put on and fresh coffee is made; the table is uncovered and my waiting supper is exposed. I sit down and eat and tell about the mirage and about being lost. Then a book is taken from the "book shelf," and I read aloud to my dear ones. Little eyelids begin to droop and little heads begin to nod.

The reading is finished and then the dear wife gets another book—"the Book of Books" and carefully opening says:—

"We read the seventh chapter of Mark last night. We will read the eighth to-night."

Then tired heads are laid upon waiting, downy pillows and the world and the mirage and all are shut out until morning.

When I have been lost in this way how I have pitied my city brother who was at that moment perhaps, riding up Fifth Avenue in his coupe. He had such a poor chance to "come out strong" and show himself a man.

CHAPTER XII.

BENEVOLENT DESIGNS.

WANTED TO BE A MILLIONAIRE—A TRIP TO COLORADO—THE "PHŒNIX" AND THE TREE OYSTER—NATURAL PHENOMENA—"THE LIGHTNESS OF THE ATMOSPHERE"—A TENDERFOOT'S FAILURE—THE GRANDEUR OF THE MOUNTAINS—THE GOOD OF DESIRING TO DO GOOD.

IT is to be fairly presumed that almost every human being that lives has at some time in his life been moved by a desire to do good to those beneath him, if such there be. Indeed it is hard to conceive of a human being so degraded and base and so bereft of all feeling that he is not moved at some time in his life to pity the miserable condition of others.

Doctors are the most benevolent people. The doctors in the United States do more charity than all the other people combined. This seems like a strong statement, but it is nevertheless true. You may take any city, town or village in the United States, and make as accurate a calculation as you can of the money expended for the benefit of the poor by all the people, banks, corporations and charitable institutions of the place and I will get a fair statement of the charitable work done by all the physicians of that town, figured by a reasonable schedule of fees, and I will show you that the doctors do more charity than all the balance of the city. Some doctors are no more charitable than other people, but most of them are. A grocer can refuse food on credit, a clothier may refuse clothing and so may all men in any branch of business, but such are the pressing needs of the poor when they call upon us that we must give our services. "Public opinion" (which is another name for the concurrence of the mob) may overlook the action of the grocer and the clothier but it will not do it in the case of the doctor who refuses his services when the poor body is racked with pain.

I started out to say that doctors are sometimes stricken with fits of benevolence. I had such an attack once myself. It was during the "carbonate silver" excitement at Leadville, Colorado, in 1879. I had practiced medicine about fourteen years then without ever having a thought of growing rich. The fact is, I felt that, in the presence of the responsibilities with which I was daily surrounded, to think of making money was reprehensible in the very highest degree, if not ungentlemanly.

I do not know why, but just about the time of this silver excitement I was stricken with a desire to be rich.

> "Not for to hide it in a hedge,
> Nor for a train attendant,
> But for the glorious privilege
> Of being independent."

I desired to do good to others, and I confess to the weakness of desiring to be rich for the sake of doing good to myself and to mine. It was the first impulse of the kind, so far as it referred to self, that I remember to have ever had, and I am heartily ashamed of it. God seems to have created some people poor in order that they might illustrate the higher virtues under difficulties, and the writer has settled down to the conviction that the Lord has been using him all this time for a wood cut and is content.

However, associated with a desire to do something for self in this instance was the higher and nobler one to help the helpless. There was a little orphan school for girls in my state which I had a great and burning desire to endow. I conceived the idea of going to Colorado and making a million dollars. I wanted just one million. Now some people would have wanted two millions, but I was never a hog about such things. I made up my mind and made a vow that if I could make a million I would give two hundred thousand of it to the orphan school.

Such was the excitement in regard to the news just at that time that men actually went out there expecting to shovel up the money in a grain scoop. I was not so foolish as that. I would have been content to use a common spade.

I went.

As I passed up the Missouri Pacific R. R. my heart

was filled to overflowing with two emotions:—with sorrow at leaving my wife and babies, and joy at the thought of growing rich and being able to do good. As I passed through Kansas City I looked over toward Camden Point, where the little orphan school was located, and chuckled to myself to think what a surprise I had in store for the trustees of that school. I was so full of it that I could scarcely keep my designs a secret. But I did. I started out with the idea that my left hand should not know what my right hand was doing, and I determined to stick to it, excepting that I intended that both hands should industriously shovel "silver carbonates" (with a spade), and when the million was obtained I would come home and make the orphans glad, and their mothers in heaven would love and bless me.

Our train moved on toward the great plains. As we passed through western Kansas people continued to get on and off the train at the stations less frequently as the stations were farther apart and the country more sparsely settled. Finally we passed the last station and entered upon the "plains," then people ceased to get on and off. There were no more towns for two or three hundred miles and all the people that were on the train were going across the plains. Then we began to be sociable and to talk, to ask each other where we were from, where we were going and what we intended doing when we got there; then we would introduce our new made friends to other friends and offer each other cigars and lunch. As we proceeded, we began to gather in groups and tell stories. The American is a great story teller. He loves to tell his best story and receive applause and hear a new one from his new acquaintance

In my corner of the car we had an excellent group of men with one exception. This was a young man with a face like a displaced interrogation point and who seemed to have failed in being a dude in about one point—the clothes. His particular *forte* lay in his ability to spoil a story that some one else was telling. He would interrupt you right in the middle of the story or just before the "point" was reached and call in question your pronunciation of a word, your statement as to the population of a city, or anything, and by the time you got through arguing with him about it, you would lose the thread of your story, everybody would be mad and the story spoiled. We nicknamed him the "Phœnix," because, after being demolished and almost annihilated, he would rise again. We handled him most unmercifully several times but it did not discourage him. He was sure to come to the front just at a time when he could do the most mischief. The fellow seemed to have been borne *mal a propos*. He had no sense of propriety, whatever.

Away out in the desert about the Kansas and Colorado line is a large hotel called Lakin. This is the half way house in the desert, and is the place provided by the railroad company where the passengers take the one meal after leaving the civilization of Kansas and before reaching the civilization of Colorado. Just before reaching the place where the train stopped for supper, the "Phœnix" ruined one of my best stories by his unwarranted interference. I was not mad, for I never permit myself to be found in such a condition as that, but I was vexed and could have throttled him.

I laid a deep scheme for revenge.

As we were leaving the train I called four or five young men to me and said:

"I have a plan laid for the final demolition of the 'Phœnix.' We must watch him until he is seated at the table and then all sit at the same table. I want you men to listen to what I shall say and, no matter how absurd it may be, agree with me. Do not only agree with me but vehemently insist that what I say is true."

This was readily agreed to.

We went in and found the "Phœnix" sitting at the largest table with an old lady near him. I had seen this old lady on the train. She was from Ohio, and was going to visit her married daughter in Colorado. She had the regulation number of boxes and bundles with which she worked incessantly on the car. She was constantly untying or tying something and taking articles out of one bundle and stuffing them into another. She had two upper front teeth out and wore the inevitable bandana around her head. As we sat down to supper I remarked:

"This is a pretty good supper for an out of the way place like this. Now if we just had some oysters"—

"Oysters!" said the 'Phœnix,' "I wouldn't give a penny a basket for oysters out here."

"Why not?" I asked.

"Because," said he, "they are not fit to eat when

they are shipped this far. They develop a nasty, fishy taste. Now, at Washington and Baltimore, where I live, you can get them right fresh out of the bay"—

"Hold on, young man, hold on!" I exclaimed. "Now, don't please."

"What's the matter?" he asked, looking up in surprise.

"You don't pretend to tell us that oysters come out of the water, do you?" I asked.

"Of course I do. Where should they come from?"

"Now, please don't, young man," I continued, while I waved him away with my hand.

"Now don't take us for a flock of innocent pigeons. I have heard some pretty tough ones, but this is too much. I don't know how these other people feel, but for my part I don't like to be taken for a fool."

"Well, if they don't come out of water, perhaps you can tell where they do come from," said he, winking across the table at a Detroit man.

"Why, I thought the babies knew they grew on trees," I answered.

"Oh, what are you givin' us?" said he.

"Why, of course they grow on trees, of course, of course, why certainly," said everybody, except the old lady who kept quiet, but seemed to be watching me out of the corner of her eye.

The "Phœnix" began to look red in the face.

"Young man," I began, "it is pretty rough on any man to be taken for a fool, but since you have seen fit to play this whole company for fools I suppose that I will have to bear my part of it. But I can't let your bald-faced assertion that oysters live in the water go without contradiction. Let me remind you that Marshall Hall demonstrated by a series of experiments years ago that warm blooded animals can not live under the water over four minutes, and everybody knows that the oyster is a warm blooded animal. But, since you persist in this flagrant assault upon well known facts, let me say that Pettis County, Missouri, where I live, is the center of the oyster producing region of the world; I know more than one man in my county who produces more oysters than the whole state of Maryland and the District of Columbia put together.

"We have Maj. G., Capt. S., and Dr. T. who have large oyster orchards."

"Why yes, certainly, certainly, of course, I know that," said everybody in chorus and repeated it so fast that the "Phœnix" couldn't get in a word.

"I've seen all those brands on the oyster barrels up in Detroit," said my Michigan man; and then everybody chimed in and asserted the same thing as to his town. The "Phœnix" was confused and mad; for he evidently saw a conspiracy in our concert of action. He turned red, spotted and green by turns. When he would attempt to speak the chorus would break out anew and drown him out. He looked around with a maddened and defeated look on his face, seized his cup of coffee and gulped it at three swallows and rising knocked his chair over and went to the door, paid his "six bits," and incontinently bolted for the waiting train. We all laughed and enjoyed his discomfiture and the old lady looked puzzled.

A jolly young German, who was my companion, thinking to continue the fun, said:

"Doctor, do oysters sing?"

"Oh, yes," I said, "they sing beautifully. I don't know of any better and more delightful way in which to spend an afternoon than to take a book and go into Maj. G's oyster orchard and sit down under the oyster trees and hear the oysters sing. It is most soothing and delightful when the old oysters sing the young ones to sleep just as darkness comes on."

"I ALLERS KNOWED THAT OYSTERS GROWED ON TREES."

This was too much for the female delegate from Ohio. She broke the bonds of silence at last.

"Well, now, do tell? *I allers knowed oysters growed on trees but I never knowed that they could sing before.*"

This was too much. Everybody roared in chorus. The old lady knew that she had started the laughter, but she didn't know exactly how she had done it. She joined in, however, and looked from one to another to "catch the point," if possible, and in turning her head, she spurted her bread and coffee through the aperature, made by the absent frontal incisors, all over the young man from Detroit.

But the "Phœnix" never rose again. He took up a lonely position in one corner of the car and held it to the end.

We approached Canon City on foot from the railroad station at daylight. There were the mountains looming up before us with the cleft of the Grand Canon, where the Arkansas river comes out of the mountains, plain to be seen. But there was no town; we couldn't see a single house although there was a level valley and not an object intervening between us and the Grand Canon. We went a little further and saw one house which seemed to be trying to hide itself under the mountain. A little further on another house stepped out from behind this one, and then two houses stepped out from behind these two and four from behind these four and so forth. In a few minutes we found ourselves in the midst of a flourishing town of two or three thousand inhabitants. I was mystified. I couldn't understand the phenomenon of these houses walking out from behind each other at daylight, so determined to probe the mystery to the bottom.

If I am hunting a stray horse I always inquire of a

boy or a negro, but when I want natural phenomena explained I look for a "prominent citizen." This I did. After I had stated what I had seen, and asked him the reason for it, he thought a moment, put on a wise look and said, slowly:

"Well,–I dunno-o-o-oh. It is generally-considered-here-e-e-to-be-caused by the-ah-lightness of the atmosphere."

At the point where we stopped the first night we had black beef and blacker sausage for supper, both being strongly tinctured with the taste of the sage brush. I called a Hibernian who waited on the table to me and asked:

"Pat, what makes this meat so black and gives it this peculiar taste?"

"I dunno, sur," said Pat, while he winked a wink that took one side of his head to do it, "unless it is, sur, that they do say that it is owin' to the loitness of the atmosphere."

We traveled up the Arkansas river two days, there being fourteen of us on the stage—sometimes hanging on to the clouds by our eyebrows, and then again almost in the "valley of the shadow of death." We had one lady, very fat, on the stage, who cried all the way from sheer fright. I would have cried but I was so badly scared that I was speechless and cryless. My heart was in my throat and prevented articulation. An Irishman, who was one of the passengers, declared,

"The next time I ride over these mountains I'll walk."

We came to a place where only a few days before two horses and a wagon had gone over a precipice several hundred feet. We were looking down into this chasm and trying to see the wrecked wagon and horses when the driver stopped and said:

"Here, I guess you folks had better get out here."

The fat woman was already crying, and with this she began to yell in dead earnest. She sat on the back

I WENT DOWN IN THE MUD AND SHE ON TOP OF ME.

seat and I on the middle one. I had been in the habit of getting out first at stations and then helping her. I got out here as soon as I could, for I could tell by her shouts that she was close upon me. Just as I turned around to receive her she jumped right on to my stomach with her whole weight—about one hundred and seventy pounds. I went down in the mud and she on top of me, of course. I do not know what I would have done if there hadn't been somebody there to take her off, for she was so badly scared that she was perfectly helpless and she had rendered me almost as helpless as herself.

Another gentleman and I got under her arms and almost literally carried her to the station—a half mile distant—where the stage had stopped. I was almost paralyzed with the effort to carry her and had the backache all the balance of the day.

When we arrived at Leadville it was ten o'clock at night. A man came and opened the stage door and looked in by the light of a lantern. She made one desperate spring, yelled "Oh, John," and fell on his neck. He staggered under her ponderous weight and she swung on. They went staggering and whirling off amongst the bushes and I have never seen her since. If he gets her out of Leadville I feel sure that he will have to blindfold her and back her down the mountains like stock men load unruly horses on to railroad cars.

There was house room enough in and around Leadville to accommodate five thousand people and there were twenty thousand to be accommodated. Such a crowding mass of humanity I never saw before and hope never to see again. The ground was covered with snow, the weather was too cold for mining except where the mines were already in operation, and nearly every body spent their time in walking around the streets, herding up in the gambling rooms (which were open on the streets and furnished the only free accommodation in town), or cutting logs and building huts in preparation for the spring mining.

As I couldn't go to spading up my million until the snow went off I decided to practice my profession and make a few thousand just to pay expenses. I put on my best clothes (and they were the best that I saw in Colorado), put up at the best hotel and hung out my shingle. I stayed there one month and never received a call.

I don't know why—couldn't explain it then, and can not now unless it was because I was so well dressed that people thought I was proud. Men came to me every day with specimens of ore and desired to sell me rich mines, but no one came to have his wounds healed. All seemed to think that I was a millionaire who had come there to buy up all of the good mines and who was disguising his real object under the pretense of practicing medicine. There was no use to protest. It did no good. It had gone forth that I was a Boston millionaire (I had never seen Boston) who represented a syndicate that controlled millions. I was treated with great deference, and the ore continued to pour in on me day by day; but no one wanted me as a doctor.

I would look at the specimens and the assays and ask the most innocent questions about them—for I didn't know "carbonate" from "horn silver"—and they would look at each other and wink as much as to say, "ain't he a sly old coon? But he can't fool us."

I tired of this kind of thing at last and decided to come home. When I got everything on the stage and myself into it I called the hotel clerk to bid him good bye, and said to him:

"Charlie, answer me a question; I've been here a month trying to get something to do in my profession. I am the best dressed man in Colorado. I don't think that I am either an ignorant, or a bad looking man. I've seen lop-eared, ignorant, "Jim Crow" doctors going around here as busy as bees. Now tell me; what is it that drove people from me as a physician? Why is it that I couldn't get anything to do?"

Charlie put his hand up to the side of his mouth, looked mysterious and leaned forward and whispered in my ear:

"I don't know, doctor, unless it is *on account of the lightness of the atmosphere.*"

And so I came home.

But I saw the grand old mountains as I had always longed to see them. The grand, gloomy and silent mountains that God has builded as witnesses of the great throes and upheavals through which this earth has passed in days gone by. I looked upon these grand old mountains "on whose summits the clouds gather of their own accord even in the brightest day. There I saw the great spirit of the storm, after noontide, go and take his nap in his pavilion of darkness and of clouds. I saw him aroused at midnight as a giant refreshed by slumber, and cover the heavens with darkness and gloom; I saw him awake the tempest, let loose the red lightning that ran along the mountain tops for a thousand miles swifter than an eagle's flight in the heavens. Then I saw them stand up and dance like angels of light in the clouds to the music of that grand organ of nature, whose keys seemed to have been touched by the finger of Divinity in the hall of eternity that responded in notes of thunder that resounded through the universe. Then I saw the darkness drift away beyond the horizon and the morn get up from her saffron bed like a a queen, put on her robes of light, come forth from her palace in the sun and stand tiptoe on the misty mountain top, and night fled before her glorious face to his bed chamber at the pole."

I STOOD AT THE MOUTH OF A GREAT CANON AT EVENING.

I stood at the mouth of a great canon at evening, where the water had, by the attrition of the ages, worn its way through hundreds of feet of solid granite. The beautiful river, whose waters came from the melted snow on the mountain tops, came leaping and dashing down through the great canon, sprang into the valley and went singing on to the sea. The valley below was covered with cedars, arranged as artistically as if they had been planted by the hand of man, and the mountain sides were covered with stately pine. And far away up and beyond all I could see the lofty, snow-capped summits that in their towering grandeur seemed to pierce the upper skies. I stood here at sunset when it was already dark in the valley, but still light upon the mountain tops. The sun was setting and I saw him pierce the mists that ever hung about the mountain's brow with his broad lances of light. I stood in the darkness and looked into the light; I stood in the night and looked into the day.

> I could see with a simple glance of the eye,
> To the place where the day bade the night good-bye.

Appalled and awe stricken by the beautiful picture I raised my eyes that I might catch a glimpse of the hand that had wrought the wonderful scene, and there, high up on the granite rocks, I beheld traced in letters of living light the beautiful legendary inscription—"*Buy Frazer's Axle Grease.*"

And so I did come home.

"Was your trip entirely devoid of good?" you ask.

Oh, no. Nothing is devoid of good which has good intentions behind it. I went out all oppressed and sway-backed with a big desire to do good to others, and as I came home I looked over toward the little orphan school and felt down in my pocket and found about three dollars.

I didn't write the check.

But it did me good. The next best thing to doing a good deed is to want to do it. No man ever felt a great, honest desire, deep down in his heart, to do something for the betterment of others who didn't grow and broaden and become a better man.

"A noble deed is a step toward God."

And a noble desire is very nearly akin to a noble deed. It is desires like this, and deeds when we can do them, that constantly develop us in life and lift us up and make us feel our kinship with Him who so loved the world that he gave his life for it.

> "Heaven is not gained at a single bound,
> But we build the ladder by which we rise
> From the lowly earth to the vaulted skies,
> And we mount to their summits round by round."

CHAPTER XIII.

DEATH BED REPENTANCE AND CONFESSIONS.

GENERAL CONSIDERATIONS—"CAUSE OF BILL SIMPSON GOING TO H—L"—THE "COLONEL" AND THE METEORIC SHOWER—"UNCLE MIKE" AND THE STORY OF THE STONING OF STEPHEN.

THE doctor sees men and women at their weakest and their worst. Some people come to their sick beds, and, perhaps, to their death beds with all the arrogance, bravado and hauteur of their every day life. But not many. The sickness that threatens life and that betokens approaching dissolution causes most of them to unbend.

The man who has the most strenuously denied the authenticity of the Scripture when well, and who would walk any distance and sit up unusual hours in order to argue with a preacher, and, if possible, overthrow his faith and convert him to his agnostic theories, will, after being sick a day or two, cease to argue, and as the case advances, quit swearing. As the case grows more serious his friends suggest that he ought to begin to prepare for the other world, but add that they suppose he don't care as he has "always talked against religion." He turns his head to the wall and says he "was just talking to hear himself talk." If he makes this declaration, my word for it, within twenty four hours he will have either priest or preacher, and will either confess or have prayers.

I have seen many of these cases of confession and attempts at reformation by parties supposed to be on their death beds. The doctor is frequently consulted as to the advisability of sending for a minister. It is a ticklish point for the doctor. His patient may be in a condition which makes him fearful that the excitement attendant upon religious exercises, questions, answers and confession may turn the scale against him. On the other hand if he refuses to permit a minister to enter and the patient becomes delirious or unconscious and dies without regaining consciousness the doctor will be blamed for the fact that the deceased must suffer the pangs of torment throughout the unending ages.

That is a pretty strong accusation for a poor, harassed country doctor to carry about with him. As if he was the author of all the sins of the deceased.

An ignorant fellow, who had been abusing another doctor to me once, wound up his inventory of the doctor's sins and short-comings with the statement:

"He's the cause of Bill Simpson goin' to hell, too."

"The doctor the cause of such a thing!" I exclaimed. "How could he be?"

"Why he wou'dn't let him have any preacher.

They wanted to have readin' and singin' and prayin' before Bill got outen his head, and the old blatherskite kicked agin' it and said it wouldn't do to excite him. Fust thing they knowed Bill was as wild as a Texas hoss and couldn't tell singin' from thunder, and he never knowed nothin' after that."

Here was a wicked and ignorant fellow who really had that kind of faith in the efficacy of "readin' and singin' and prayin'" that caused him to expect another man, as wicked and ignorant as himself, to be read and sung right into the gates of Paradise. Many people, less ignorant and not wicked at all *feel*, if they do not *believe*, the same thing.

The doctor must decide all such questions for what he believes to be to the best interest of the sick one. The doctor may be himself an infidel. I have known not a few physicians who tried to preach their infidelity at the bed side of the sick. This is a very wrong and a very foolish thing to do. It is nearly as bad to try to change the sick one's faith, and win him over to some new, novel or different faith. The doctor has to do with the body and not the soul, and it is best for him to leave the inculcation of religious faith and religious ideas to those who are trained for the business.

But he must decide as to the admission of a minister. I confess that it is sometimes a hard problem to solve. I have generally kept myself on the safe side by permitting what was asked, but limiting the number to be admitted and warning against all excitement.

There are some people who mistake bodily exercises for religious exercises, and who call upon their God as if he were deaf or far away. With such the doctor must be very exact in his limitations. I am sure that I have had one or two people killed by this kind of thing.

But does it do any good?

May be so; may be not. I have known a few persons who made professions of repentance and reformation when sick, who kept the faith after recovery. But the great majority return "as a dog to his vomit, and a sow that has been washed to her wallowing in the mire."

The case of the quarrelsome old lady who thought she was about to die very fairly illustrates this class of cases. She called in all of her neighbors with whom she had quarrelled and forgave them and was forgiven. As they departed she called out,

"Now neighbors, remember, if I die this stands good; but, if I get well it don't."

So it is with these people. They intend for their professions to count if they die, but to be void if they recover.

If it be worth while for a man to make preparation for another world—and if this were a work on theology I should say that it is—he had better make that preparation when in good health and in his cool, sober senses. The death bed, with the pulse at one hundred and fifty and the brain on fire, is a poor place to consider questions of such tremendous moment. It is like a man trying to execute his last will and testament while falling overboard from a ship—it is apt to be hurriedly, and probably, bunglingly done.

I have heard and known of some very ridiculous things in connection with the actions of wicked people who expected soon to "shuffle off this mortal coil."

There have been many stories written about the conduct of people on the night that the "stars fell" in 1833. This one has never been in print that I know of:

There was an old Kentuckian who was uneducated and rough, but naturally a very shrewd man. He was a horse trader and a hog drover and was a mean and stingy money getter. The one redeeming trait in his close fistedness was *that he gambled.* He exhibited here enough liberality to risk his money, and to give others a chance to win it if they could. But he was hoggish in his nature, was brutal and overbearing and generally quit a winner. He played cards because he loved to win money, and when he won it he kept it The gambling fraternity, who, whatever else may be said of them, are liberal, almost to a man, both feared and hated him. They hated him for his brutality, and his meanness generally, and they feared him because he was rich, and it is in gambling as it is in almost all other lines of business—the fellow with the big pile generally has his opponent at a disadvantage.

On the night of the great meteoric shower this old rascal (whom I shall call Colonel John) was playing with two young men. They were playing poker "without limit," and while their fortunes varied as the night wore apace, the Colonel had "hogged" most of the big bets. He would put up so much money that the other fellows were afraid to "call," and he raked it in without a "show down." In addition to this he had been caught cheating and nothing but his superior strength, his brute courage and the general awe which his reputation inspired kept him from being mercilessly handled.

He had just raked in the last dollar that the other two fellows possessed when some one opened the window blinds and noticed an unusual light without. The meteoric shower had probably been in operation for some time, but the blinds had been closed and they had not seen it.

The attention of all was now arrested by this celestial phenomenon. The Colonel held his paw on his pile of money and leaned over and strained his eyes in watching the unusual sight. He was ignorant of astronomy, and, of course, this could mean nothing else to him than some terrible visitation of the Lord.

One of the other gamblers was an educated fellow and had some idea of what the nature of the shower was and was not much alarmed. But he thought he would take advantage of the occasion to make the Colonel disgorge his ill gotten gains.

"Colonel," said he, "I believe the world is coming to an end."

"Yes, Jimmie," said the Colonel, "I reckon it is, I reckon it is. It looks powerful like it, dont it.

"Yes, the world is coming to an end and you have got to face the Lord in Judgment with this money, which you have just as good as stolen, in your hands. What are you going to do about it?"

"I–I–I dunno, Jimmie, I–I dunno. What do you think I ought to do?"

"Why, you ought to give it up. There can be no repentance and no forgiveness in a case like this without restitution. Don't you think you ought to give it up?"

"Well–well–well, Jimmie, I expect I ought—I expect I ought. It's too bad, ain't it? too bad–bad–bad–bad!"

"Well, if you think you ought to give it up, why don't you do it? You may be snatched before the Judgment bar at any moment, Colonel; give me back that money."

The Colonel leaned forward a little more and looked out at the falling meteors, with eyes protruding and a face ashen pale; then pushing the money along the table a few inches repeated in a faltering voice:

"Yes, Jimmie, I reckon I'd better give it up. It does look as if the world was comin' to a eend, and I reckon you'd better take it. It's too bad–too bad–bad–bad–bad."

"Colonel, you sit there and hold on to that money like an old miserly hog. Why don't you hand it here if you expect forgiveness? You know you stole that money and that you are no better than a robber. You have taken the money that should buy bread for my wife and children. You cheated and got it unfairly. The Lord is preparing for the Judgment now. In a few minutes the heavens will be rolled together like a scroll and then it may be too late. Give me that money."

The Colonel leaned forward and took another look, his eyes protruding more and his face growing still more pale, but he held his hand on the money.

"Yes, Jimmie, I–I–I reckon you'd better take it. I know I've been bad. I know I have; but I don't want to meet the Lord with this money, Jimmie. I reckon I'd better give it up."

"Well, why don't you do it then? Don't you see that the whole universe is being consumed by fire and that everything is being dissolved by fervent heat? Colonel, don't go before the Great Judge with this stain upon your soul. Give me that money."

And thus they had it.

At each time that the Colonel would confess that he ought to give it up he would shove it over toward Jimmie a little farther, but still kept his hand upon it.

Jimmie took hold of the Colonel's hand and tried to get the money but the Colonel clutched it nervously and held on.

Finally, Jim made a last appeal. He described the Judgment to the Colonel and told him that if he did not give the money up he would be sent to hell and consigned to apartments where he would be burned with fire, but never consumed.

"Now," said he, "Colonel, I don't want you to go to hell, and I know you don't want to go there. Will you give me that money and save your blackened soul from perdition."

DEATH BED REPENTANCE AND CONFESSIONS. 245

The Colonel was still watching the sky with protruding eyes and ashen face.

"Well, yes, Jimmie, I guess I'd better give it up. I *don't* want to go before the Lord in this fix. I guess you'd better take it. I know I as good as stole it and

"I-I-I THINK IT'S A CLARIN' UP A LITTLE BIT."

I'm afraid the Lord won't forgive me. I-I-I guess you'd better take it."

"Well, then, why don't you let me take it?" said Jimmie as he clutched the Colonel's hand.

Just then there was a very perceptible diminution in the number of meteors that were falling.

The Colonel saw this, and leaning forward a little farther toward the window, his face brightened as he drew the money toward himself and exclaimed with great excitement:

"*Hold on, Jimmie, hold on a minit! I–I–I–think it's–a–clarin' up a little bit.*"

And so he kept the money.

I have seen a great many who thought they were near to the Judgment and who professed great repentance and reformation, but when they saw "it clarin' up a little," they changed their minds.

The case of the Colonel illustrates the "ruling passion strong in death," but I have one which occurred in my own practice illustrating the same point, but where the ruling passion was not the love of money.

There was an old man in my county who had come there in a very early day—so early in fact that there were few whites in that region except the Presbyterian Missionaries to the Osage Indians at the old Harmony Mission on the Maries des Cygnes river.

His name was Mike.

At least Mike was his first name and that will do. Mike came from old Tennessee in his young married life and settled down here in the wilds of western Missouri with little except his strong arm and his determined courage with which to hew out his fortune.

He had a long back, short legs, long, muscular arms and a head as round as a cocoanut.

His weakness was fighting. Mike just dearly loved to contest disputed points with his fellow men with his two knotty fists. He was built for fighting and was a hard citizen to handle. If you happened to be in the county seat on a public day and would keep your eyes open along about three o'clock in the afternoon you would see men coming from all directions toward a certain point. Hurrying to this point you would see great clouds of dust rising so thick that you could see nothing but legs and arms whirling promiscuously in the air. After a while you would cease to see the legs and then if you would listen you could hear a sound like a dog chewing gristle.

Then the constable and a hastily summoned posse would rush into this mountain of dust and after a little while one man would come forth leading Mike and four others would come out carrying the other fellow. Mike would go and wash his bleeding nose or skinned cheek and then would be ready to "argue the question" in the same way with some one else. If they didn't "double teams" on him (and that was rare in those days) he was almost sure to be a victor.

Sometimes he would meet with a big fellow who would go at him with a rush and get him down and maul his cocoanut head into the dust or mud until he wore himself out and lost his wind, when Mike would get a thumb in his mouth, twist out, get on top and in a very few seconds after he begun to "work his machine" you would hear the muffled "Nuff" come from his opponent.

Mike never said "Nuff."

I do not think that he ever quoted or ever heard that "The Old Guard dies but never surrenders," for he was not a man who crystallized his thoughts and principles into short sentences of this kind; but he lived and fought on that principle. You might have pounded the life out of him but he wouldn't say "Nuff."

After one of Mike's fights he would go home and sober off (I forgot to say that Mike drank) and stick some pickings from an old fur hat on his wounds and go about his farm as quietly as a deacon. He was a good, quiet neighbor and was generous to a fault. His herds grew on the unlimited prairies and Mike prospered. He got to be one of the largest and best farmers in the county. After one of his fights he would not go to town for two or three months; but when he did go he was almost sure to get drunk and have two or three fights. This continued until Mike began to grow old, and, like all great fighters, he had to yield the belt to some one else. He gave up the championship grudgingly but he had to do it. He got used up badly once or twice by stronger men and so, concluding that "discretion is the better part of valor," Mike quit fighting. But he would come to town and get drunk and quarrel and incite others to fight; for Mike was not hoggish—if he couldn't do a thing himself he liked to see others do it.

After I had been practicing in this county several years Mike came to town on a public day in a two horse wagon and got drunk, as was his custom. He started home after dark, and, it is probable that he went to sleep on the spring seat of his wagon.

One of the front wheels ran into a rut and he tumbled over the wheel to the ground. His arm fell across the rut and the wagon wheels on that side ran over it and fractured it between the elbow and the shoulder. The horses took the wagon and went on home. Mike was too drunk and too much hurt to travel, so he lay upon the ground and slept and shivered through a frosty September night.

His family found the team at the front gate the next morning and at once came back in search of Mike. A friend of mine was sent for and went out and set the fracture. Within a day or two Mike developed a pneumonia and it was not many days until he seemed to be on the verge of death. A consultation was asked for and I was called in. I found the old warrior in great peril. His right lung was consolidated, his respiration bad, his pulse irregular and faltering and his temperature high.

Mike was sixty-five years old and the prognosis was unfavorable. My friend asked me to give my opinion, which was also his own, to the wife and mother of the household.

She was a good, kindly woman, a warm hearted Methodist and a splendid wife, mother and neighbor.

She had lived with this great fighting man and his tiger nature for more than forty years, had cooked his meals, done his washing, and bound up his wounds received in his "arguments" with his fellows. Nor was

Mike mean to her. He was too brave a man to strike a woman. Time and again had she urged him to quit his evil ways and try to be a Christian. Mike had always met these exhortations with grunts and got out of the way as soon as his legs could carry him.

He respected religion, and thought it was a good thing for women and children who were weak and couldn't fight; but for a strong man who could defend himself, Mike thought it was nonsense.

It was too much like "begging the question" and crying "Nuff" for him to have anything to do with it.

After I had given the good wife and mother my opinion of Mike's case, she asked me if I would not frankly tell him of his danger. She added:—

"I have tried time and again to get him to be a Christian. Since he has been sick I have asked him several times to let me read the scripture to him, but he will not let me. Doctor, please try to impress him with a sense of his danger. I don't want him to go in this way. He has always been so wicked and yet he has been a good, kind husband to me, and if he would only seek the Lord so that I could meet him in Heaven I would be so happy."

Then she burst into tears. After talking with the other doctor it was agreed that I should frankly tell "Uncle Mike" what we thought of his condition.

I went in and said:

"Uncle Mike, you are a very sick man."

"Yes, sir; I suppose I am."

"Well," I said, "I feel it my duty to tell you the

truth. You are sixty-five years old, you have a broken arm and after an all night's exposure you have pneumonia in one lung and there is a suspicion in our minds that the other is about to be invaded. If you have any unsettled business, either pertaining to the here or the hereafter you had better attend to it at once. We think that the chances are that you will die. Now, I don't want to scare you"—

"You can't scare me by——sir, you needn't say that."

"Pardon me, Uncle Mike, I know you are not a coward, but if you wish to make a will or have any unfinished business you had better attend to it at once."

With this I left him.

His wife—"Aunt Jane," as she was called—met me on the porch and asked me what he said.

I told her and she turned sadly away with disappointment in her face.

I continued to attend the case with my friend, and "Uncle Mike" grew better day by day. After his recovery was assured "Aunt Jane" told us the following story, and she laughed through streaming tears while telling it:

"On the afternoon after you had told my husband of his dangerous condition, I was sitting near his bed and watching him. He lay and looked up at one spot on the ceiling for about an hour. Then he turned his head and said:

"Jane, come here."

I went to his bed side and asked:

"What do you want, dear?"

He lay still a moment and then said in a choking voice:

"Jane, you-may get-that-book——and-read-some to me——if you—want to."

I was so pleased that I almost flew to the stand where the Bible was. I picked it up and went and sat down by the bed and wiped my spec's. I began reading from the first place I opened—for I have always heard that it was lucky to do that. I happened to open at the account of the stoning of Stephen. I read and spelled the story through as best I could—for I am not a good reader."

When I had finished, I noticed that my husband's face was flushed and the muscles were working. I felt happy, for I thought that, may be, the spirit was at work in his obdurate heart. He looked at me and said:

"Jane, read that again."

I slowly and carefully read the story again. As I went on and read about how the mob put upon Stephen and beat him, I could see my husband work his under jaw and draw his shoulders up and get more flushed in the face and I felt sure that he was about to be converted. When I came to where Stephen knelt down and prayed it seemed as if he could hardly keep himself in bed, and when I had finished he turned over on his splinted arm and raised the other up and clenched his fist and gritted his teeth and said:

"Jane, they were a set of d——d cowards to all

jump on to one man like that. If I'd a been there I'd a whipped a half dozen of the d——d, white livered cowards."

This was in accordance with Mike's principles, for, if he ever took part in other men's fights he always fought for the "bottom dog in the fight."

"Uncle Mike" recovered in spite of our unfavorable prognosis. Within a few years he joined the church, and for the last few years of his life he lived a quiet, sober and religious life, which made "Aunt Jane" so happy that she almost felt that she had been translated in the flesh.

They are both dead now and their bodies rest side by side, and it is reasonable to presume that, notwithstanding "Uncle Mike's" stormy and belligerent life here, he may be able to get along with the saints without a row. We have a foundation for this hope, when we know that "Uncle Mike" can not get drunk "Up There." And it is my sincere prayer, and the reader's,

"JANE, THEY WAS A SET OF D——D COWARDS."

I hope, that "Aunt Jane" is happy with this once stormy old warrior, but now quiet and blissful companion "on the evergreen shore."

CHAPTER XIV.

SHAM SUICIDES.

A STARTLING STATEMENT—THE YOUNG WIFE—THE JILTED GIRL AND THE DEADLY FLOUR—DR. EGGSLINGER—STORY OF THE WIDOW MINOR—THE REJECTED LOVER—HOW TO DETECT THE FRAUD.

IT may, perhaps, seem like a strong statement, coming as it does from a physician, when I say that out of the great number of cases of supposed poisoning—poison taken with a suicidal intent—to which a doctor is called, not more than one in four has really taken poison. I have run over all the cases to which I have been called within about twenty-three years and I find that the cases average about one each year, and out of these twenty-three cases there are five cases in which poison had really been taken with suicidal intent.

The reader will naturally inquire,

"Then what motives impel people to pretend to have done such a thing when the result could only be hurtful to themselves?"

The motives are as numerous and as foolish, dear

reader, as are the motives which impel poor, weak human beings to do other wrong and foolish things.

Let us see:

Here is a young woman whose parents are in moderate circumstances in life. She is reasonably well educated, is pretty, emotional, weak, vapid and hysterical, and to add to the difficulty, she reads the trashiest of trashy novels. In other words, she has cultivated a morbid element in her nature and you can not expect anything but morbid processes in morbid conditions.

A young man comes to see her—courts her in fact. He is young, handsome and, perhaps, bad. His station in life is above hers, so that whether he be true or false, some people will feel warranted in questioning his motives.

The poor girl loves him. She builds an air castle for the future which he and she are to occupy. They will have nothing to do, according to her romantic ways of thinking, but bask (these poor fools are always "basking" in something) in shady bowers and watch the sun throw rainbow tints through spurting fountains while they suck eternal and everlasting bliss through double straws.

Suddenly the young man quits coming. This is not the worst; he goes to see another girl and she finds it out. He avoids her on the street and at the sociable. This is a terrible disappointment to a weak and emotional nature. It is an awful shock to a romantic young girl who has builded so many rose-tinted air castles.

What shall she do?

She must win him back. He must return.

She puts her poor little wits to work to devise means by which she can influence him, and, foolish girl that she is, does the very thing that she ought not. But she is sensational and romantic, or nothing, and whatever she does must have the elements of a tragedy in it. She goes down town and purchases ten cents' worth of strychnia or morphia. Then she goes home and changes the poison for flour and, going into the presence of her mother and sister, she empties the flour into her mouth, takes a drink of water, and throwing herself into a tragic attitude says, "Oh, dear mother and sister I must die. I have taken poison," and then flops down on the sofa, shuts both eyes tightly and goes to foaming at the mouth. Of course the mother and sister are alarmed. The family physician or "any physician," is sent for in hot haste. He comes, and, whether ignorantly or not depends on circumstances, fills the miserable thing with whites of eggs and rancid grease and sits by her bedside all night. After a while she begins to show signs of returning consciousness; she rolls and moans and finally exclaims,

"Oh Henry! My Henry! Oh, don't let them kill my dear Henry! Bring him to me and I will die in his place."

Now this is a fine case of private theatricals. Perhaps Henry is sent for and perhaps not. At all events Henry is a rascal and he feels that he is in his very bones.

The morning paper announces that,

"We regret to learn that Miss Maude Cushaw, the beautiful and accomplished (these people are always beautiful and accomplished) daughter of our esteemed fellow townsman, Col. Cushaw, took a deadly poison with suicidal intent, but Dr. Eggslinger was called and after using the stomach pump (bah! Dr. Eggslinger never saw a stomach pump in his life) and the usual remedies her numerous friends will be glad to learn that the young lady is in a fair way to recover.

Dr. Eggslinger goes about quietly and bears his honors meekly, feeling that it is not every country practitioner who can save an accomplished young lady from the deadly effects of a full dose of XXX flour with a stomach pump (which he did not have) and the "usual remedies."

A young and childless wife grows jealous of her husband. He remains out late at night and seems to be growing cold and neglectful, and when she falls on his neck and takes the starch out of his shirt collar with her tears, he pushes her away and says "Oh, pshaw, Mary, you are foolish," and goes and gets a dry collar and then goes down town. She reads in the papers about the faithlessness of other men and she concludes that John must be faithless, too. The poor, loving thing almost breaks her heart in thinking and weeping, and her poor life becomes thoroughly miserable. She begins to cast about her for a remedy with which to win John back to his first love; and if she is emotional and reads trashy novels, it is ten to one she will try the "poison racket" as the remedy.

Sham Suicides.

Another woman has been doing wrong. She has gone in "by and forbidden ways" and at last gets caught. The newspaper writes her up without mercy and the town rolls the scandal as a sweet morsel under its ponderous, wagging tongue. The poor, guilty woman stands the strain for a day or two and then takes poison—*from the flour barrel.*

I had just such a case once. To the small town where I was practicing there came a widow of the grass variety—a regular hay mow. She was young and dashing, and while she was not beautiful, she was good looking and outdressed all the other women in town. She connected herself with a prominent church, plunged right into the middle of " our best society " with a " hop, skip, and a jump," and, in a short time, cut a swath like a self-raking reaper.

There were two young widowers suing for her hand, apparently, but a red nosed grocer got away with the prize. He had an enormous nose which always had the appearance of having been recently painted and varnished, and his eyes always looked as if they had been lined with red flannel and stitched on the sewing machine (*marginal blepharitis*).

The widow had rooms (in which she kept her millinery) at our principal hotel and George (the grocerman) was in the habit of spending his Sundays in the widow's "office." The jealous widowers peeped through the glass in the door and saw things too horrible to relate. Within an hour it was all over town and formed the theme for a ten day's gossip. On the next day a young man rushed into my office and breathlessly informed me that "Misses Minor has tuck pizen and they want you to go just as quick as you can get thar."

I went.

It was my first case of poisoning and I cudgeled my brain on the way as to what I should do.

Arriving at the room I found the widow on the bed with eyes shut tight and foaming at the mouth. She was surrounded by the kind hearted hotel keeper, his wife, and several other ladies—all wringing their hands and lamenting that such a thing should occur in our quiet and moral town. I felt of her pulse. It was seventy-six, soft and regular; pupils normal and responsive to the light. It was my first case and I was young, but I was wise enough to know that the widow was "actin' up." I asked who would most probably have brought her the poison, if she had really taken it. They all accused the grocer in one unanimous and concurrent breath. I sent for George and he came. His nose had taken on a real inflammatory hue and the red flannel hung over the edges of the free borders of the lids a little more than usual. I questioned him and he swore by the memory of all the saints that he had brought her nothing. This confirmed my diagnosis. But I must save the poor widow's reputation. She had suffered enough for permitting George, with his erysipelatous proboscis and his carmine optics, to take off his shoes and coat and lie down on the bed (for that was all that had been seen) while she sat and lovingly kept the flies off him. The flies were always lighting on and inspecting

George's nose and looking into his flaming orbs, and any good milliner might have been permitted to keep them away without compromising herself. George's nose might spoil if they were permitted to invade it and that would be terrible.

I said, so that all could hear me (and I especially wanted the widow to hear me):

"I don't think this lady has taken anything. I am not acquainted with her, but she looks like too sensible a woman to commit self destruction. Her mind and nervous system have been put to a great strain in consequence of these ugly stories, and it has thrown her into a state of catalepsy, but she will come out all right. However, I always give the patient the benefit of the doubt and shall, therefore, give her an emetic."

I mixed up a solution of *Tartar emetic* and *epicac* (a most abominable compound) and put a teaspoonful in her mouth. She worked it out. I put in another, covered her mouth with my hand and held her nose between my thumb and index finger. The milliner hesitated and then—swallowed. I repeated the dose every five minutes. After the third dose the milliner began to turn white around the mouth and great beads of perspiration stood on her forehead. She got limber and then she made a plunge for the bed side. I was prepared for this and received her with applause and a wash basin. It was not long until the first act was *encored* and the *encore* was repeated. Then the milliner began to mutter. I knew she was "coming to." I would have given her more of the vile stuff, but she had already thrown up her immortal soul and I thought enough was enough. My partner having arrived I sent everybody else out of the room. As the widow had been paddling for more than an hour in the disagreeable and uncertain waters of assumed unconsciousness I wished to give her a chance to come ashore. She muttered some more, and then talked:

"Oh, father, dear father,"

"Come home with me now," I added in an "aside" to my partner.

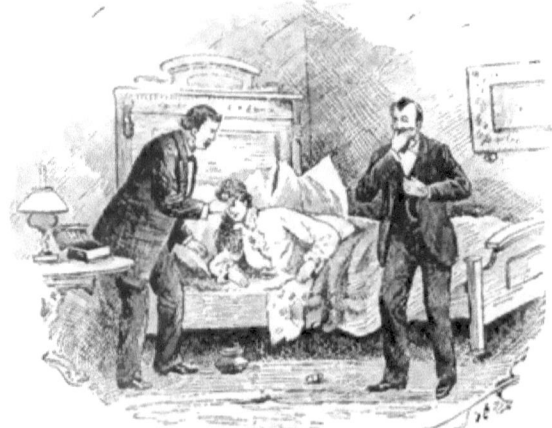

I RECEIVED HER WITH APPLAUSE AND A WASH BASIN.

"They have been pilin' big rocks on your Ophelia."

"Ophelia! ye gods, this is high tragedy," in another aside

"Oh, father, come"

("where my love lies dreaming," aside)

"And take your poor child home."

Then she did the finest piece of acting I ever saw on or off the stage.

As I was lifting her back after one of her ineffectual attempts to *start the plantar fascia*, she suddenly opened her eyes and then, with a startled look and drawing in her breath and lifting her hands deprecatingly, she exclaimed:

"Oh, you are not father; who are you?"

'No, I am not father, I am just father *pro tem*. Lie down, my dear, you'll take cold."

The widow recovered, sold out her millinery in bulk and went out in the country to remain a while with a kind family which belonged to that branch of the church which had championed her cause. About a month afterward they began to tire of her and informed her that they could not keep her longer. On that night I received an urgent call to go out and see her as she was supposed to be dying. I knew that she was not, but I went out. On arriving at the place I was met at the door by the kind hearted lady of the house (a most noble and beautiful character of a good, religious wife and mother) who was trembling and weeping. She hurriedly told me that she had that afternoon told the widow that she could not keep her longer; soon afterward the widow had dumped herself on the lounge, set her teeth and foamed at the mouth, and, she had not spoken a word since and the good lady was afraid she would die. I soon calmed her fears and went into the presence of the supposed to be dying woman.

I wished to do what talking I had to do in the presence of the patient. The lady asked:

"Doctor, do you think she will die?"

"Oh, no," I answered, "she is in a peculiar nervous condition called catalepsy. You remember that she had a similar attack at the hotel, but I soon brought her out of it. I have a remedy which will vomit and relax her, and, in a few minutes, she will be all right. Now I knew that I was not going to get to repeat that nauseous dose in the widow's case. No person ever wants to take that dose twice.

But I began to mix the dose and then the widow began to grind her teeth and mutter. I knew she was preparing to come ashore before taking the medicine. I continued to stir the dose and talk to the lady of the house about catalepsy and the rapid action of the drug. After a few minutes she opened her eyes, gazed wanderingly around, fastened her gaze on me and asked with a surprised voice:

"Why, good evening, doctor, where did you come from?"

"Oh, I dropped right down from Heaven—came to minister to the suffering."

I announced that it would not be necessary to give the remedy since she had come out of the cataleptic state without it.

The widow soon flitted away beyond my horizon and went—the Lord only knows where. But, if she be living and her eyes ever read this story I wish to apologize to her for having given her the abominable dose. I had been taught by older heads that it was the proper thing to do in cases of hysteria and of persons making pretense when there was nothing the matter. The advice was very bad and my action altogether wrong. Doctors should be ministers of healing and therefore have no right to administer punishment. No matter how reprehensible the action of the patient the doctor should remember that it is his province to come with healing in his hands, in his voice, in his every act.

We should learn to look leniently on all such cases, for they must necessarily come from morbid conditions of either mind or body. I would much rather be loved for my kindness and tenderness toward a poor, miserable wretch than to be hated for my cruelty. It is our duty, when alone with such patients to speak very plainly to them and to give them to understand that we are not deceived (for none of us like to be taken for fools) but whatever we do and whatever we say should be said and done in great kindness.

Poor weak women are not the only ones who are capable of and liable to do such foolish things. Men often persuade themselves that they can move upon the feelings of a loved one or excite the sympathy of the community by foolishly pretending to have taken a deadly drug.

I was called one night to see a young man who was supposed to have become suddenly insane. I found him in an open lot adjoining his father's residence, with this history:

He had come home from the residence of a most excellent young lady, who had repeatedly told him that she could not marry him. On this night she had emphasized the statement and had succeeded in convincing him that she was in earnest. Feeling provoked in some way he suddenly swore at his mother and then informed her that he had taken poison, and when the father arose to go after me the young man drew his revolver and fired at him. He then retreated into this open lot where he remained in seeming great agony, but kept every body at bay with a revolver.

I found an excited crowd surrounding this lot, parleying with the young man and trying to devise ways

I MADE THE MOST GALLANT AND HEROIC CHARGE OF MY LIFE.

and means for his capture. He would listen to nothing, but kept the crowd terrorized by occasionally firing over their heads. Lariating him was suggested, forming a company of cavalry and riding him down, etc., etc.

During all this time the young man seemed in great agony—doubling up and groaning, lying down and rolling and eating ice and snow which he scraped up with an oyster can. I finally said that if the crowd would attract his attention I would go around the back way and charge him from the rear. This I did, making the most gallant and heroic charge of my life, as I then supposed, to save an erring fellow mortal. He heard me, however, fired at me as I came and then arose to a knee and hand posture. I fell over him and sprained my ankle and hip. He got up first and seizing my "plug" hat which had fallen in the fray, he cast it up and neatly put a bullet hole in it while I was getting up. I got my perforated plug and made a hasty retreat. I then became satisfied that he was shamming. A few minutes afterward he assumed a sitting posture and raising his left arm he pointed his pistol diagonally across his breast and fired; the bullet perforating the uplifted outer border of his left *pectoralis major muscle*.

He was quickly carried to the house and, upon close examination, I decided that he had taken nothing. He at once inquired for the young lady. That settled it. He continued his threats to the family, however, and the father turned the case over to me to deal with as I thought best. I put him in jail without a warrant "in one time and three motions." Twenty-four hours made him as docile as an Alderney heifer, and, upon his promising to behave, I let him out. He left the country, married another girl, and did well.

Sitting in a drug store one Sunday afternoon a branch water man came in looking for a doctor. The druggist directed him to me. He represented the extreme type of the branch water man. He looked as if he had just bought a complete outfit from a rag man. His hat was greasy, old and torn and his trousers sagged miserably at the base. He was unacquainted with soap and an entire stranger to disinfectants.

He informed me that he wanted me to go and see a sick man at the "Junction House" just as quick as I could "git thar." I inquired as to the man's symptoms. He didn't know anything except that the man was "awful sick." I further insisted and informed him that I might want to take something with me.

'Well," said he, at last, and as if he was being compelled to divulge a lodge secret, "ef I must tell you, they say he tuck assnic."

"How much arsenic did he take?"

"Well, they say he tuck a half pint."

I informed him that if his friend had taken a half pint of this deadly drug I thought he would be ready for the compost heap in a short time. I instinctively knew, however, that the man had done no such thing. The "Junction House" was a regular hive for this class of people and I never knew one of them to commit suicide in my life. It is a pity they do not.

Reaching the house I found the lower halls and stairways lined with women and children. Entering the room I found it full of worthless men, and "Nat, the fiddler" on a rickety bed. As soon as he saw me he arose to a sitting posture and blaring his eyes and throwing his hands up and down he uttered an "oo-ah, oo-ah, oo-ah, oo-ah." Two men jumped on him and bore him, by main strength, to the bed and there held him tight and fast.

I interfered and ordered them to let him alone.

" Why," said one, " ef we don't hold him he'll butt his brains out."

"Let him butt them out," said I, " he don't need them."

If hysterical men and women, who are putting on airs, were left alone they would soon subside ; but, it seems that there never was a man who acted the fool who didn't have a fool to hold him. And the same may be said of women.

I learned, incidentally, that Nat had recently gone away with a newly organized variety show, in which a young woman, noted more for the scantiness rather than the richness of her apparel, was the principle attraction. Nat went along to furnish the music. The company had taken in about four towns when it collapsed. This left Nat with his violin high and dry, without a cent and ninety miles from home. He pawned his fiddle and coat for victuals. He got a " tie pass " and when he reached home found another fellow occupying his place in his household; and his wife, feeling that Nat had been too much of a worshipper at the feet of Bessie (she of the scanty apparel) refused to permit him to enter. Nat beat about the bush and " slept with the out-hogs " for a few days and then went on a spree.

This pretended attempt to take poison was the result of the spree.

The newspapers wrote him up in good style, basing

their strictures of his conduct upon my statement that it was not poison. Nat went to the office and tried to convince the editor that he had taken poison. I then had the paper state that Nat had the same reasons for committing suicide now that he had before with the additional reason that a majority of the people in town thought that he had made an ass of himself ; that I had ten grains of strychnia weighed out which I would give him upon application, and would agree to lock the doors and keep everybody out until it acted.

He didn't come and get it.

It may be said that a physician should not expose a patient under such circumstances.

Under some circumstances, no; under others, yes. When a certain kind of men and women try to play a sensational role and lacerate the feelings of a sensitive and kind hearted people by a pretense and a fraud, then I think that no good and honorable physician is bound to lend himself or become a party to such frauds. Let the truth come and hit them hard.

It is easy enough to detect these frauds, as a general thing. Any physician ought to know that a poison which is so deadly and instantaneous in its effects as to cause the patient to fall down immediately after swallowing it, should kill at once, and before he could possibly reach the patient. Again, a poison which affects the general system so suddenly and so seriously should put almost every muscle in the body in a state of semi-paralysis. In such a case the eyes would be open or partly open. In most cases the pupils should be affected—

either dilated or contracted. The pulse should, as a rule, be weak and rapid. In many cases there should be vomiting or retching. It is also important to know whether the patient fell on a bed or lounge, or on the floor or ground. Real suicides do not choose soft places on which to fall.

If the patient is pretending he or she will, almost surely, shut the eyes very tight and when the physician attempts to open them for inspection, there will be *voluntary muscular resistance*.

Now, with close-shut eyes, pulse at seventy or eighty, no dilatation or contraction of the pupils, the extremities warm and the addition of a *motive* for this kind of acting (if you can get at the motive) you may rely on it that, in nine cases out of ten, you will be safe in saying that the patient has taken nothing that will kill her. It may not always be best to say that the patient is pretending, and this more especially in the case of young girls. It is not necessary to tell the crowd anything, except that she will not die. But, do not hesitate to tell her parents; and, as soon as the girl will consent to talk, make her understand that you are not deceived—for she will respect you the more when she knows that you are not. It may not be out of place in such cases to deliver a kind, but firm lecture to the young woman regarding the wickedness and foolishness of her conduct. If done right it will do good.

CHAPTER XV.

LIARS AND THEIR LIES.

GENERAL OBSERVATIONS ON LYING—CLASSIFICATION OF LIARS—BILL WHITTINGTON AND A SAMPLE OF HIS LIES—SIM'S UNFAIR TRICK—THE STORY OF THE BULLIES—JACK, THE BARBER, AND RAFFERTY'S FUNERAL—A GREAT SHOT AND A FAST TROTTER—DO DOCTORS LIE? SEVERAL SAMPLES WHICH ANSWER THE QUESTION—AN ASYLUM FOR LIARS.

IT is a puzzling thing, to any one who has studied humanity to any extent, that there are so many liars in the world. Children are taught in school that "truth is mighty and will prevail;" that lying is sinful and that his Satanic Majesty—the engineer and fireman who runs the heating and drying department in the basement of the Hereafter—is the father of liars. Notwithstanding this the world is just swarming with liars all the time. We are a nation of liars, and I had about concluded that we were the only nation in existence that enjoyed this unenviable distinction, until I made the acquaintance of many people of other climes, and then I changed my mind. All nations have their liars and many of them.

It is curious to note the reasons and motives that men have for lying. One man will tell a lie from a motive and a standpoint that will make his neighbor ashamed, and yet that neighbor will turn around and tell a lie from some other motive and never feel ashamed at all.

Women are not great liars. That is, the proportion of women who lie is not as great as that which pertains to the male population. Women are more refined, and more timid—many of them are afraid to lie, and yet when a woman does lie she makes it count. She means to hurt some one and the chances are that she will.

Did you ever note the different kinds of liars? Here are some of them:

The *accidental liar* is a man who tells a lie because he forgets the truth. He is telling a story or relating a circumstance and, suddenly, his memory fails him on a given point. There is a gap that must be filled or the story is ruined. He goes to work at once and fills it with something larger than the thing he forgot. A lie is generally bigger than the truth; that is, it seems bigger, or, in other words, a lie about a given thing is bigger than the truth is about the same matter.

Then we have the *malicious liar*. He or she is the fellow or fellowess who tells a lie to injure some one's reputation. Fortunately for the world there are not many of them. It is a rare thing that any man or woman invents a lie, "out of whole cloth" for the purpose of injuring another. But it is done, and sometimes with success. If a woman lies—and she does not often do so, God bless her!—she is more apt to be a *malicious liar* than is a man. Some of the most hurtful lies I have ever encountered have been told by women.

Then we have the *selfish liar*. He tells lies for selfish reasons. He does not wish to hurt others, but he desires to help himself along in the world. He will lie about business matters; he will lie about politics; he will lie about anything that will give him pennies or position. He may be a good fellow, but he is greedy and craving, and just throws in a lie now and then to help himself along and keep things moving.

The *boasting liar* is the most numerous and the least harmful of the lot. This is the fellow who has done such wonderful things in his time, and has seen such miraculous performances "back yonder, where I came from." He has worked at everything and done some things in all trades and lines of business, and has always excelled and startled his friends with his superior skill and tact, and yet he is poor. I have sat down and heard these fellows tell of the different trades they have worked at and the different lines of business they had been in, and the number of years they had followed each one and have quietly taken down the number of these years, and I have then gone off and added the figures together and found that the man was, by his own admission, at least one hundred and sixty-five years old. In the presence of the boasting liar you can not speak of a dog fight, a big fish, a strong man, or a big tree without the fear of hearing one of his lies. It does no good to protest against the lies of this fellow, for, if you do so, you only put him to the trouble of going through the form of swearing to them without the notary. The redeeming feature of this man is that he is nearly always a pleasant man in his profession of champion liar. You may go to work and make up as big a lie as you please—just concoct a "whopper," in order to beat him and he will sit and listen to you with all the patience of an attentive and interested auditor—never indicating by sign, word or look that he does not believe you. Nor does he interrupt you, and when you are done he will ask you for a chew of tobacco, clear his throat, change his position a little, and smile—then say: "That reminds me."

Now you may look out. He has been pleasant and deferential to you. He expects the same treatment from you. You may now prepare for defeat, for the boasting liar will never suffer defeat so long as he can get to tell the last story. Strange to say, the boasting liar tells many of his lies until there is no doubt that he finally believes them himself. This liar has his stock in trade which he retails—and wholesales if occasion requires—at all times, but he will invent a special lie for a special occasion. He will invent a lie this way and, perhaps, never tell it again.

For instance, I was in a group of gentlemen once and the subject of the conversation was the curious results of wounds—of men wounded so seriously that it would seem they must die, and yet they would get well; and of others wounded so slightly it seemed scarcely worthy of attention and yet they would die. As an illustration I gave an instance of a Federal Cap tain who was shot through the right lung with a grape shot at the battle of Lexington, Mo., and who recovered, and of another man who got a small pistol ball in the wrist and died, "and," I added, "the extremes are even greater than this, for men have died from getting a tomato seed in the *appendix vermiformis.*" There was a man standing by whom I had never seen, and whom I would not have judged to be a liar, who spoke up and said,

"Yes, stranger, it is just as you say. It is queer how those fellows will get well after such serious accidents. Now I was standing in our town (it was the capital of his state) talking to some gentlemen once. There was a fellow painting the roof of a five story building just across the way and we were watching him. All of a sudden his foot slipped and he skeeted off that roof and came toward the side-walk like a flying squirrel. When he struck on the hard granite you could have heard it a quarter of a mile. We all rushed to his assistance but before we could reach him he got up and shook himself, climbed back up the ladder and went to painting again. He wouldn't even stop to tell us how he felt."

There was a moment's silence and then the little crowd quietly dispersed. They were all good Christian men and no one struck him. I really believe the fellow thought I was lying about the grape shot and the tomato seed and was trying to "lay over me."

I knew one of those fellows once amongst the western pioneers. He was a branch water man. He lived in a cabin that would have made a Digger Indian ashamed of himself, and if he ever worked any nobody knew when he did it. Yet, with the aid of his rifle and his wife he lived, and was one of the happiest mortals I ever knew. His wife wove and spun the wearing apparel of the family and she generally managed to get her jeans out in the spring—being five months late—and her home made linen in the autumn, so that Bill (his name was Bill Whittington) always wore his linen through the winter and his white undyed jeans in the summer. The shifts that family would make as to clothes was remarkable. Bill had a grown son, and one winter, I remember, he was not able to buy but one pair of men's shoes. So he and his son each took a shoe and tied up the other foot and went lame all winter. Bill was lame in his left foot and his son in the right.

BILL WAS LAME IN HIS LEFT FOOT AND HIS SON IN THE RIGHT.

Bill was not accomplished in but one industry and that was lying. He hunted a little—just enough to keep the family in meat and to take a deer skin to "the store" occasionally to get some article of family necessity. He had really never done anything but lie and hunt in his life, yet he would tell of the most marvelous things that he had done. He had been a merchant, a steam boat captain, a Mississippi pilot, an architect and builder—in short, almost everything. He would sit down and tell with the most astonishing gravity about having built a house for a wealthy friend in the state from which he came. The man had unlimited wealth and just gave him *carte blanche* for materials without regard to cost. When Bill finished the house, in which there were twenty-five rooms, it was a marvel of perfection and beauty. The wood-work could be used for mirrors and the floors were polished so that they reflected the walls and all that hung upon them.

The fellow couldn't put a papaw handle in a garden hoe and do it well. Bill would sit up and tell these stories in the presence of his wife (who had known him from his childhood) and never smile.

The subject of wells was mentioned once. Some one spoke of a very deep well which he had seen. This was a "starter" for Bill. He said the deepest well he ever saw was dug by himself and his brother "back yonder where I came from." A man had hired them to dig a well during a dry year, when the water was scarce, and had agreed to pay them so much per foot until water was struck. They started in and dug and dug, and yet no water. They put in better hoisting machinery and continued to dig, but still no moisture. After several months' work they got so deep that it consumed a great portion of their time in going down of mornings and coming up at night. Then they arranged to remain in the well day and night and had their provisions let down to them by the returning tubs which hauled up the dirt. They had a convenient arrangement of ropes, bells and signals by which they made all their wants known to those working on the outside.

"After we had been in thar for several months," said Bill, " we was workin' along one afternoon—I guess it must have been about three o'clock—and all at once when I struck my pick in the bottom it sounded holler I spoke to my brother about it and he tried it, and, sure enough, it sounded holler agin. We thought we was a comin' to a river and so we got down and listened and what do you reckon we heard?"

"Running water," said everybody.

"No, sir!" said Bill, "No, sir! I wish it had a been; but, I'm dad blasted if we didn't hear people a talking on the other side of the yeth."

"What were they saying, Bill?"

"How could I tell? They wasn't like us, and was a talkin', some sort of outlandish jingle.'

"Well, you dug right through on to them, did you, Bill?"

"No siree. You wouldn't ketch me doing no big fool thing like that. I couldn't understand a word they said, but I could tell by the way they was a ravin' around that they was all-fired mad about somethin' and I didn't want to drop down on 'em when they was mad. They might a killed a feller."

"No sir. We just pulled the rope that rung the bell for 'em to haul us up and they did. It took an awful long time though for 'em to get us up."

"What did the man do with the well, Bill?"

"Filled it up, of course. Me and my brother got the job and made a lot of money out of it; for you can just bet they was acres of dirt piled around thar."

I never knew Bill to get beaten at his own game but once and then a mean advantage was taken of him. He had a neighbor named Sim—something. Sim was industrious but full of fun and mischief. He and a neighbor were "swapping work" in corn planting time. On this particular occasion the neighbor was over at Sim's helping him put in his corn. Bill Whittington had a habit of going around where his neighbors were at work and detaining and entertaining them with his lies. Along in the afternoon as Sim and his neighbor came to the end of the row whom should they see but Bill, sitting on the fence? They had been pushing things all day and were tired, so they sat down for awhile and Bill at once began to tell lies. The subject of strong men— great fighters and wrestlers—happened to be the theme. Bill had told of some marvelous feats of strength performed by himself, his brother or some relative.

"I have seen stronger men than that," remarked Sim.

"You have?" said Bill in surprise, "what did they do?"

"It was in Kentucky," Sim began, "when I was growing up. There was a man in our county that they called "the bully." He had thrown down and whipped every man who laid any claims to strength in our county. He was "the bully" of the county and no man lived there who dared to meet him. There was just such another man in the second county from us. He had cleaned out everybody in his county. The friends of those two bullies had been at work for a long time trying to arrange a "pitched battle" between them. At last they got it arranged and the day set for the two men to meet in the county that intervened. They were to meet at the county seat on a certain day and the thing got advertised all over the country for several counties around. Expectation was on tiptoe and everybody was going to see the fight. All the male population of our county went over to back our man. They arrived at the town where the fight was to take place the evening before and camped out. The other fellow and his county men camped on the opposite side of the town and the people from other counties were camped all around for two or three miles. It was like a big army. Oh, there was an awful lot of excitement. Everybody was up and had breakfast bright and early so as to get into town and get a good place where the fight was to be. The time was arranged when both should start into town so that they should meet at the Court House about the same time. Our man took the lead and walked into town and our whole county followed him. The other did the same. As they went in our man began to bellow like a bull and the other fellow heard him. Then you ought to have heard the other fellow bellow. Why it just cracked the window lights. That made our man mad and then you may just reckon that he did bellow. The chimneys began to fall down. When the other fellow heard him he was just opposite where an old mill had burned down and the mill stones

'AND THREW HIM CLEAR OVER THE COURT HOUSE.

were lying there. He was so mad that he just grabbed a mill stone in each hand and came up to the Public Square knocking them together over his head. His men were yelling and our fellows began to feel bad. Just then our man came up to where a farmer was exhibiting an imported English bull that weighed twenty-one hundred pounds. He had seen the other fellow knocking the mill stones over his head and he was roaring mad. He jumped at this bull and before anybody had time to think he grabbed him by the tail and just jerked him up and swung him around his head three or four times and threw him clear over the court house and knocked off the second story of a saloon on the other side."

Then Sim paused.

Bill had been listening with rapt attention all the time, and you couldn't have told by any movement, nod or gesture that he made, but what he really believed it all. This is the courtesy that a big liar always pays another big liar. Sim stood up and didn't seem to be going on with the story. Bill grew anxious, and asked,

"What did they do then, Sim?"

"Well, a mule got between them and me just then and I couldn't see 'em," said Sim. "Git up Ball," said he to his old horse and away he went across the field "laying off" his furrow.

They left Bill sitting in the corner of the fence almost paralyzed with surprise. In all his lying life no man had ever treated him so before.

After a while he seemed to recover a little and he slowly got up from his sitting position. He climbed on the fence in a bewildered sort of stagger; then looked wistfully after Sim and the neighbor for a moment, slid off the fence and went shambling away. He was so disgusted that he actually absented himself from society for two weeks.

We meet this kind of man everywhere, and he is not confined to any particular stratum in society.

There used to be a barber in the town where I lived who was one of the worst of the boasting liars that I ever met. His name was Jack. Jack used to soothe me with his marvelous lies while shaving me. Jack had one abiding weakness besides his lying and that was that he harbored the delusion that he had once been a government scout, a detective and finally a Chicago policeman. He had been three times captured by the Confederates during the late war (it is doubtful whether he was in the war at all), had been tried, condemned to be shot—the hour set. Each time, by some marvelous interposition or some shrewd act of his own, he had escaped. I used to listen with a great deal of quiet attention to Jack's lies and, occasionally put in a question which would compel Jack to tell more lies which he used as a sort of "rip-rap" to preserve the foundation of the original lie. I used to speak of Jack's wonderful lies in the presence of my little boys, until one of them conceived a desire to hear Jack in his great *role*. I took him down with me one afternoon when I was going to be shaved. He pulled up a chair near where I sat while being shaved and seemed to take a great deal of interest in watching Jack work.

I knew how to set Jack off. It was much easier than work I had to do every day. All I had to do was to make a remark, a suggestion, or ask a question.

There was a funeral procession passing the shop and I remarked that Judge So-and-so was having a very largely attended funeral. I knew that would be sufficient and so it proved to be.

"Large!" said Jack, in astonishment. "Do you call that a large funeral?"

"Yes," I said, "that is quite a large funeral for this town,"—and so it was.

"Oh, but you ought to have seen Rafferty's funeral in Chicago," said Jack.

Jack was getting up steam and the machinery was beginning to move. It would only take a few questions to set him running in good style.

Who was Rafferty? What did he do to entitle him to such a remembrance?

Jack steadied himself, strapped his razor, and started in.

"Rafferty had once been on the 'force' but had been dismissed for drinking, or something else, and, while he was very brave and had once been very popular, he had got to drinking and had become a bad and dangerous man. One day while bordering on a fit of 'tremens' he had run amuck at a saloon and had either stabbed or shot two or three men. One had surely died and perhaps two—I forget now, but Rafferty made his escape."

Jack continued:

"I was on the secret force at the time and the Chief told me to take one man and go out in a certain direction, along a certain line of railroad. I went out about four miles and couldn't hear anything of him. I sat down on the end of a tie and was thinking as to what I should do, when a farmer's wagon came along. I asked the farmer if he had seen such a man as Rafferty—describing him. The farmer said that he hadn't seen any such person; but, there was something in his maṇner which, to my experienced eye, made me suspicious."

"I presume that a person like me would never have noticed it, would he, Jack?" I asked.

"Naw," said Jack, "You'd a let him go; but, I went up to the wagon and looked in and there lay Rafferty in the bottom of the wagon bed. As soon as he saw me he threw up his hands and said:

"'It's all right, Jack, old boy; I give up, for I know it's no use to resist, but there ain't another man in Chicago that can take me.'"

"He would have resisted me?" I suggested.

"Resisted you!" said Jack with a flavor of contempt in his voice, "He would have killed you before you could have cocked your pistol."

Thus encouraged, Jack went on:

"We took him back to town and put him in jail. There was an awful prejudice against him among a certain class, but still he had lots of friends. He lay in in jail a long time. Finally his case came up to trial. He had three of the best criminal lawyers of Chicago for his counsel with Bill O'B—— at their head. They hung the jury and there was a long wait and then another trial and another hung jury. This was repeated the third time and then the prosecuting attorney took a change of venue to Milwaukee, Wisconsin. There the jury found him guilty of murder in the first degree. The day was set for him to be hung and they brought him back to Chicago to hang him. By this time the popular indignation had about died out and Rafferty's friends were hot. They appealed to the Governor, but it did no good. They finally hung him and the day was set for the funeral. There were seven hundred big carriages and eighteen hundred buggies in the procession."

I do not know that I give the number of carriages and buggies just as Jack gave them, but, I remember that I went home and, with the assistance of my little son, figured up the length of the procession. By assuming that each team and vehicle covered a certain number of feet, and, allowing so many feet between each, it made the procession a little over twenty-seven miles long. At the ordinary funeral pace it would have taken the procession two days to pass a given point.

"Brush here," yelled Jack, and he no doubt, told equally as big a lie to the next customer. Jack was an artist.

Every grade of humanity—educated and uneducated, rich and poor—has its liar. The boasting lies only seem the more ridiculous when coming from a man like Bill Whittington—the branch water man—who seems too trifling and unimportant to do any of the things which he claims to have done.

I was called to see the family of a wealthy farmer once with whom I had only a slight acquaintance and of whom I had heard very little. I remained all night. There were several people at his house besides the family, and, as the patient was resting well and in no danger, we all gathered in the capacious sitting room and talked unreservedly about anything and everything that came up. The old farmer began by telling about his remarkable shooting; of how he had "taken fellows down" who came out from the city to shoot. He killed birds on the wing with the rifle after they had missed with the shot gun, and had put twelve shots in succession, with a colt's revolver, through an inch auger hole, at a distance of forty yards.

Here I began to doubt. The subject changed to horses and the question of trotters and fast records came up. He stated positively that he brought a colt from Tennessee, when he came to Missouri, which he trained himself, and which trotted a mile in 1.14. This was at the time when Dexter's 2.17¼ was the fastest recorded time. I was posted on the trotting question, and so asked the old gentleman if he was not mistaken—wasn't it 3.14? He was indignant in a moment.

"Don't I know what I am talking about? Didn't I lay the line that measured the ground? Didn't I hold the watch when the horse made the record?"

I apologized and went to bed, convinced that my new patron was a gifted, able and monstrous liar, as well as one of the best of husbands, fathers and neighbors, however inconsistent this statement may seem.

"Do doctors lie?"

Well, yes, occasionally. That is to say, natural

liars sometimes study medicine. The liar gets into the medical profession, as he gets into all professions and trades. Heaven is, perhaps, the only place where the liar can not enter, and, I am led to hope that some of those good natured, big hearted and harmless liars may enter even there. The liar spoken of in the scriptures may be the man who tells lies that do harm and make mischief.

When you do meet a doctor who is a liar (and I am proud to say that a somewhat extended and intimate acquaintance with the profession leads me to the declaration that the profession of medicine has as few liars as any other) but, I was about to say, when you do meet a doctor who lies, he generally takes it out in telling lies about the wonderful things he has done in the fields of medicine and surgery.

A young doctor in hunt of a place stopped in my town, a few years ago, and made my office his lounging place for a week. I was led to suspect, from some statements he made, that he was probably not an ardent devotee of the truth; but as our acquaintance was short I had no chance to verify my suspicions. He settled in a small town only a short distance from me and only a few weeks after he was located I met him on the street in my town in a slightly intoxicated condition. I asked him how he was getting along in his new situation.

"Oh, everything is booming. No trouble at all about getting practice; had a couple of surgical operations a week ago in which I would have liked to have had your assistance, but didn't have time to send for you."

I asked,

"What were the operations?"

"One was a disarticulation at the hip joint and the other was an ovariotomy. Both cases are doing well and are progressing rapidly toward recovery."

I asked him who assisted him and he answered,

"Two old women in both cases."

He didn't even own an amputating case.

He lied himself out of that town in just nine weeks.

One man, who was otherwise a good fellow, told me of having performed the Cesarean Section in a lonely cabin without professional help, at midnight and with no other instruments than a pocket case, and saved both mother and child. He would not even open an ordinary boil, nor lance a felon, and yet he desired to be considered a surgeon. This desire to be a surgeon by men who do not know anatomy and who have no mechanical tact, is the one crowning weakness of the profession. It is better, however, never to attempt a grave operation when you are not qualified, and just take it out in lying about it, than it is to attempt it, do a bungling job and then feel *compelled* to lie about it. There is a choice even in the kind of lies a man ought to tell. *Lying on the safe side is best.*

The war of the Rebellion turned out a great many of this class of surgeons at its close. It is true that there were many good surgeons in both armies. But there were a great many who learned to cut off arms, legs, toes and fingers—and sometimes cut them off when they might have been saved, I fear—and most of this class came home full fledged surgeons—in their own minds. I remember that it was a very common thing, just after the war, to see this appended to a doctor's card or newspaper advertisement: "Special attention given to surgery;" and this by a man who did not know a *lipoma* from a *carcinoma*, and who could not tell the differential diagnostic signs between a dislocation at the hip joint and a fracture of the upper third of the thigh bone. Some of these men did a great deal of mischief in their surgical pretensions, and it has taken the twenty-five years that have elapsed since the war to demonstrate in many such cases that there is a decided difference between a butcher and a surgeon.

One of these would-be surgeons told me once that while in the army, and just after a battle, he came across a soldier lying on the road side and bleeding dangerously from a wound about the face. It was of a character that satisfied him at once that nothing less than ligating the *common carotid* artery would do any good. He was without assistance of any kind; but, he got down and, single-handed and alone, without help or anæsthetics, he ligated the *common carotid*. He sent some soldiers to see about the man and then, in the multiplicity of important duties, forgot the case. Six days afterward he met the man carrying his gun and doing duty.

There was a pause at this point in the story. I suggested that the appearance of the atmosphere indicated a change of the weather. This was dangerous ground too; for I was really afraid that he would tell a lie about the weather. But he didn't. I think he took the hint, however.

I was sitting in my office a few years ago with an old physician who was looking for a location, and four other gentlemen, when the question of *animal ligatures* was mentioned, and the visiting brother told the following remarkable story:

"When I was about twenty-one years of age and just out of school, and, before I studied medicine, I manifested some weakness of my lungs. Upon the advice of our family physician my father determined to send me south. In order to make the expense as light as possible and that I might improve the faster, he procured a position for me with some Government surveyors. I improved from the start and was soon strong and hearty. After a while we got far out from the settlements about one hundred miles west of where the city of Waco now stands. One day a companion and I were out hunting—he being on foot and I on a pony. We became separated along in the afternoon, and, while wandering around looking for game, I heard the report of a gun about four hundred yards away. I galloped up to the top of the nearest hill in the direction of the sound. When I reached a point where I could command a view of the surrounding prairie I beheld my comrade, about two hundred yards away, engaged in a hand to hand fight with a stalwart Indian.

I put my horse to his full speed and went toward them. I soon took in the situation. They had met and the Indian had made some threatening or warlike demonstration and had drawn my comrade's fire. He had fallen, or dodged a bad shot, and had then attacked him with a large knife. The contest which I witnessed consisted simply in adroit efforts of the Indian to stab him and in desperate efforts of my comrade to keep him off and avoid his blows. I yelled at the top of my voice as I went toward them and the Indian, hearing me, gave a last desperate lunge at him and then ran away. I fired at him as he ran, but missed him.

"I soon saw that my comrade was badly cut, and upon examination I found a deep cut in his left side, about six inches in length, through which the gashed intestines were protruding. I tried to put him on the pony but he was too weak to ride alone. I then tried to get him up before me but could not do it. I finally got him across the saddle (head on one side and heels on the other) and lashed him on with the lariat. I led the pony, and after a weary tramp, landed him in the camp about three miles distant. Arriving there a consultation was held. As we were so far from civilization we decided to send to a Catholic Mission ninety miles away for a priest who had learned something of surgery while preparing for the office of a Missionary priest. It was our only hope, for we had no idea as to where we could find a surgeon. Two men were sent on foot who were instructed to do most of their traveling at night and their sleeping in the day time on account of the Indians. We took care of the wounded man—gave him water, fed him and kept the flies off him, as best we could, while the boys were gone. On the fourth day they returned with the faithful old priest. After a little rest the father examined the wounded man and then said to me,

"'My son, go down to the dry branch, which we crossed as we came here, and turn over the flat rocks, which you will see in the bed of the stream, and under these rocks you will find a great number of large bugs —a kind of beetle, with horns; gather a number of those in a tin bucket and bring them to me.'"

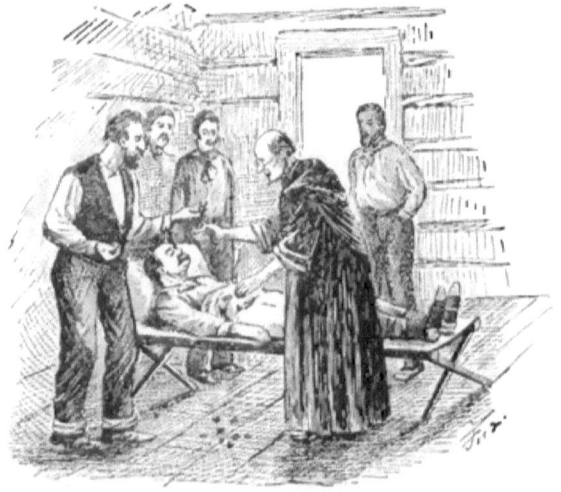

'HE THREW THE BIG END AWAY AND REACHED FOR ANOTHER BUG."

"I did as he directed, finding a great number of large beetles with large, lateral horns on their heads. I brought him several dozen. By the time I returned he had taken a cloth and warm water, and after picking the grass and weeds off the wounded man's bowels, had washed them quite clean. He then caught up the wounded intestine, and, instead of trying to put the cut edges together he laid the two sides of the cut intestine side by side, as you would bring the edges of your coat sleeve and your cuff together. He then called for a bug and, taking it gently by the body, he straddled the two horns over the doubled bowel. He then gave the bug a squeeze which irritated it and caused it to clasp its horns together. The horns penetrated the bowel from side to side. He then, by a slight twisting motion, wrung the bug in two at the small part of its waist, threw the big end away and reached for another bug. He proceeded in the same way—putting his stitches about a half inch apart—until he had closed a cut in the splenic flexure of the colon about four inches long. He then returned the bowel and closed the wound in the abdominal wall with flax thread in a common sewing needle. The fellow never had a bad symptom and was out carrying the chain in about six or eight weeks."

A profound stillness prevailed after this story was finished, and the old man seemed to grow restless and got up and went out. Silence still prevailed until he was out of ear shot, when all looked at each other and then burst into uncontrollable laughter. One wittily suggested that whatever else might be claimed for the story it could not be said that "there were no bugs on it."

In considering the subject of liars it has occurred to me that there ought to be an asylum or a reformatory for them. Why not? The disposition to lie is evidently a disease with some men. It is true if a man tells a lie just for mischief or to conceal a crime then we can see the motive. But there is no motive in the boasting liar's action. I have seen these fellows when they just seemed to lie involuntarily. Now, if we could have a reformatory for these men great good might be done. It is true it seems that their lying does little or no harm. But it does harm to the liar. No matter how good a fellow the boasting liar may be (and I have known them to possess most excellent qualities as husbands, fathers and neighbors) he is always in more or less disgrace; and, besides this, he may transmit it to his offspring; and a transmitted *diathesis*, or tendency may be made stronger in those to whom it is transmitted than it was in the transmitter, and these tendencies may be, and are, modified, no doubt, so that the *hereditary liar* may develop into a mischievous and harmful liar.

We might send these people to a reformatory and send along with them their histories, in which might be included some of their most prominent and unreasonable lies. Classes might be formed of the different kinds and grades of liars; and, at certain hours on certain days, one class could be assembled for a lecture. Here a professor of Truth could lecture them on the enormity of the sin of lying; could refer to the great truths from great men which had lifted mankind up and done them so much good; and to the great lies of great liars which have held humanity back and done it so much harm. The Devil could be referred to, by the professor, as the Father of Liars with excellent effect, and finally, he could read to the class some of the lies of some member (which had been sent up as a part of his history) and comment on it before his face.

The greatest trouble that I can see about an institution of this kind is, that I fear that there would be so many relapses amongst those who had served out their first terms and been sent home that it would tend to discourage the professors.

CHAPTER XVI.

CONSULTATIONS AND THE CODE.

REASONS FOR THE CODE—RELATIONS OF DOCTOR AND PATIENT—THE NEW COMER AND THE EMERGENCY CASE—SMITH AND THE CAT SKIN POULTICE—JONES, HOT CORN AND BURNT FEATHERS—"OLD PILL GARLIC" AND THE DYING GIRL.

HERE is nothing connected with our profession concerning which there is so much dense ignorance among the masses as the "Code of Ethics." People, as a rule, both the ignorant and the intelligent, regard it very much in the same light that they would the constitution and by-laws which should govern a band of robbers. They look upon it as being the fundamental law which governs a class of men who are banded together against society, and, in some way, this law is the expressed intention of the manner in which the conspiracy is to be carried out. The organization of medical societies and their active work only shows the active workings of the conspirators under this law.

So deeply rooted is this idea in the public mind that not a few of the quacks whom I have known— quacks who knew more about the prejudices of people against "code doctors" than they did about practice—have taken the pains to proclaim through the newspapers and in cards and pamphlets that "the doctor does not belong to the medical societies and is not bound by the Code of Ethics." Many men have temporarily gained a good practice by pandering to this prejudice.

Now, candidly, is the prejudice founded in reason?

I answer, no; and I am prepared to further assert that, if the people generally understood the Code as every good physician ought to understand it, they would all be strong advocates of it.

They would advocate it for the very reason that, while the Code is intended to hold doctors to a strict accountability for their conduct toward each other, it holds them just as firmly to a strict accountability for their conduct toward their patients and the public generally.

The Code is to the doctor the highest law in the universe outside of the Bible, and, if he does not recognize the Bible, then it is the highest law. What the discipline is to the Methodist, the Confession of Faith to the Calvinist, and the Articles of Faith to the Baptist, the Code is to the doctor. It is the expressed law which is to govern him in his conduct toward his brethren, his patients and the public. It may be urged that a gentleman does not need the Code. This is true. Neither do the healthy need a physician; nor do the saints in heaven need a Savior. Unfortunately for our profession, we were all men before we were doctors.

Men as varied in our instincts, education, intelligence and desires as any other class of men. If we could make the *ideal doctor* first and then make the *man* to fit him then we would need no Code. Unfortunately for doctors, some of them are not all that a doctor should be. The opportunities offered to take advantage of a fellow practitioner, and especially to take advantage of and to cheat a credulous and confiding public, are so many that many a doctor, not morally strong, but naturally weak and avaricious, takes advantage of them.

For such the Code is made.

We can not compel them to accept it any more than you can compel a man to be a Mason, an Odd Fellow or a Christian. But you can refuse a man Masonic or Christian fellowship if he is neither and we can refuse a doctor our fellowship if he refuses to be one of us in spirit by subscribing to the fundamental law which holds us all to a strict accountability for our conduct as medical men and gentlemen.

And yet we are blamed for this every day. Intelligent people who would never think of recognizing a man as a Christian who does not subscribe to the fundamental law of Christians—the Bible—will abuse and blame us for refusing to recognize and affiliate with a man who publishes his condemnation of our fundamental law—the Code.

"And yet doctors quarrel," I am answered.

Yes and so do Christians; so do Masons, so do everybody.

Man at his best is a quarrelsome creature. Of all

the creatures that live he is most jealous of his rights. The doctor is, perhaps, the most jealous of his kind.

The question is often asked me,

"Why do doctors quarrel more than other professional men?"

I am scarcely willing to admit that they do; but, if they do there are good and sufficient reasons for it. There are good and sound reasons at the bottom of all puzzling questions, if we can only get at them. Let us see what they are in regard to doctors' quarrels:

Other professional and business men, as a rule, have only a commercial interest in their clientele. The merchant measures his goods across the counter to you, is glad to have your custom—and your money, and if he sees you enter the store across the way he "does not take it to heart." Some one else comes "from across the way" and takes your place. The lawyer writes your deeds, examines your titles and defends you in court and the next week will take a case against you if you do not see him first. And so with all professions and lines of business except ours. We occupy a different relation to our patrons from that of any of these. We are brought in direct contact with the family in a relationship the most intimate as well as the most serious and sacred that falls to the lot of man.

Suppose, if you please, that I have done the practice of a family for fifteen or twenty years. I have been present at the births of all the children of the household, have taken them through their teething, the measles, mumps, whooping cough and scarlatina. I have stood by the mother in the most serious times, when a mistake or bad management on my part would have left a helpless household bereft of its dearest and best friend—the mother. I have sat night after night in the dangerous illness of the children with my finger on the pulse and have administered the remedies with my own hand, and remained and carefully noted their effect. The mother and father hold me above all others in highest esteem and teach the little ones from their first lispings to believe that "Dockie" is the greatest and best of earth's noblemen. There is nothing in that household too good for me. The little ones climb upon my knee without fear and ask me to explain all about the mystery of how, when and where I found them, " when oo bwought me to mamma." Is there nothing between me and that family, think you, excepting a cold business relationship and the commercial matter of fees? Oh, my friend, he who thinks so knows little about the best fees that a doctor receives—the love, affection and esteem of those whom he has helped in the direst extremity of their lives.

Now, just here a fellow comes along with a plug hat and chin whiskers. He moves in. He is one of those fellows "who knows so much that it seems to make him unhappy."

He is a cousin of the mother or a remote relation of the father; or, he belongs to the same church that they do or is a member of the same lodge with the father. He is one of those ingratiating fellows. He is poor and needy and anxious to do practice and especially anxious to do the practice of this very family—thinks he ought to do it, for they are his kin, or his church or his lodge brethren and sisters. His wife plainly tells the mother of their poverty and says that, "if the doctor don't get something to do I don't know what will become of us."

The father and the mother talk the matter over and kindly conclude that they ought to call him in—" when there ain't much the matter."

I thus find him gradually wedging himself in between me and those who are dear to me, and who hold me still dearer. Now, in spite of his poverty, that old human desire to unceremoniously kick him besets me. I can not be in his presence without feeling the hamstring muscles of my right leg involuntarily contract.

He is robbing me of that which I hold above all fees and above all else—the love and confidence of a good family—that love and confidence fairly won on the battle-field of my profession when life was the prize for which I fought. Is it any wonder that doctor's quarrel; more especially when we consider the fact that all doctors are "not as good as they ought to be?"

Many of the bitterest quarrels of doctors arise from the second doctor being called in an emergency while the regular attendant is absent.

You are attending a case and you leave town to see another. An emergency arises. The patient is taken with a sudden pain in some part of the body—a pain which has not been present in the case before—or has a hemorrhage or faints. The family, in their excitement, send for "anybody," which is a bad rule—for "anybody" is not always competent. They get some man who is not altogether scrupulous and who is angling for good paying families.

He comes.

After making himself as agreeable as possible he gives his attention to the patient. He gets the history of the case, and especially the history of the new trouble, and is informed that you are attending the case.

He asks,

"What does the doctor (you) say ails the patient?"

He is answered that you said it was "malarial fever." He says not a word, but turns his face away from the person who is answering his questions and smiles—simply smiles a bland, incredulous smile.

Now, it does not seem that a simple smile ought to cause any trouble, and yet there is a cause for a big war and the expenditure of millions of blood and treasure in that smile.

What does the smile do?

It simply throws doubt on your ability and your diagnosis. It says, as plainly as signs can say it, that you are treating the patient for something he hasn't got, and that, in short, you are a donkey and don't know what you are doing. When pressed for something further he, perhaps, shrugs his shoulders and says,

"Oh, well, madam, I wouldn't like to say. We must be particular about these little things, you know."

He asks what you are giving and when shown the medicine he turns his head away and smiles again. This adroit fellow, with two smiles which cost no effort, and without saying a word, has, perhaps, shaken and almost destroyed a confidence which you have been years in diligent and honest effort in building up. When you hear of his smiles you momentarily feel like a murderer, if you have any temper—and you probably have if you are good for anything and belong to my race.

Consultations, too, are often the cause of quarrels. There is a disagreement. It may be an honest disagreement, but it leads to trouble. The family, in some way, find it out—which they should never be permitted to do. They find it out and the consulting physician is sought out and questioned. If he is an honest man and knows his duty he will not talk. But he may not be honest; or he may not know his duty. At any rate the family get very different ideas from the two men, when in fact, they ought to get all they should know from the family physician and from him alone, as he is the one to give the family all directions, and all indeed that they are entitled to know. There may be cases where the calling in of a third man is necessary. Under such circumstances the family physician may be permitted to state plainly why a third is wanted.

And yet consultations are very necessary in many cases, and the physician should be the first to call for it when the necessity arises. I have known some otherwise very good physicians to make themselves very unpopular, both with the profession and the public, by their persistence in refusing consultations. Such men generally have an overweening confidence in their own abilities, or very little in that of their professional brethren. The physician who permits any precious human life to be lost without first calling to his assistance all the help that is needed or is available does not know half his duty.

But it is trying, sometimes, to feel compelled under a pressure of circumstances to call a man whom you know to be ignorant, unscrupulous or mean. There are so many ways in which a consulting physician can display his littleness if he is mean enough to do so. I once knew a doctor who was never called in a case without doing something which was calculated to undermine the attending physician. He would volunteer directions about the diet, or how to administer the medicines; and I have known him to purposely leave his gloves, and return for them from his buggy, and while in the room, fix the cover and give some extra directions or cautions about the case. This seemed so kind and so good upon the part of the doctor to the family that they involuntarily fell to worshipping him.

"He took so much interest in the patient," they said; and yet, for all his seeming interest, he thought of himself (of whom he was passionately fond) a dozen times where he would think of the patient once.

I have heard of and have seen some very amusing things in consultations. When I began practice I went out on the border, partly in order to quickly secure practice which I needed, and partly to get away from the old doctors, whom I very much feared. I committed the very common mistake of believing that grey hairs and wisdom were synonymous words. I was young and ignorant and knew it. I did not wish to expose my ignorance to anybody and so decided to keep out of the way. When I got settled I practiced for several months without calling counsel. I knew it must ultimately come, but I postponed it as a man postpones the lancing of a felon. I thought it would be painful and I wished to put it off as long as possible. If I could have been chloroformed (like the man with the felon) and could have held the consultation while under complete anæsthesia I know I would have felt better.

But it came.

I finally had a prominent citizen on my hands with pneumonia. He didn't improve. The right lung became *consolidated* and I suspected invasion of the left. His pulse was rapid, his breathing shallow, and his countenance cyanosed.

The family asked for a consultation, and, as an honest man, I could not refuse it. They wanted an old man whom I shall call Smith (because that was not his name) and I consented.

I had heard much of Smith. He had practiced in that country ever since he was let out of the Ark, and according to tradition, had done some wonderful things. He generally selected a remedy "which went right to the spot." If I had any such remedies I didn't know how to select them and there, I thought, was where my weakness lay.

Smith came. He was riding an old rail backed horse with a chawed off tail, and a saddle with a cantle so high that it struck him under the scapulæ and a horn about as high in front. He rode with a part of a barrel hoop and when he would strike the old horse in the flank he (the horse) would kick up behind and his tail would go round like a coffee mill handle. Smith had a bushy head, beetling eye-brows, and wore the old fash-

AND HIS TAIL WOULD GO ROUND LIKE A COFFEE MILL HANDLE.

ioned, green leggin's tied on with the hems of his wife's petticoat, and thought sat perched on his massive brow like a lone crow on a country hog rack.

He examined the patient very superficially—confining his examination mainly to asking questions of the wife—and we retired. With trepidation and modesty I detailed the history of the case and my treatment, and then braced myself to receive the cannonading of solid wisdom which I supposed would come. I expected him to so overwhelm me with his technicalities that I wouldn't be able to be out for a week. Smith looked at me sharply from under his eyebrows and asked:

"Doctor, did you ever try black cat skin poultices in these cases?"

I admitted that, in my ignorance, I never had.

"Well," said he, "it is a good thing if you can get a *reel* black cat. It acts like a charm."

I was astonished. Seeing a loop hole, out of the case, I informed the family that, as the patient was in great danger, and as Dr. Smith was older than I and had once been their family physician, I thought he had better take the case. They were delighted and Smith unhesitatingly took charge.

That was an awful and calamitous night on cats—especially black cats. The boys killed nearly all the cats in the neighborhood and the prominent citizen died early the next morning.

Smith said that "if he had gotten there a little sooner and could have found a *reel* black cat he thought he could have saved him." There is another matter connected with this case which may delight the reader. *Smith is dead, also!*

I was called once to meet in consultation a man whom I shall call Jones. I rode fifteen miles on a dark night, over a rough country before I reached him.

When I reached the place I found the typical home of the squatter—log cabin, one room and no yard fence. As I entered the room I inhaled an odor so pungent that it almost gave me an attack of spasmodic asthma. Jones arose from one corner of the room and came forward to meet me. He was six feet two in his stocking feet and had a nose that looked like the red lantern in a political torch light procession. He had only one eye and the other looked like a fried egg. When he stood up by me and towered above me and beamed on me with his good eye I felt that I had at last met the mythical Cyclops. He said he had a case of retained placenta.

"Well, what is it that smells so, doctor?" I asked.

"I am burning some chicken feathers in a pot under the bed. I have always heard that that is a good remedy, though, they say that Dominicker feathers is the best," said Jones.

We moved the pot on account of my threatened asthma.

When I came to examine the patient I ran across a hot and wet ear of corn leaning against her side and others on her abdomen and around her limbs. I took out about a half bushel altogether.

Jones said that he had "always heard that that was good in such cases," and I stood there and waited for the Lord to smite him and didn't kill him myself. I relieved the woman of the placenta, but she died. I am sorry to state that Jones was living at last accounts.

A medical friend of mine tells me a funny story

illustrating the character of a shrewd country quack. When my friend returned from the Confederate army (where he had been an assistant surgeon) he settled in the county seat of one of the wealthiest counties of our state. He was young, but had had some experience, was a close student, and had that kind of energy and grit that finally enables a man to rise in almost any calling.

Living in the country some ten or fifteen miles from town was one of those shrewd fellows, who practiced on the slam-banging, fire-away-without-taking-sight method. He was often compelled to call in a consulting physician, and, generally called my friend. Just why he did so my friend was not able to guess, unless it was that my friend was young and the old fellow thought would be less able to expose his ignorance. They were on quite good terms, but one thing my friend could never succeed in doing and that was to get the old man to tell what he was treating the patient for until he (my friend) first examined the patient and made a diagnosis. Then the old man would agree with him, compliment him on his ability and say

"That is just what I've been doctorin' him fur."

He was somewhat afraid of the spreading popularity of the young doctor, and would often say of him,

"A. is a d—d fine young doctor; d—d fine. In *fifteen or twenty year from now* he'll be as good as any of us."

That was a safe declaration, as he—the old man—would in all probability, be out of the way by that time.

At last my friend made up his mind that the next time he was called in he would compel the old man to tell what the matter was or he would refuse to do so. He was soon called to see one of the county Judges in a remote part of the county. The old man was treating him and A. found him there. When A. went in the old man greeted him cordially and when A. asked him how the Judge was the old man answered,

"Purty sick, purty sick; A. warm yourself and go in and examine him."

"What seems to be the matter with the Judge?" said A.

"Go in and examine him for yourself," said the old man.

"Well," said A. "I will; but can't you give me some idea of what the trouble is, so as to save time and that I may not expose him too long on such a cold day?"

"Go in and examine him and then tell me what the matter is; I don't want to prejudice your mind. Find out for yourself, young man; it'll do you good."

With all the pressure A. could bring to bear he couldn't wring the old doctor's diagnosis out of him. He went in and examined the Judge and found him in the second stage of pneumonia. He came back and after pumping the old doctor again and proving the inefficiency of his pump he gave it up.

The old man's turn came now.

"What do you say's the matter with him, A.?"

"He's got pneumonia," said A.

"Head's level again. You hit 'em right along, my boy. I tell 'em all you are the comin' man in these parts. Have you ever seen the new instrument that they examine the lungs with?"

A. didn't know that he had. The old man then went down into a very long pocket in a very long overcoat and triumphantly brought out a Camann's binaural stethoscope. Where or how he ever came across it A. did not know.

"Look at that," said the old man. "Look at that, young man. That's what'll tell you what's the matter with the lungs every time. Put these two eends in your ears and go in thar and put this other eend on the Judge's chist and listen."

A. thought he had the old man cornered, and so asked:

"What shall I listen for doctor?"

"You go in thar and put that on the Judges chist young man, and then come back and tell me what you heard."

"Well, doctor," said A. "I can do that, but can't you give me some idea of the sounds that I shall listen for so that I may make better use of the new instrument and that the examination may be the more instructive to me."

The old man showed signs of being hard pressed, but at last recovered himself and said.

"A. go in thar and put these two eends in your ears and put the big eend on the Judge's chist and listen, and if you don't hear the d—dest rumblin' and roarin' that you ever heard in your life then you may call me a liar."

Dr. A. gave it up.

I know of nothing that better illustrates the fact that the ridiculous often treads closely upon the heels of the serious than the following which occurred in one of my own consultations:

I was called by telegraph several years ago to go to a town on the railroad some distance from where I was then living. I knew something of the history of the family to which I was called.

A mother and three daughters—the mother made a widow when the youngest was a babe. They were poor but good people and the daughters were all pretty. The poor mother had held them together by dint of hard work—a little millinery, a little dress making and other sewing—in her humble house. The youngest, and the fairest and the most loved was now fifteen.

I never knew so much that was amiable and beautiful and cleanly and lovely, in a family so poor.

When I arrived at the house I was taken through the little sitting room and parlor and up a narrow and steep flight of stairs to a bed room above. Here I found the youngest in the throes of death.

She was attended by one of the queerest beings that I ever met in consultation. He was near sixty years of age and wore a wig and dyed his beard with nitrate of silver. His beard always had that peculiar arrangement of colors which Warren gives to the hair of Tittlebat Titmouse in "Ten Thousand a Year," the color which Bret Harte calls "the purple black of a dyed mustache." He was at enmity with the world on two counts: First, the world did not accept his religion, and second, it did not take his pills. In fact he had kept the world from taking his pills by insisting too strongly on its taking his religion. The citizens called him "Old Pill Garlic."

The history of the present case was that the beautiful girl had, on the Friday preceding, eaten some wild persimmons. At night she was taken with a sudden and severe pain low down on the right side. "Old Pill Garlic" was called, and, instead of giving the suffering child an opiate and putting on a poultice, he gave three of Cook's pills. That failing to accomplish anything, he gave three compound cathartic pills, then three blue mass pills, then three doses of calomel. After he had run the gamut of the magic three he then gave salts, castor oil, seidlitz powders, etc., finally ending with a few drops of croton oil, which he often repeated per orem and per anema. The girl had torsion, impaction, intussusception or some obstruction of the intestinal canal, and, of course, "Old Pill Garlic's" medication had only added fuel to the fire. He was standing by the bed a perfect picture of routed helplessness. The poor child was cold as ice to the knees and elbows, was pulseless and was tossing in the agonies of death. After hearing the history and examining the patient, I stepped aside with the doctor.

"Well, what do you think of her?" said he.

"I think she is dying," said I.

"What! not so bad as that, is it?"

I answered that she would not live an hour.

She did not live half that time.

Here was a man with some education, and who had also had the advantages of a medical education, who had practiced medicine nearly forty years, and yet did not have judgment enough to know when a person was dying. I was given the most painful task of informing the mother and sisters that the child was dying.

Painful task, I say, because of all the painful duties that a doctor is called upon to perform, this has, to me, always been the most painful. There was agony, screams and tears. Oh, the agony it cost to surrender the beautiful, the gentle, the loved and petted one of this little band.

When she had breathed her last a lady (whom I had known from my young manhood) asked me to help her take the mother and sisters down stairs. We did so, and leaving old P. G. behind, passed down through the little parlor, and into a little bedroom. Here my lady friend broke down and said,

"Oh, can't some one pray for these poor, suffering women? Brother—will you pray?"

This last was addressed to a good old deacon who had just come in. We all knelt down and the deacon petitioned the Throne of Grace. The prayer was somewhat rambling and ungrammatical but he talked as if he was talking to the Lord face to face. There were no attempts at lofty flights, but in the simplest and plainest of human speech, he told the Lord of the wants of the widow and the orphans, called him "Heavenly Parent" and "Beloved Father," and with his simple speech, tender pathos and strong faith, lifted us all up to the Pearly Gates.

The stricken ones seemed to be soothed by the prayer and ceased their loud wailings.

Just as the Deacon said "Amen," there came a sudden overturning of something at the top of the stairs, a wild exclamation, and then r u m p i t y, b u m p i t y, bump, bump, b u m p i t y, bump—swash '-h-h-h. The last sounded as if some one was swabbing a Krupp gun with a Dutch peddler.

I SAW THAT HIS HEAD SHONE LIKE A LOCOMOTIVE HEADLIGHT.

"There," said my friend, "the old doctor has fallen down stairs."

I seized the lamp and ran into the little parlor and there found "Old Pill Garlic" on his knees and left hand while he felt out in a spasmodic and uncertain way with his right for something in front of him. I saw a black object on the floor, thought it was a cat and kicked it. Then turning the light full upon the doctor I saw that his head shone like a locomotive headlight. I knew then that the black object was his wig. I picked it up, and, having a light in the other hand, I put it on hind part before.

When the doctor arose he had bangs clear down to his eyes, and he turned around like a blind horse three times before he got his wig straight.

I asked if he was hurt much.

"Oh, no, no," said he, in a way that indicated that he was in the habit of falling down stairs just for the exercise it gave him.

We soon had the wig straightened, however, and, bidding all good-bye, I took the train for home within an hour. I was so impressed with the sorrows of the family and the deacon's prayer that "Old Pill Garlic's" tumble did not seem amusing or ridiculous. In fact it made so slight an impression on me that I forgot it.

Six months afterward a facetious fellow from the little village came into my office and reminded me of it. There was no sorrow present then, and no tender prayer to lift me up and it did really seem ludicrous.

CHAPTER XVII.

PEOPLE WHO ANNOY DOCTORS.

PATIENTS, HOTEL KEEPERS, ETC.—THE HOMELY CRANK—
"THE HON. MRS. SKEWTON"—MR. GUTZWEILER—THE SICK GIRL,
THE DEAF LANDLADY WITH TIN TRUMPET, AND THE MILLINER.

I PRESUME that people of all professions and trades have their annoying customers and patrons. The lawyer is annoyed, no doubt, by the persistent client who wants to sue but has no case; the merchant by the customer who looks at everything in the store and buys nothing; the minister by the sinful penitent who is always sinning and always repenting and is never satisfied; and so I might go on through them all and we would find that there is no business to transact, which brings us in contact with the masses, which has not its trials and petty annoyances.

Some people seem to have been born to trouble others. They seem to feel that they are burden bearers and they are everlastingly trying to shift the burden. Some people are born *mal a propos*—breech presentations, so to speak—and they go about the world wrong end foremost, and no reasonable, well organized person can come in contact with them without being more or less upset. I know people, to avoid meeting whom, I would willingly walk around a whole block.

It is not the sick alone, of whom the above observations are made; for, any good and humane physician will learn to bear and forbear with the sick. Some of our patients, however, annoy us enough—those who "get their disease in their heads;" who are never any better; who tell us that the last medicine made them worse; patients who come oftener than we desire and who wish to go over all the details of their physical ailments each time, and who throw in all of their little family troubles, squabbles and broils, as a sort of relish; those who wish to hold a consultation with the doctor about their cases, or come with a diagnosis already made and a remedy selected, but seem to want the doctor to take the responsibility of the treatment. Such as these give us trouble enough; but, there are others who seem to make it a part of their business to worry their family physician, or any one whom they may select for that purpose.

I think there are some women in the world (and they are most all good, God bless 'em!) who, when arranging for a trip down town, really cogitate and tax their brains as to how much real annoyance they can inflict on the dry goods man, the dress maker and the milliner, and who finally wind up by saying to themselves something like this:

"And, ah–yes, well, after that, I guess I'll go around and worry the doctor awhile!" and they do.

I remember one miserable case that gave me

enough worry to have made Job totter on his good resolutions.

Before I had made her acquaintance I had noticed her sailing around our streets, in a cranky sort of way—always pulling a little girl by the hand, and walking so fast that the poor child was often almost pulled off its little feet.

She was a slender, stoop shouldered, tallow faced and cadaverous looking little woman, with a hawk-bill nose and pop eyes. Oh, she was so homely! I have heard of people being so homely that they had the face ache. If such a thing were possible how this woman must have suffered. It really gave one a pain to look at her. She came into my office one afternoon dragging the little girl by the hand and planked herself down in a chair, and, after arranging some bundles she had in an old maidish sort of fashion, she looked at me and opened up thus:

"Air you Dr. King?"

"Yes, madam."

"Well, I've heard of you, and they say that you air a purty good doctor. Now, I want you to tell me what's the matter with anybody when they feel jest like somebody was a gripping of their thighs and pulling all the flesh off and like somebody else had both hands a holt of their bowels and was jest a twistin' and a wringin' of 'em and like somebody else had a rusty nail tied onto a string and was jest a pullin' it up and down on the inside of the spine of their backs."

I smiled, almost audibly, at this array of unusual symptoms and answered:

"Well, madam, those are not symptoms of anything that I ever heard of."

"Shet your mouth, you mean thing," said she, snappishly, "I jest know you air a laughin' at me."

Then I couldn't keep from "laughin' right out in school."

Well, I examined her case and prescribed for her, and had her on my hands as a standing horror for four years. She just wouldn't have anybody else. I took it as a great compliment and again thought of trying to trace my genealogy back to the "Man of Uz."

She was dissatisfied with the whole earth and the planets and the space and things beyond the planets; but, her one crowning trouble was that she was lean, and her one desire in life was to get fat. She would say to me:

"I'll take anything; I'll eat sticks, I'll eat boards, I'll eat hay if you will only tell me it will make me fat."

I would as soon have undertaken the task of putting fat on a hoe handle or a pair of tongs as to try to put it on her. You had only to see her to *know* that to make her fat was an impossibility.

She had a good looking husband and was jealous of him, and, in addition to her other troubles, she used to load me down with her suspicions about "my man."

She wanted beer—as she had heard that would make fat. I ordered it—a glass at each meal. She would get a half dozen bottles, drink them all in one day, get gloriously drunk, be sick three days and then come down to the office and tell me that the beer was not doing her any good. I believed her.

She finally died of acute mania; but, oh, my! the trouble she did give me in the last four years of her life! I am glad now that I was patient with this poor nervous and unfortunate woman. Perhaps I added a little to her happiness—if it could be said that she knew any such thing as happiness; or, to put it better, it may be that the kindness I showed her and the patience with which I bore her many most aggravating annoyances made her less unhappy. If so, then I am glad, for, perhaps she will remember it up there, where she is, perhaps, as pretty and as fat as any of the others of the redeemed.

Another class of people who annoy doctors is the class of persons who send for you in a great hurry—want you "right away"—and are never ready for you when you get there. They keep you waiting at the door for half an hour and then a servant admits you and directs you to take a seat in the sitting room, where you wait another half hour.

I attended a comparatively poor family once where it took almost as much time and red tape to reach the patient as it ought to take to procure an audience with the queen of England.

It may be that the lady of the house is sick and that after you reach the front door she takes a bath, changes her night dress and perfumes herself (this kind of people are great perfumers) fixes her hair, and, if she is not too sick, paints and powders her face. After this she admits you. This sort of people are always sacrificing the convenience of somebody else in order to have their own way and their own time about matters. They are supremely self important, not to say selfish. I do not know how my professional brethren act under such circumstances; but, no family ever puts me in a waiting attitude but once. After that there is a plain, fair talk, which everybody can understand, and the moral to it is: Don't make the doctor wait; be ready for him; his time is precious and there are other sick people in town who need him, perhaps, while he is waiting. After this talk, if the offence were repeated, I would either go away or kick in the front door, and my action would probably, be determined by the strength of the door. I believe that there is such a thing as outraging the feelings of a saint. This is one way in which to do it.

I had a most annoying case of the kind once. A distinguished old couple from another state visited the small town where I was then practicing. The gentleman was a most excellent man in all respects—had succeeded in making a great deal of money in his time, and his frivolous and weak wife had succeeded in spending it for paints and powders, frills, flounces and furbelows almost as fast as he had made it. She was between sixty and seventy years of age at this time and was as pronounced a specimen of the type dudine as I ever saw. She had never been beautiful, and at this time she was old and bony, with sunken, wrinkled cheeks and scraggy jaws; in short, she was a regular *mardi gras* figure. They were people somewhat distinguished in the locality from whence they came, and this reputation had preceded them, so that almost the entire little town was put under contribution for their entertainment. This, I suppose, is the reason why I bore with the annoyances of this silly and frightful old ogress without " giving her a piece of my mind "—a very large piece.

She grew sick. Change of climate, water and diet brought on a violent trouble and I was sacrificed for the occasion. I never got to see her under an hour after I called and it was often longer. She had the most elaborately wrought night dresses and wore more loud jewelry than a Senegambian princess. She wore spit curls, pasted and painted all over and into the dips, spurs and angles of her scraggy old face, and perfumed until the air was rank with the odor of Mellier extracts, attar of roses, musk and so forth.

She would generally permit me to catch her in the last act of this business of upholstering her physiognomy, and would simper and giggle and make pretense of hiding her boxes and bottles under the bed clothes, like a silly, bashful girl, who is caught kissing a boy, the giddy old thing. She would sit up in bed and go through this nonsensical performance when she was so sick that it was all she could do to hold up her weak and empty head. I nicknamed her " The Hon. Mrs. Skewton." The reader will remember " The Honorable Mrs. Skewton " (in Dombey & Son) who used to have such flirtations with Capt. Joe Bagstock, and who ordered the attendants to " draw the pink curtains," when she was dying, in order that she might have the pink glow on her check. This woman was a complete counterpart of her.

One thing that makes such persons so unbearable is the fact of the utter uselessness of the life that the person has led or is leading. A person whose whole life is devoted to spending what some one else makes; who never does anything commendable; who never earns anything, is always contemptible. We don't like to be annoyed by worthless, useless people. I would willingly sleep in a hog pen (and lie next to the hogs) with a John Howard, or with any man whose life has been unselfishly devoted to the great work of relieving the pains, miseries and wants of others, if it gave him comfort, while I can not bear patiently for a moment with the selfish annoyances of people who live for and think only of themselves. This is the difference, and it is a great difference.

Another class of people who annoy doctors is the class who wish to get sick people out of their houses. To this class belong, notably, hotel keepers, boarding house keepers, real estate landlords, and, sometimes others.

Here is a case:

I am called to see a young man who is stopping or boarding at a hotel. After the second visit I pronounce the case to be typhoid fever. To the friends, attendants or others about the sick person I announce this fact and order that certain things be done and that certain precautions be observed. This news spreads through the hotel and the landlord hears it. He at once sees disas ter staring him in the face. He, therefore, lies in wait for me at my next visit. As I pass in he hails me. I know at once what he wants and tell him I will see him when I come down. On coming from my patient's room I find him faithfully on guard. He speaks very low, takes me to a private room, shuts the door and sits down facing me and the following dialogue takes place:

"Doctor, you are waiting on Mr. Johnson in room 11 are you not?"

"Yes, sir."

"Well, er-ah–what's the matter with him?"

"He has typhoid fever."

"*Typhoid fever!* You don't say so?"

"Yes, sir, it is an unmistakable case of typhoid."

"Umph hoo! Well, I am sorry to hear it."

Then there is a short silence and I know just what this silence means. He is summoning all the impudence from the innermost depth's of his selfish nature and getting ready for the onslaught. He breaks silence:

"Well, er-ah, Doc., when can you take him away from here?"

"Get him away?" I ask, in astonishment.

"Yes," he answers, somewhat confidently, now that he has broken the ice, "when can you move him?"

"*I* move him?" I ask again, affecting still greater astonishment.

"Yes, when can you take him out of the hotel?"

"I can't take him away at all," I answer.

"You can't? Why not?"

"Well, in the first place, I didn't bring him here;

and, in the second place, I am not in the transfer business. You seem to think that I have gone into the transfer business, but you are mistaken."

"Well, but–er–ah–he's your patient."

This is his clincher, and I answer it—

"Yes, but he is your guest, and he was your guest before he was my patient. Do you think I am going to fritter away my time moving people around from place to place and getting sick people out of hotels in order to please frightened landlords? You must be going insane?"

"But what am I to do?" he asks, with much excitement.

"Don't do anything. Keep quiet and behave yourself and then you will not get into trouble."

Then he thinks awhile and this is the result:

"Well, er-ah, can *I* move him?"

"Well, as to the physical act of moving him I presume you could; but you will not."

"I will not? Why not?"

"Because I will not permit you to move him."

"You will not permit me! Well, now, that's pretty cool. We'll see."

"That's a good idea. You see about this matter before you do anything rash, for if you move this sick man without my consent and any harm comes to him in consequence of the removal I will have you arrested. Let me advise you to see your lawyer before you move this sick man."

This frightens him; but he tacks and comes again.

"I'd like to know what he is to you? He's a perfect stranger to you."

"He is everything to me, sir. He is very sick and has sent for me and entrusted his life to my care, and, so long as he is sick and helpless, and I am acting in the capacity of physician in his case, he is not only entitled to the very best care and treatment at my hands, but he is entitled to my protection and I will defend him against a world in arms, if need be, and the man who injures him must first place me *hors du combat*."

This is a poser. The landlord thinks again, and, in his mind, sees his best guests packing their trunks and fleeing from the contagion of typhoid. It is dreadful and the very thought of it sits upon his heart and weighs him down like a nightmare. Then he gets pathetic and pleads. He begs and cajoles me; but, I am defending a sick man and am obdurate. Then he goes and sees his clerk and his wife and comes back full of the spirit of compromise: Can he move him into a small room at the top of the house? I go with him and look at the room; and, if it suits me I say "yes." If not I select one that does suit me, and permit the landlord and his help to move my patient. I remain and watch the process to see that he is not hurt, and, since matters seem to be moving on so nicely, I quietly inform the landlord that, if everything goes well, at a certain time I will permit him to move my patient to another place—I to first see and approve the place and he to take all the trouble of moving him under my directions. For the time I am absolute master of this man's house, and I enjoy it. I enjoy no part of it more than the fact that I have impressed on the mind of this ordinarily imperious autocrat the fact that *I am not in the transfer business.*

Here is another case. I am attending a poor young married woman, in a small, frame house, which belongs to a thrifty, but close fisted German. The husband is a railroad man, earns small wages which just about enable him to keep his little family and pay the rent, and the young wife is stricken down with a pelvic hemorrhage, (*pelvic hæmatocele*) not a fatal trouble by any means, but one which requires quietude for several weeks, and which, if the patient were moved or allowed to make exertion in the erect posture, might result fatally. The German has, perhaps, already experienced trouble in getting his rent when it was due, and now that the husband must quit work for a while and lose time in consequence of his wife's sickness, the thrifty Teuton sniffs trouble and losses in the air.

He does not know me, but he comes to my residence at an hour when he knows he can find me. He introduces himself and says:

"Vas you ductor Ging?"

"Yes, sir, that is my name."

"Vell, you haf one batient on my house at —— East fort street—Meeses Morgan."

"Yes, sir, that is correct."

"Vell, ductor, oxkuse me, but vas she very seck?"

"Yes, Mr. Gutzweiler, she is very sick."

"Vell, oxkuse me, ductor, but ven can you get her my house oudt?"

"I can't get her out at all."

"Ish dot so? Vy you can't?"

"Because she is too sick to be moved, and because I am not in the transfer business. You have certainly made a mistake Mr. Gutzweiler, you think I am in the transfer business."

"Who said dose dings, dot you in de transfare peesiness vas? I don't said nodings like dot."

"No, you did not, but you wanted to know when I could move this woman and I didn't think you would ask such a question unless you thought I made it a business to move sick people."

"No, no, no, I don't dink no such dings like dot; aber he vas your batient."

"Yes, 'aber' she is your tenant.

"Mine Gott! I know dot alretty, und I haf heap of droubles dot rent to gollect alretty, und now I gets nodings."

"That's bad and I am sorry, Mr. Gutzweiler, but the woman can't be moved. That is the long and the short of it, so please do not bother me any further about the matter."

"I doned gare von tam by dem long und dem short, aber I vant dose beoples moved my house oudt, und I'll git 'em oudt, by yeminy! You'll see. I get some law und move 'em oudt; dot's vat I do."

"That's right, Mr. Gutzweiler, you get some law, but don't move them without the law, because, if you do, and that woman should die, they will get you in jail, sure."

"Who get me in chail?"

"Why, the grand jury and the sheriff."

"Oh, mine Gott! Dis vas der meanest beoples und der vorst laws vat I efer seen," and the bowlegged, jug bodied and disconsolate fellow waddles off home.

He evidently consults a lawyer. He comes again the next day and opens up after the same fashion— "oxkuse me, ductor, aber ven can you move dose beoples my house oudt?"

I call his attention to the fact that I am not in the transfer business, which seems to excite and aggravate him. He begs, argues, scolds, gets mad and raves, and occasionally gets so excited and exasperated that his small stock of English is not sufficient to express his overwrought feelings, and he halts, gasps, strains and tugs at his memory, and draws hasty drafts on this small stock of English which are not honored, when he gets so outraged that he wrenches great, irregular masses of jaw fracturing words and parts of sentences from his German store, and literally *flings* them into the sentence with an audible crash, and a wild, insane gesture, which finishes the sentence, and with his heart pressure thus relieved, he stands and pants and mops his head like a man who has run a hard race or laid down a heavy burden.

I sit and smile and look up at the ceiling. I despise stingy people and, therefore, am never more at my ease than I am when I see one of these nickel squeezing fellows worrying about his losses.

He comes again the next day and the next and the next. He makes all sorts of propositions, which all include the idea of moving Mrs. Morgan and all of which I reject with a quiet, firm shake of the head, and with the air of a man who knows that he holds the situation in the hollow of his good right hand and intends to have his own way—not just for the love of power, not to be wilfully overbearing, but for the sake of poor little Mrs. Morgan, who lies helplessly flat on her back, and for the sake of the little girl who would be motherless, should Mrs. Morgan die. That is enough to justify a man in being firm, even if some shrivelled souled, nickel squeezer does not feel well. I lost no sleep on Gutzweiler's account, but I was intensely amused at his agony. It was as bad as a case of cramp colic.

But, he came too often. He was occupying too much of my time. I couldn't afford to have a circus in my house every day even if it did amuse me. I lost patience with Gutzweiler and so, when I saw him coming one afternoon I met him in the front yard and, in a few words, told him that he must not come to my house on that business any more.

He threatened to move my patient and I quietly told him to move her, and that it would kill her and then he would go to jail. Then he got madder and animadverted in very tortuous and torturing mixed English and German on the laws of this country.

I said to him in a quiet, suggestive and somewhat aggravating way:

"I'll tell you what I'd do if I were you, Gutzweiler."

"Vat you do?" he asked.

"I would go back to Germany. You can go back to Germany and work for fifteen cents a day and eat spoilt kraut and have a real good time—almost as good as the hogs do out here!"

This was too much. Gutzweiler got steaming hot and grew insulting. I seized a garden rake which had been left against a tree in the front yard and made a feigned desperate pass at him and said:

"I DON'D SKIN SOME FLINTS, NUDDER."

"You miserable old skin flint, if you don't get out of my yard I will break you up so small that there will not be enough left of you to address a letter to!"

"I done vant no letters! who said I vant letters vas

a pig lie; und I done skin some flints, nudder! You go — — — gubbledy, gobbledy, gibbledy, rar-r-r-r, rar-r-r-zt-zit"—as he disappeared around the corner, his mixed English and German sounding like a combination of the noises of escaping steam and a wooden sorghum mill.

I don't know whether Gutzweiler ever collected his rent or not, nor do I care. I know that I did not get my fee in the case. Don't care for that, either. Mrs. Morgan got well and the little girl was not left an orphan and that was enough to satisfy any good man.

Here is a still more peculiar case:

A young girl whose father had died when she was a child and whose mother married again—married a man who took a dislike to the little girl and drove her away from home at the age of twelve—gets sick. She has been a sort of *protege* of mine for some time. She had seen much trouble for a young girl, but through her own exertion, with some aid from good friends, had succeeded in obtaining a fair education. She was a good girl, but was sick a great deal. I had attended her for years, at times when she suffered greatly.

Through the influence of friends she got a position in the post office, and just at a time when she was congratulating herself that she was beginning to see the long looked for and much longed for daylight, she, as I said before, was stricken down with a bilious fever. She was rooming with a young grass widow who worked in a millinery store—the milliner furnishing the room and Clara occupying it with her to save expenses. They were in the house of an old widow lady who was so deaf that she could not distinguish between the noise of a cannon and a church choir. She wore wool in her ears and carried a tin trumpet about three feet long.

Miss Clara was very sick. Her sickness was not dangerous, but painful.

At my second visit the old lady met me in the hall—tin trumpet in hand and ears full of wool. If she had had the best ear trumpet that was ever invented she couldn't have heard thunder through those dense wads of wool.

She had the flat voice peculiar to deaf people and used the staccatoed interrogatory, "hah?" after everything that was said to her.

She came at me sidewise, with that exaggerated dinner horn to her ear, and almost knocked me over with it before I could make out what it was.

"Doctor, you are tendin' on Miss Clara, ain't you? hah?" (staccato "hah!")

"Yes, madam," I answered.

"Hah?" and she ran at me sidewise with the abominable old horn again.

I dodged it and said, "Yes, madam, I am attending her."

She shoved that horn at me again (always as if she were trying to jab me in the face with it) and said,

"Doctor, I'll hab to ask you to talk through by truppet, ads I ab quite deef. Dow ted be." (Now tell me.)

I timidly caught the long tin tube by the big end and peered down it, saw the bunch of wool in her ear, and asked:

"What is it you want to know?"

"Hah? What ab I goig to do?"

(Very loud) "No, ma'am, what is it you want to know?"

"Oh, yes; what is it I want to do? Wed, det be see; oh, yes, ids she very sick?"

"Yes, ma,am."

"Hah? a dittle douder, please.'

"*Yes, ma'am.*"

"Hah?"

"YES, MA'AM."

"Oh, yeds. Wed, det be see——oh, yeds, do you thick she'll be sick very log?"

"I don't know."

"Hah?"

I scream "I don't know."

"Oh, yes, wed "——

And while she is getting ready to fire another question I drop my end of the horn and run up stairs.

I found the poor girl quite sick—high temperature, bounding pulse, headache, backache and vomiting. She told me with tears in her eyes that she was afraid she was going to have trouble, as the old lady didn't want her in her house while she was sick, as she was afraid it would interfere with her renting other rooms, and, worse still, the milliner was pouting because she (Clara) had groaned and retched all night and had kept " her grass-ship " from sleeping.

I calmed her fears, prescribed for her and went

away—escaping the old woman, the tin horn and the wool, on my way out.

The next day the old woman was on the look out for me, trumpet in hand, and more wool in her ears than before. She sidled up, like a hog going to war, and scared me by jamming the flanged end of her old tin horn in my face again.

"Doctor, that gad is awfud sick, do't you thick she ids?"

"Yes, ma'am."

"Hah!"

"*Yes, ma'am.*"

"Hah?"

"YES, MA'AM."

"Wed, doctor, whed do you thick you cad boove her?"

"I can't move her at all."

"Hah?"

"I can't move her at all (very loud)."

"You wid boove her id to the hawd (hall;) ids that what you said?"

(*Sotto voce*) "Oh, you old mummy! how I would enjoy throwing you into the horse pond, tin horn and all," and she jammed the flange under my mustache again, almost knocking out my frontal incisors, and said,

"Hah? What did you say?"

I seized the horn with both hands and yelled,

"Nothing!"

"Hah?"

"*Nothing!*"

"Whed did you say you could boove her? Hah?"

All this time I had held the big end of the horn in both hands and the old lady had the small end to her ear with one hand and we had been going around and around in the hall like two fighting roosters, she looking at me all the time with that intense *listening* expression on her face, and I getting red in the face and yelling like a fire chief at a big fire.

I CAN'T MOVE HER.

"I can't move her," I yelled.

"Hah?"

"I CAN'T MOVE HER," I screamed.

"Hah? Dalk a dittle dowder."

I grasped the thing tighter, jammed it into the wad of wool, tip toed and ran my mouth, moustache and nose into the funnel end and screamed almost loud enough to rupture her tympanic membrane,

"I CAN'T MOVE HER!"

She looked at me with that intense, greedy, listening look and said,

"Hah? *Dalk a dittle dowder!*"

I dropped the horn and it struck the hall floor with a whang, and looking at the old woman with a frown and a deprecating gesture, I shook my head until I almost loosened my teeth:

"Oh, go 'way! go 'way!" and ran up the stairs. As I did so she raised her trumpet with a beseeching look and said,

"Hah?"

I reached my patient's room and sat down and mopped my face, for I was perspiring profusely and was as tired as if I had been wallowing in a puddle with a rhinoceros.

My patient was badly demoralized. She was still very sick and she told me, with much agitation and many tears, that the old lady wanted her to get out, fearing that if she remained it would injure her house; and that the milliner had grown obstreperous and said,

"She must get out, for she just could not stand it to work all day and lay awake all night."

I told her that they could not and should not move her; that I would see to it personally that they did not, and that she might calm her fears on that point. I advised her to be quiet, take her medicine, say but little and bide her time.

She raised up in bed on her elbow, and with her big, blue eyes swimming in tears, said:

"Please, Doctor King, look after me and protect me; for I am *so* sick; and you know I have been raised almost entirely by myself and I don't know a thing about girls. This is the first girl I ever roomed with."

"Well," I said, "my dear child, I have very little advantage of you there, for I never roomed with but one girl either."

She broke into a hearty laugh and I left her. As I went through the hall I dropped this note into the old lady's room:

"MRS. ——

Please do not talk to Miss Clara. You worry her. Keep out of her room.　　THE DOCTOR.

Then I drove to the millinery store. I went in and inquired if Mrs. Bangles worked there. Yes, she worked there and was in. I asked to see her and she came out looking somewhat surprised.

"I am Dr. King, Mrs. Bangles and I —"

"Oh, yes, you are the doctor that's 'tending on Miss Clara —— and you are the very person I want to see, for I want to know when you can move —"

I raised a hand and said,

"Just one minute, Mrs. Bangles, please; you are laboring under a grave mistake; I am not the transfer man; I am not engaged in moving people; I am a physician."

She looked at me in wide eyed wonder.

"Well, you will have to take her away for I did not get a single bit of sleep last night, for she just groaned and —"

I raised my hand and checked her again, for she was growing excited and talking loud,

"S–s–sh," I said, "don't talk so loud or people will find out that you have a temper. Now, I came to say this: The girl is too sick to be moved. She can't be moved. It is impossible. To move her now may kill her. If you force her out of that room and away from that house and she should die, her death will be laid at your door. It will be in everybody's mouth, the newspapers will get hold of it and they will write you up as the most inhuman wretch that ever lived. They will call you 'The Woman Fiend,' the 'Female Murderess,' and you will have to flee from public indignation as you would from a contagion, and wherever you go the story will follow you, and you will ever hereafter lead a pursued, helpless, hopeless, blasted life, which will be worse than death."

I watched her countenance while I was making this terrible array of the things that would occur in case she turned the sick girl out. Her face took on a ghastly pallor and she made several ineffectual efforts to swallow something which seemed to have come into her throat, and after staggering up and resting one hand on the counter she asked in a choked voice,

"Well, what am I to do?"

"Do anything, Mrs. Bangles," I answered, "except to be cruel. Cruelty is no part of your nature. You are a good woman, but you just haven't thought. Think this matter over seriously. Think how you would like to be treated if you were in her place. If you ever pray go and say your prayers to-night, and after you get through sit down and imagine that the great God is looking right into your heart, and then think what you ought to do and decide what you will do. Remember, I insist that you are a good woman, and you will have to prove to the contrary before I will believe otherwise."

I left her. When I called the next morning I found my patient without fever and full of surprise.

"What do you suppose has come over Mrs. Bangles?" she asked.

"I don't know," I answered, "why do you ask?"

"Why," she went on, "when she came home last night she brought me some lemons and made me a lemonade. She gave me a sponge bath and then sat by me and bathed my face and put cool cloths on my forehead and changed them every few minutes. She talked just as kind and called me 'dear' and kissed me. Why, I never saw such a change! When I went to sleep she was still by the bed ; and, I must have slept very sound for when I awoke this morning I found that she had lain down beside me and was asleep with her face right against mine. She must have been crying, for my face and hers were both wet with tears from her eyes."

"Oh," I said, "Miss Clara, at first she thought of herself only; then she acted selfishly, as people who think of themselves only always do; then she thought of you, and then she acted unselfishly. Her true woman's nature came to the rescue and she acted her true, good self. She has learned a good lesson and it will do her good. You must be grateful and love her and let her know that you do."

So my patient did not move at all.

These are the exceptional cases. My experience has been that most people are kind to the sick. The very best that is in human nature comes to the front when we are in the presence of the sick, the suffering and the dying. This is especially true when we see the helpless and the unfortunate sick and suffering, who need our care and sympathy.

Human nature is very good after all. There is much that is brave and good, tender and true in men and women, if there is only an opportunity to bring it out. Some people need opportunity and occasion to bring out their good points just as others may need opportunity and occasion in which to display their courage or some other great quality. When once brought out, it grows stronger all the time. In other words, the better part of our natures —charity, forgiveness, liberality and all—need to be exercised in order to be strong, just as our muscles and our brains need to be exercised in order to develop and grow strong. In this life the things that lie still must perish; the things that are active, that move, are the things that live and grow.

I have never seen the milliner since, but I know the circumstance must have been of lasting benefit to her. I hope it may land her safely in Heaven. I do not know what the effect was on the deaf old landlady. She couldn't hear enough to learn much. She was, practically, a dead stump. But when she gets to the pearly gates, if she must undergo an examination before she can enter, I do hope that she will not put up that old tin trumpet and say,

"Hah?"

CHAPTER XVIII.

DID HE KILL HIS WIFE?

HELPING THE DOCTOR OR OTHERWISE—A SECOND MARRIAGE AND A MOTHERLESS CHILD—THE RESULT OF DEVELOPING ONE SIDE OF THE FAMILY—JANUARY AND MAY—DID HE KILL HIS WIFE?

IN our practice, ordinarily, we have the helpful assistance of the family and friends of the patient. This is necessary to the well-being and ultimate recovery of the sick one, as well as to the success of the doctor. But this is not always the case. As strange as it may seem there are cases in which we find opposing forces. Somebody does not desire that the patient shall recover; and while, as a rule, they are not mean enough, or are too cowardly to administer anything which would hasten the patient's taking off, yet they oppose you in little ways. They saw something during your absence which contra-indicated the medicine and they did not administer it. They are slow to do the little things which you order to be done, and which are often so essential to success.

Here is a case:

A man marries the second time. He has one

child by his first wife—a little, sickly, cross, pitiful thing. The second wife is a selfish woman, and let me say right here, that no thoroughly selfish woman ever loved another woman's child. She has a nose which is high across the bridge, a strong under jaw and a projecting chin, thin lips and a mouth slightly turned down at the corners. She keeps her mouth tightly shut, except when at war, and, when in ill humor, she shoves the under lip up in the center, which results in giving the mouth a crescent curve. She is straight up and down on the back of her head, or, in other words, she has not that great anterio-posterior length of crown which phrenologists say denotes the motherly instinct.

In time she has a baby of her own. She would not do this except for two reasons: First, she wants something which will furnish an excuse for pushing the child of the first wife aside and at the same time win the affections of the husband and father from his first born; and, secondly she could not help it. The step child is at once driven to the kitchen and there it remains. It is neglected, starved, abused and beaten. From exposure and neglect it at last grows sick. It is still neglected, but finally reaches such a condition that "a decent respect for the opinions of mankind" compels the cruel step-mother and the pliant, nobody of a father, to send for a doctor. Now, here is a case in which you are handicapped from the very beginning.

The step-mother desires that the child shall die. It is in the way—in the way as to its actual presence and every day needs, and will be in the way of her child when the property shall be inherited. The father is passive, mentally myopic, stupid and reasonably obedient. The prospect is that you will lose the little patient. The angels pity the poor little thing and mercifully come and take it home to its own dear mother's breast.

Here is another case:

An old and wealthy citizen grows sick. He has been a grinder in his day and has accumulated wealth enough to ruin his sons and to invite heartless rascals to marry his daughters. The sons are shiftless spendthrifts, the sons-in-law are greedy and the old man is miserly and tough. He should have died long ago according to the natural course of things, but he is tenacious of life and refuses to die—the ungrateful old wretch.

The daughters may be good and dutiful, but there will be a row if they attempt to assist you in an intelligent way. The sons and the sons-in-law sit around and scowl; are not in favor of anything in particular but are opposed to everything in general. I can not conceive of anything in human shape that is more contemptible than a stout, able-bodied man sitting around waiting for somebody to die.

If you expect to save the old man you had better hire a nurse and order everybody else, in plain terms, to "Hands off."

Case III:

A couple get married when they are very young. They are matched in every way as to education, property and social advantages. They are in moderate circumstances, but they toil on together. The husband has a good brain, becomes a student and developes into a strong man mentally. He may choose a profession and even become distinguished amongst his fellows. What has the wife been doing all this time? She has been doing household drudgery and bearing children— one every eighteen months. The strain on her constitution has been great. The rapid revolution of her maternal functions has taken all the life out of her. She grows sickly, loses her teeth, is wrinkled, slab-sided, jaded and worn out generally, and withal, is ignorant. The husband has gone forward and upward in letters; she has gone backward and downward. She never goes into society and sees nobody. He goes everywhere and sees everybody. She has grown prematurely old and homely. He is yet young, and handsomer than when they were married. Nobody admires her. Everybody admires him. The men say,

"Charlie is as smart as a whip and a splendid fellow."

The women say,

"Oh, so intellectual and handsome, and such a homely old wife. I wonder how he ever came to marry her?"

Now, this may be a rare case. It is rare, in fact; but the writer, in his limited experience, has seen more than one like it. At last the poor, worn out wife and mother grows sick. She has done her duty, served her time and the angels are calling her, too.

Now Charlie is rich and ambitious and he knows

that he can marry again. He can marry a young, handsome and well educated woman; one who will be more in sympathy with him, whom he can take into society and "show off," and who will help him in his ambitious schemes. He could not do this with his poor, worn out first love. The reader now raises an objection and says I make humanity too bad. I am not writing about the rule, dear reader; I am giving the exceptions. Humanity is not all bad, thank God. I believe that men and women are falling upward every day; but many are falling the other way. The burglars and thieves are not all the bad ones that this world holds, and some of the worst of humanity never see the inside of a jail and are never punished. There are murderers who never wield a knife, pistol or bludgeon, but who commit murder by *looking on and wishing.*

Now, if he is a thoroughly worldly, ambitious and selfish man, do you think he will struggle very hard to "pull the old woman through?" I fear not. If he is a good man he will still love and cherish her and desire her recovery; but if he be the first you will not have his moral support in your battle for the life of the wife and mother.

I have seen other cases like this:

A young girl marries a decrepit old man for his money. She is young, foolish and poor. He is old, foolish and rich. Here's a match. He wants a young wife against the peach bloom of whose cheek he can lay his withered and scraggy old jaw. He dotes on her, buys her everything and pets her. She tolerates and waits for death to come and claim his own, when she expects to enjoy life. Death does come at last and calls upon the poor, foolish old codger to "kick the bucket." I have seen those heartless and almost headless young fillies flit about the house in a restless way and look in occasionally as if to note how near they are to "pay day"—the "pay day" for which they sold themselves in their beautiful and gushing young girlhood; and, when the last hour came and the toothless old mariner was heading for the "shining shore," I have seen those same heartless things stand around and hump and shrug their shoulders and try to squeeze the bag of their affections for just a little lachrymal moisture; but never a tear.

DEATH DOES COME, AT LAST.

I have never had but one case in which I felt sure that my patient was killed outright while under my treatment; but I am so sure of it that I am going to tell about it.

In my early practice in a southwest Missouri town I made the acquaintance of a man whom I shall call

Jack. Jack came west from Pennsylvania in the great immigration after our late civil war. He was a shoemaker by trade and a born villain. He was born and reared in the slums of London. He was about five feet four in height, bow-legged, hump shouldered, snaggle toothed, and had a face as mean as old Quilp's. He was up in dog fights, cock fights, prize fights and all manner of brutal and inhuman meanness. He took the lowest class of illustrated papers and sat and gloated over their bloody records and obscene pictures by the hour. He kept one of those white, English bull dogs for his inseparable companion. The dog had a head on him like a sausage grinder, a split in his upper lip through which his teeth shone, and his tail looked like an animated and abreviated crow-bar. When you entered Jack's shop and found him on his bench with "Bill" (that was the dog's name) sitting by his side, you mentally exclaimed: "Twins! as sure as I am alive."

There was a prize fight in our county once. The parties had come over from Kansas to avoid arrest. The news got out the day before in some way, and while there were several who would have enjoyed the fight, Jack was the only one from our town who reached it in time. He arose early in the morning, mounted a pony and went, by what could be called nothing else than brute instinct, direct to the spot.

His wife was just his opposite. She was a large, splendid blonde, taller than the average woman, weighed one hundred and sixty or seventy pounds; had blonde hair, large, beautiful blue eyes, and as fair a complexion as man ever beheld. She would have been called a pretty woman anywhere on the earth.

She was not highly educated, but had had some advantages, for a poor girl, in the public schools of her Eastern home, and was not wholly ignorant. The first time I ever saw her she was suffering from " a fit of gravel "—the passage of a *nephritic calculus* from the kidney to the bladder. It is a painful trouble and as it was the first case of the kind that I had ever seen I took some credit to myself for having made a correct diagnosis—the pain ceasing suddenly when the calculus reached its journey's end, as I had predicted. After this I became Jack's family physican. I do not remember to have had much to do in the family until the summer of 1870. This was a year in which we had an unusual amount of sickness in the South-West. The country was new, much prairie had been broken, the streams all overflowed their banks in June and the summer was intensely hot.

I was riding day and night, the prevailing sickness being just what one would expect from the conditions— severe types of bilious and intermittent fevers; the latter taking on the pernicious or congestive forms. Mrs. Jack was stricken down right in the midst of my busiest season. Her case did not differ in any material degree from other cases that I saw every day—a day or two of *malaise*, backache, headache, boneache, a sudden chill followed by a rapid rise of temperature and bilious vomiting. One to three visits generally sufficed for the worst case. A dose of anti-bilious powder or pills, followed by heroic doses of quinine did the work in short order.

But Jack's wife did not improve. I gave her the same treatment, in the main, that I had given others, but there came up vague and indefinite symptoms which I could neither meet nor comprehend. After this state of things had continued for several days I was baffled and asked for a consultation. Jack did not want a consultation; had all confidence in me and desired me to continue. Thus flattered and encouraged I fought on. As I left the house one afternoon Jack asked me:

"When will you be back, Darc.?" (He always called me "Darc." for "Doc.")

I answered that I would try to be there at nine o'clock the next day.

I was called to the country during the night, and being detained did not reach town until eleven o'clock the next forenoon. Dusty and hot as I was I drove direct to Jack's residence. In approaching the house I saw no sign of life or living thing about the premises. When I entered I found Mrs. Jack alone, unconscious and speechless. She was cold as ice to her elbows and knees and was bathed in a profuse, clammy perspiration. Going quickly to the bed I took hold of her arm and found it pulseless, I went at once to a cross fence and called two or three neighboring ladies, sent a boy for a consulting physician, and, learning that Jack was at "the shop," I sent another for him. The women began making mustard draughts under my direction while I tried to get some diffusible stimulus down the patient. In this I failed as she either could not or would not swallow. In a few minutes I saw Jack coming through the gate with that slipping, shambling, uncertain gait which was characteristic of him. He came in looking pale and anxious and, instead of going directly to the bed and speaking to his wife, he sidled over to an old

"HA, HA, HA, HA-A-A-A-A!"

stool, with an inquiring, guilty look on his face. (Oh, how plainly I can see it now!) and sat down.

"How is she, Darc.?"

I informed him of her dangerous condition.

When she heard his voice she seemed to be momentarily aroused from the state of unconsciousness in which I had found her. She turned her head and glared slowly about until she located him, then seemingly gathering all her waning strength in one last effort she threw her feet out of the bed, and before any of us had sufficient presence of mind to arrest her, she came to a sitting posture, slid out of bed and walked straight to him. She stooped and shook her finger in his face and laughed the wildest, weirdest and most blood curdling laugh that I ever heard or ever expect to hear again— " ha, ha, ha, ha-a-a-a-a ;" and then, staggering, would have fallen, had I not caught her. Two of the ladies assisted me in getting her into bed again, while Jack sat like one frozen to his seat.

She died in less than two hours.

Well, the woman was dead and the strangest thing about the case was that I had not been able to understand it.

Within a week or two Jack came to me with one of the blanks of the Charter Oak Insurance Co., of New York. He had a thousand dollar policy on her life for me to fill out and sign. I filled it out and signed it and still did not suspect Jack. The idea had never occurred to me that I knew a man who was bad enough to kill his wife. I had read of and knew there were such men, but I thought that it (like the lion which bites the man's head off in the menagerie) always occurred at some other town.

While filling out the blank I incidentally asked Jack if the company was a good one.

"Oh, yes," said he, "it is first class. I know, because I had a thousand dollars on my first wife, who died in Williamsburg, Penn., and they paid it without a word."

And still, young, innocent " greeny " that I was, I did not suspect him.

Within a few weeks I heard, incidentally, that Jack was abusing me. Said I had neglected his wife—promised to come at nine o'clock and did not get there until eleven; did not understand the case and had poisoned her.

This was painful, but as I knew that every doctor must bear this sort of thing when ill success attends him, I tried to grin and bear it. My inclination was to break Jack's head with a stick, but to do so was to advertise my own failure, and give prominence to and perhaps, excite sympathy for a scoundrel. So I gulped down my rage and waited.

Jack's conduct is plain enough now. If a thief steals your horse, although you may not know it, he is your enemy the next day. Often when men commit great crimes, although the world may yet be in ignorance of it, they at once go about measures whereby they may shift it on some one else. In doing so they often proclaim their own guilt. This is the secret of much successful detective work.

On September 20th, 1870, I started to New York to remain all winter. I went *via* Fort Scott, Kansas, and *via* the Gulf Road to Kansas City. I had to lie over at Fort Scott for a train, and learning that there was a play at " the hall " with the " local talent " of the town in the principal characters, I went with some friends, to see it. As I took my seat who should I see but Jack? He was maudlin drunk and arose with a grin and an obsequious air and offered his hand.

"How are you, Dare?"

I took his hand and he arose and departed. During the play there was a commotion behind me near the top of the stairway. I was informed that the officers were putting a drunken man down stairs. When the play was over and I started to leave the hall I was met at the door by two carpenters from my town who informed me that Jack had presented a cocked revolver at my back with the declared intention of perforating me, but his hand had been staid by a policeman who disarmed him and put him out. Upon his promising to behave his weapon had been restored to him and he had been given his liberty. My informant did not know where Jack was at that moment, but thought he might be looking for me. This was not pleasant. I prepared myself as best I could from my scanty armory and went down, expecting to find Jack lying in wait for me, and to be compelled to die at his hands or skillfully sever his carotid and let him die for me.

But Jack did not materialize and I went on to New York. A few days after arriving there I received our local paper in which I found the matter referred to somewhat after this style:

"We regret to learn that our fellow townsman, Dr. Willis P. King, came near losing his life at the hands of the notorious Jack ———, at Fort Scott, on the night of the 20th, inst. As our readers know, Dr. King started to New York on that day, to be absent all winter. Being compelled to lie over for a train at Fort Scott he went to the theatre with some friends and while there met the notorious Jack ——, of this place. Jack entertains some sort of grudge against the doctor in regard to the doctor's treatment of his wife in her last sickness. Becoming enraged when he saw the doctor he presented a cocked revolver to the latter's breast, but it was knocked aside just in time to save his life," etc., etc.

This was not correct as to details, but as near the truth as the local reporter often gets it. Jack's guilt dawned on me at last. I compared his pretended sorrow over his wife's death with the cold, formal and business manner in which he attended to the collection of her life insurance. I searched for a motive for his enmity toward me, and found an answer in his own guilt. I was now satisfied that this villain had deliberately poisoned his wife while she was under my treatment in order to get the insurance money. I wrote a statement of the whole matter to a friend, in which I openly charged Jack with wife murder, and requested my friend to have it published; but he, being a cool and cautious person, and fearing that I might lay the foundation for a suit for damages, refused to do so. I "nursed my wrath to keep it warm," and waited. I returned home in March, 1871. After kissing wife and babies and eating my dinner I went up town. I met many friends on the street with whom I must shake hands and pass a word; but, shaking them off, one by one, I finally made my way to Jack's shop. Jack was sitting at his work with the "twin" in his accustomed place, looking more like

Jack's brother than ever before. As I entered Jack arose with an abashed air, and grinning and smirking, offered me his hand.

"How are you, Darc.?"

I put my hand behind me and said,

"No, Jack, you can't shake that hand until you have explained some things."

Then drawing the clipping from the home paper, before referred to, from my pocket, I handed it to him with the question:

"What does this mean?"

Jack looked at it, colored, grinned, twisted and squirmed and then delivered himself after this manner:

"Oh, well, Darc., you know, after my wife died I was almost crazy. Hi didn't know w'at I was doin' 'alf the time, you know. Of corse I thought you didn't come has soon as you hought hon the day she died; hand I don't know w'at hi done at Fort Scott. Hi was drunk, you knaw, and don't remember hany-think. Darc., you must forgive me hand look hover it?"

I asked him to sit down. When he did so the "twin" took up his position alongside and I was more than ever struck with the remarkable resemblance between them. As they grew older they grew more and more like brothers.

I opened my long pent-up batteries after this fashion:

"I heard a good deal about what you were saying about me before I went away; but I paid no attention to it. I also heard of your attempt, or pretended attempt to assassinate me at Fort Scott. I admit that I did not understand your wife's case, but it is all plain to me now. You have said that she was poisoned and that I did it. I agree with you in one part of that statement. I think your wife was poisoned, but I didn't do it. I know who did. You poisoned your wife, Jack, in order to get the insurance money, and then tried to throw suspicion off yourself by publicly blaming me.

Now, if you open your mouth about me again; if you even so much as crook your finger at me, I will either have you arrested, or I will blow your brains out; I don't care much which. I am prepared to blow your brains out now, if you are not very quiet."

In all my life I have never seen such an exhibition of guilty cowardice,

"Oh, now, Dare., you don't think hi would do that, do you?"

"I do not only think you would, but I feel sure you did," I answered.

He begged and implored. He didn't want such a scandal. It would be bad for both of us, and he thought we had better say nothing more about it.

And so we parted.

And now the pale faced young person who has been reading this chapter rises up and asks:

"And did you have him arrested?"

No I did not.

"Why not?"

There were many reasons: Our county was in the district that had been burned and depopulated during the war. Our treasury was empty and poor. It would have taken at least one thousand dollars to exhume Mrs. Jack, and send her stomach where a reliable chemical analysis could be made and then bring the chemist to our court to testify. I knew that our court could not make the appropriation. I was too poor to undertake it; and to have undertaken it and made a failure—which we most probably would have done—would have set Jack at liberty with the sympathies of the community in his favor and I would have been disgraced and hurt beyond recovery.

Jack was already married again, but his wife was so sickly that I am sure he could not obtain a policy on her life. She soon died and Jack was also "gathered to his fathers," (if he ever had any) and to his victims whom I am sure he had. I say "victims" because I am fully persuaded that he had also poisoned his first wife at Williamsburg, Penn.

I do not know what became of "the Twin," but considering the time that has elapsed and the average age of dogs I am led to hope that he also has been "gathered to his fathers." I think this narrative sufficiently answers the heading of the chapter in the affirmative.

"Did he kill his wife?"

I think he did.

CHAPTER XIX.

GOING BACK TO COLLEGE.

NECESSITY FOR MORE EDUCATION—THE SOUTHWEST—MY OWN TRIP—MY ILL FITTING CLOTHES—MY PLUG HAT AND THE OLD MAID—MY REVENGE—THE OYSTER SUPPER WITH OBSERVATIONS ON THE HEATHEN.

THERE is nothing that the aspiring country doctor looks forward to with more eager desire than that of being able to once more attend college and "brighten up." He has received his medical education, perhaps, at some point where clinical advantages were not good; and while he had medicine in all its departments pounded into him day by day in didactic lectures, yet, he has not seen much practice until he first approached the bed side unaided and alone. He has practiced for years, has poured over volume after volume of medical lore and thereby learned a great deal. There are weak points in his practice, however; there are great mysteries attached to the cases of people who have died which he desires to have cleared up. He wants to learn surgery and something of the specialties. So, year after year he promises himself that he will go East and take another course.

Finally he does get ready. He packs his clothing and his books and starts for the nearest point on the nearest railroad. He feels queer. He knows that he is going amongst a people who have always lived in the metropolis. They are supposed to be learned about the ways of the world, to be dressy, and smart in all things which pertain to life and business. As he approaches the great city to which he is going he feels more and more queer and out of joint with the world. He discovers that they do not wear clothes like his, and, if he looks closely he will find that people on the cars are pointing at him and smiling occasionally. He thinks he will go out on the platform of the car and avoid criticism for a while for he knows that he is being criticised. As he rises he treads on the spittoon and, in trying to recover himself, he stumbles and almost falls over an old woman's satchel and his hat falls off. In trying to recover his hat he runs the end of a car seat into the capacious pocket of his linen duster and tears it out, He goes out and stands on the platform and hates himself for being so awkward.

It is amusing to sit in the lecture rooms of the great schools in those Eastern cities and see the new fellows come in. You can tell those from the far West and Southwest the moment you see them. Their dress is so outlandish and their manners so awkward that one would think that they could not possibly learn anything. And yet you will find many brainy fellows amongst them. Tennessee and Arkansas and south west Missouri used to send the hardest looking lot on first appearance of any states in the Union; but in two months they would have their hair cut, put on Eastern style clothing and generally proved in the end to be the smartest men in the class. They almost always worked like beavers and when the time came to be examined they acquitted themselves with the very highest honors. As soon as the awkwardness of home and country life wore off, they were as polished in their manners as so many French counts.

We don't know whether our clothes fit or not until we have a chance to compare them with other clothes that do fit. Where nobody's clothes fit, everybody's clothes fit. I suppose that a Chinaman thinks his clothes fit, and, no doubt they do—in China. At least, no one has a chance to know that his clothes do not fit until he sees clothes that do fit.

I remember well my first trip to New York. I had been practicing in the rural districts remote from a railroad for many years. The styles didn't change with us very often. When I was getting ready to go away, I had my tailor cut and make me a new suit. I learned afterward that my tailor was a discharged section hand from a railroad a hundred miles away.

The suit was very fine, I thought, so fine, indeed, that I secretly contemplated entering Gotham in a fashion that would set up an epidemic of paralysis among the best dressed people there. I also bought me a new "Plug" hat—"the latest out" my hatter said.

I discovered long before I reached my destination that there was something wrong with my clothes. I attracted almost as much attention as Sitting Bull or the Chinese Embassador. At first I was vain enough to think that it was my personal beauty or my commanding figure that was attracting all this attention. I soon discovered my mistake. It was my clothes.

I reached Jersey City at last and crossed the ferry. I told the hackman to drive me to the Astor House. This was the only hotel in the city that I had ever heard the name of. After going through the trial of getting my supper and going to bed, I slept soundly, notwithstanding the great noise of the great city, for I was tired.

I arose the next morning, bright and early, and descended to my breakfast. I noticed people looking at me and talking low. I supposed they were pickpockets who were preparing to rob me.

I had my money in one boot and a bowie-knife in the other. I expected to make the knife leg defend the money leg and then let the money leg buy the knife leg out of the difficulty. I went on the street for the purpose of inquiring the way to Bellevue. There was an immense crowd; such a crowd as I had never seen before. The side walks were packed on both sides as far as the eye could reach with a moving mass of humanity, most all of them going south. The streets were filled with vehicles of every kind. I asked an old gentleman if there was a fire anywhere. He explained that these were business and working people going "down town" to their places of business and labor. I attempted to cross the street, through this moving, interminable mass of vehicles. I started, faltered and then turned back. It will confuse any man to pick him up from the deep silence of the great prairies and set him down amid the rush and hurry of Broadway in about sixty hours.

I waited until a big policeman conducted some ladies across and fell into their wake and crossed in safety. I was so confused and excited by the effort, however, that I ran into a sharp faced, sour looking man as soon as I reached the other side and almost upset him.

"Great Heavens!" said he, "what ails you?"

He was gone before I could explain.

Then some very elegant and benevolent looking gentleman grabbed me and insisted on taking me into a store and selling me some "cheap clothing." I had had a suspicion for a day or two that my clothes didn't fit as they should. I now became painfully aware of the fact that they didn't fit at all. My pants were too short and when I sat down they drew up at the bottoms in front half way to my knees, and the side seams ran directly down over my knee cap. My coat was long in the waist, short in the tail and the collar insisted in reaching up and holding on to my occipital protuberance, and my vest was baggy and unreliable. My new hat—"the latest out"—was just seven years out of date. The rim was narrow and stuck straight out all around and the body—which was unusually long—tapered toward the crown. The hat touched my head in just three places—at the frontal eminences in front and at the occipital protuberance behind. No Swedish emigrant that ever landed in Castle Garden could possibly present a more ludicrous appearance than I did. I struggled valiantly with the kind hearted clothing man and finally got away. I had heard of these fellows and didn't want to trade with them. I slunk around and tried to dodge the crowd until I met a policeman. I asked for an American clothing house. He kindly showed me the way. Here I was fitted out in a good, neat, well fitting suit. I put them on then and there. The good gentleman from whom I made my purchase took me across the street to a hat store where I bought a new plug which was *a la mode*. Then I asked for a barber shop and was shown that. My hair was dense, long and shockey, and I had two little spikes of a goatee, one on each corner of my chin.

When I took my seat in the chair the barber asked me if I wanted my hair cut and I answered that I did, badly. How would I have it cut?

"Clean this stuff off my chin and cut my hair in the New York style. Skin my head, scalp me, do anything you please; but be sure it is in the style," were my orders.

After he was through with me I went back to Broadway, took the right side of the street, walked fast, popped my heels on the side walks and plowed the people on either side like an ocean steamer and in two hours was a thoroughly converted New Yorker. At least, I thought I was; for the gazing stopped.

What a glorious time the country doctor has in the great city. He sits under the droppings of the sanctuary—at the feet of the masters in his profession—and has the cobwebs brushed away from his beclouded mind

The mysteries are cleared up in the clinics and he goes to his room every night filled to the muzzle with new facts and new ideas. On Sunday afternoons he "takes in the sights" about the great city and walks his country legs off on the hard pavements. When he goes home in the spring he is, to all intents and purposes, another man in his knowledge and in the self confidence which that knowledge brings. He is another man in his dress and, perhaps, in his manners.

He goes home all "dressed up" and his own family scarcely know him.

I wore my new hat all winter and, when I went home in the spring I bought me another—the finest and best I could buy on Broadway. I just made the dressy men sick with my new hat in my poor country town where the styles never came until they had gone out everywhere else. Everybody envied that hat, and I only wore it on high occasions and then, I confess that I harbored a secret pleasure in making other people feel bad.

"Pride goeth before a fall," and so it did in this case. I thought too much of that hat.

I wore it one night in May to a strawberry festival at "the hall." It was a church festival and the whole town was out to enjoy it. The church people had sent the boys to the woods and had them cut and bring in young green trees and had set them up all around the walls.

I found a nice place amongst the branches of the bushes to put my hat, and so, put it away. After eating strawberries and cream and promenading awhile, my wife desired to go home. We went around to get my hat.

There were two old maids from Boston who were teaching writing school in our town at the time and I found them sitting on a bench just under the place where I had hung my hat. They were typical New England old maids—tall, slender, angular, sarcastic and grave. They had both reached that period in old maidenhood when a woman gives up the idea of marrying and so puts in a goodly portion of her time for the remainder of her life in hating the brute man. I think that the sight of a pair of pants on a clothes line would have thrown either one of them into a fit of hydrophobia. They were sitting on this bench as stiff and prim as wooden images and looked like a pair of exclamation points at the end of a sentence. I reached for my hat and it wasn't there. I felt uneasy as I saw one of the old maids begin to twist and wriggle about a little. I remarked that one of the boys had probably worn my hat out.

"Are you looking for your hat?" asked the one with the wriggle.

I answered that I was.

GOING BACK TO COLLEGE. 371

She raised up and deliberately put her hand behind her, and, without looking back or down, brought out a shapeless mass of back fur and stuff which no one but an expert would have recognized as even the *remains* of a plug hat.

"Is this it?" said she with a voice and air which seemed to mean that she had been saving it for me;— and she had. She had saved it sure enough. She had pressed it, and, if she had had time, I suppose would have pickled it. The top of the crown was crushed down into the rim and the rim broken clear across on both sides. I

"OH, NO, IT IMPROVES A PLUG HAT TO SIT ON IT!"

inspected it with blood in my eye and a frog in my throat.

"Why, it's ruined, ain't it?" she asked.

"Oh, no," I answered "it improves a plug hat to sit on it."

She manifested no further interest in the matter,

but projected her iron jaw a little and continued to inspect and criticise the promenaders. I had never laid violent hands on one of the opposite sex, but it would have done me good to have mopped the floor with this old, animated telephone pole. I went down the hall steps in three jumps and the next morning gave my hat to a negro to saw a half cord of wood. I had not even then surrendered the idea that that hat had some sort of value attached to it; but now, I feel that I cheated the poor negro.

What on earth the woman wanted to sit on the hat for I have never been able to divine. If the hat had had a galvanic battery in it I could understand it; but it had none. However, she seemed to enjoy it, and I suppose she really did. I made up my mind then and there to have my revenge. My first thought was to wreak it on old maids in general; but I soon saw that that would not do. It would not do to make good and kind-hearted old maids suffer for what this miserable old scare-crow had done.

There was nothing left but to take it out of festivals. It was at a festival that my hat and heart had been crushed. It was the delusive temporary forest that had tempted me to hang my nice hat where I did. So from that day I became a "festival fiend." I went to all the festivals. I went early and late and went early and remained late. I would dart in on them at most unusual hours and seek opportunities to do something that would spread consternation amongst the prime movers of these snares and, if possible, make everybody feel bad. I never missed one when I could get there.

My revenge came at last. In another town I found the time and means of wreaking my revenge.

I ran in to a festival in a church basement one night about midnight. It was late and most of the good things were gone.

There was still a considerable crowd; and all the ladies who expected to see their names in the papers next morning as "presiding at the table" were there.

I sat down at the table and thought about my hat. The crowd, the promenading, the music—everything carried me back to that loved but crushed hat. The ladies crowded around and all wanted to take my order. I wanted oysters, for this was the worst of all the festival snares—an "oyster festival."—as if the oysters were having the feast instead of the folks. A sprightly and kind hearted lady took my order. She came back and set my dish down with a great flourish. It was a big plate of thin, sickly looking soup with one little crippled oyster in it.

She went away to get some dish water for some other late comer, and I sat and looked straight across the table. I didn't vary my gaze to the right or left, but gazed steadily and vacantly in front of me. No one seemed to notice me, but I still gazed. I was determined to attract attention, and I finally did. My kind hearted friend in her rounds noticed me in passing. She watched me for a moment and then made a plunge at me.

"Why, what's the matter, Doctor? Can't you eat your oysters?" ("oysters" mind you, in the plural, and she knew she had brought but one.) "Won't you have something else?"

"No, madam," I answered. "I do not wish anything else."

"Well, why don't you eat your oysters?" "Oysters" again, you see.

"Why, I was just moralizing," I said, still gazing intently in front of me.

"Moralizing!" said she. "What were you moralizing about?"

By this time a large crowd of the ladies had gathered around to see what the matter was.

"I was just thinking," I said, "about the difference between cultivated and Christianized people and those who are not."

"Well, what is the difference?" asked a half dozen, expecting to get some compliment or fact which they could use in "converting the world."

"Well," I went on, "there are those unchristian and heathen people who keep restaurants. I go there some times, I am sorry to say. I am obliged to, for we don't have church festivals open on the streets every day. Now, when I call for oysters there they will bring me a whole dozen on one plate. They do this, notwithstanding the fact that they know oysters will fight and claw each other when two or more are put together on a plate. But what do they care? Their sensibilities have never been cultivated or heightened by a Chris tian life and they don't care if the oysters tear each other's eyes out. Na-o!

"Now, when I come here you ladies bring me one oyster, because you know if you put more than one on a plate they will fight and you can't stand it to see bloodshed, even among oysters."

"NOW, EAT YOUR SUPPER AND KEEP YOUR MOUTH SHUT."

They each seized a plate and flew to the other end of the room where the oyster soup (mostly soup) was made. Then they halted and consulted.

They stuck their chins out, and wagged their heads and I could catch fragments of sentences like this:

"Well, I don't care who he is;" "Don't care if he does—hateful thing;" "For my part, I'd let him go," etc., etc.

But my kind friend seized the ladle and went to delving down into the broth. She brought me two dozen oysters, and emptying them in my dish said:

"Now, eat your supper and keep your mouth shut."

I did. But I was revenged for the loss of my plug hat, at last.

But, to return to our mutton. It may be that my Western and Southwestern brethren may take umbrage at my criticism. If you do, dear friends, please note that I have made myself the awkwardest of the "awkward squad."

Now, in 1890, you do not find men coming from the West looking so peculiarly dressed and awkward as heretofore; for the railroads have penetrated everywhere within the last fifteen years. And where they go the styles go. The railroads and telegraph annihilate space, in a measure, and bring people a thousand miles apart almost to each other's doors.

I can not conclude this chapter without urging my country reader to go to the great centers every five or six years and take a few months of lectures and clinics. We all get into ruts and need prying out. Every man who practices the healing art owes it to himself, and more especially to those who give him charge of their sick bodies, to keep abreast of the times in his procession.

Too much honor can not be paid to the noble men in our large cities for their work in lecturing and writing and keeping the "smaller fry" in the profession from going into the "dry rot." It may be argued that they do what they do from selfish considerations. This may be true of some but I am sure that it is not true of all. But, whatever the motive may be, the work is done and we poor fellows in the backwoods reap the benefit of it—if we will—and, in the end, our patients also get the benefit.

CHAPTER XX.

QUACKS AND QUACKERY.

THE TRUE PHYSICIAN—THE DIFFERENT KINDS OF QUACKS—THE GENTLEMANLY QUACK—THE SMART PRETENDER—THE PROFESSIONAL BUZZARD OR "JIM CROW" DOCTOR—"ABDOMINAL DIGITALIS AND AORTIC REGURGITATION—DOCTOR CONNECKTIE AND DR. GULLUS.

IN order to present the quack in his true light, let us first see what manner of man the true physician is, so that, by the outlines of his symmetrical character, the former may be made to stand out in all his ugly deformity.

The true physician is a man of good moral character. His conduct is such that, with those who know him best, there is no doubt about it. His acts are the acts of a noble, true and unselfish man, who means to do right not only by himself, but by all with whom he comes in contact. He is a man of knowledge and is not content with what he already knows, but is constantly and persistently trying to know more. He takes and reads the best literature of his profession, and would at any time stint his stomach or cheat his back of a new coat in order to buy a new book, written by one of the masters in the profession. He tries to familiarize himself with every form of disease, and to arm himself with the best weapons with which to meet and vanquish the enemy. As an honest man, he feels it his bounden duty to do this. He feels that if he should do less he would be recreant to his duty and unfaithful to the trust imposed upon him by his profession. He is a brave man, and is, to all intents and purposes, a born warrior. While he is as tender as a woman with everything that is sick, and that suffers, yet, when occasion requires it, he is as courageous as a lion, and does not shrink from his duty, even though his own life be in danger. From the depths of a kind heart, made kinder and tenderer through contact with suffering, he lays his hands kindly and tenderly upon all who are unfortunate and need kindness and pity; and yet, in the discharge of his duties, he can inflict pain in order to save life, and his brave heart does not quail even in the face of defeat and death. He makes no pretension to knowledge that he does not possess, and when he does not know a thing, will admit that he does not. In times of epidemics, when death is upon every hand and the community is being scourged as by fire, while others flee to places of safety and seek refuge where the contagion comes not, he takes his place with his people, and goes quietly where others dare not enter—where the seeds of typhoid, cholera, yellow fever and small-pox are rank in the air; and yet he fears not. Duty with him is everything, and death is preferable to dishonor.

He knows the weaknesses and faults of the people

whom he treats, and, like a true man, hides them away from the world in the innermost recesses of his heart, and is not burdened—for secrets are a burden to those only who desire to tell them.

He does his work for the reasonable remuneration that is fixed by his fellows and sanctioned by law, and does not make bargains and collect fees in advance that burden the poor, and for which he may never render adequate services. He does not promise to cure anything and everything in order to get a case; in fact, he promises very little, but does a great deal where to do anything is possible. He is closely identified with everything in his community which goes toward elevating humanity, and which tends to ennoble and dignify human character. In short, the true physician is an upright and true man; a worker and a seeker after the good things attainable; is honest and unselfish, and a doer of good deeds through all his life; and when he gets old and too frail to work longer, he can sit down with the satisfying thought that he has done all that it was possible for him to do in his sphere. He meets his fellows with head erect because he is not ashamed, and when death comes he goes,

> "Not, like the quarry slave at night,
> Scourged to his dungeon, but, sustained and soothed
> By an unfaltering trust, approaches his grave
> Like one who wraps the drapery of his couch
> About him, and lies down to pleasant dreams."

But what shall I say of the quack? How shall I describe him? He presents himself in so many different forms that, like the chameleon, he is hard to describe. In order to properly describe him, I shall be compelled to divide him and describe him under different heads.

Webster defines the word quack as follows: "A boaster; one who pretends to skill or knowledge which he does not possess." We give it a much broader meaning than this. We apply the term not alone to the ignorant boaster, but to any man who attempts to practice medicine without being well grounded in the fundamental facts underlying an intelligent practice; and even when a man is competent, if he is guilty of irregular practices, and resorts to illegitimate methods to obtain a practice, we denounce him as being guilty of quackery.

The *gentlemanly* quack may or may not be a graduate, but he is a gentlemanly man. He starts out in his professional career with good prospects; but he is like a wasp—larger when he is born (graduates or begins) than he ever is afterward. He is a person who attains to the full height of his intellectual and professional manhood early in life, and afterward, instead of growing and broadening, he begins to dwarf, and soon becomes professionally mummified. He does not attend medical societies, and does not study; never buys a new book, and does not take a medical journal. He does not "believe in medical journals," and thinks that they "do a doctor more harm than good." He soon forgets everything that he ever knew; makes up a jumbled anatomy, physiology and pathology of his own, then goes into a rut and consistently stays there. When in consultation he will accept your diagnosis without a murmur, although it may overturn all that he has been compelled to say of or to do in the case ; and when you are gone he will go right back to his own treatment, and stick to it until the patient dies. He can not see why the patient did not get well, because about all the people that he ever saw recover did so under that identical treatment. "Bilious attacks" and "malaria" are the favorite diseases of this man. All other diseases he conveniently divides into "lung diseases," "kidney affections," and "liver complaints." For the first he gives compound syrup of squills ; for the second, sweet spirits of nitre ; and for the third, calomel, podophylin, or nothing, according to the school he represents. When he is not able to locate the disease, he bombards the liver on general principles. He gives calomel, day in and day out, in obstruction of the "common duct" of the gall bladder, and diuretics in retention of the urine from strictured urethra. This same fellow sits by the bed of the parturient female for four or five days, in cases of cross presentation and difficult labor from any cause, because he "believes in letting nature take its course," and sits around like a knot on a log and lets women die from post-partem hemorrhage, because he does not "believe in meddlesome midwifery." This man is a good collector; takes whetstones, fiddles, cows, calves, second-hand furniture, and tow linen and tallow for his pay, and turns it all over to the best advantage without ever discovering that nature cut him out and fitted him for a junk-dealer and a rag man.

Perhaps the best thing that can be said for this

creature is, that he goes through his whole professional life, and finally dies without discovering the fact that he has killed from ten to twenty people every year.

The *smart pretender* is a different man from the foregoing. He is a loud man. There is nothing, if you will believe him, that he does not know. He has specifics for everything and actually cures people, no matter what the disease is. He gets through college cheap, practices medicine cheaper than anybody, and is altogether a cheap man. He gets practice by sending word that he can cure the case, has cured many just like it. He makes a diagnosis off-hand and at long range, without having seen the case or even heard much about it. This man is unfitted by nature for the noble and exalted duties of the physician, because he is shallow, does not know anything, and is incapable of knowing much. He is naturally a coward and a liar, and no coward and liar ever made a good doctor. He seeks practice for the basest and most selfish reasons, and indeed is never actuated by lofty and unselfish motives. This fellow is transparent even to the laity, and is compelled to seek "greener fields and pastures new" quite often. He may take a new place by storm, but he is too weak to "hold the fort" very long.

We have also the *professional buzzard*. This is the weakly, watery-eyed, red nosed old scarecrow, who at some time in his early life has gotten hold of several recipes which he considers valuable, and he is therefore induced to give suffering humanity the benefit of them. He is poor and mangy and mean, and hangs upon the outskirts of the profession just as the coyote and the buzzard hang upon the outskirts of a battle field—picking up whatever he can. He is greasy and pinched, has a breath of benzine and a general odor of unchanged linen. He slinks naturally from the true members of the medical profession, always comes into the drugstore by the back door if he can get in that way, and learns all that he knows about new remedies from the drug clerk. He can not write a prescription, and he has a decided weakness for "yarb-medicines," which he gives in the form of "slops and teas." He pours this stuff down his dupes with about the same idea, I imagine, that a hired girl pours dish-water down a rat-hole—that of filling a vacuum and killing time. This wretched and dismal old fraud does not do much harm, however, for the reason that the people whom he kills are very much like himself—making better fertilizing material when dead than citizens while living.

The *advertising quack* and swindler is the worst of the lot. He is the black wolf, aye, the Bengal tiger of the profession. He is ignorant as a physician, but not an ignorant man by any means. He is full of shrewdness and cunning, and knows poor, weak human nature like a book. He has within him all the elements that go to make the successful gambler, three-card monte man, or burglar. He may have his little trouble, as all people do, but it is not with his conscience. His office (which is generally a fine one) is a sort of bunco-shop, into which the ignorant and credulous are inveigled and mercilessly swindled. He chooses the practice of medicine as a profession instead of burglary because the law protects him in the one, and does not protect him in the other. His office is hung with forged diplomas, and with pictures representing surgical cases upon which he claims to have operated, but did not; and his pigeon-holes are full of certificates of cure, written and signed by himself. He knows the value of printer's ink, and uses it liberally. He advertises to cure all diseases, both acute and chronic; and he makes a specialty of diseases of the eye, ear, throat, nose and lungs, diseases of the mind and nervous system, diseases of children, consumption, piles, gynæcology and fits. He fills his own prescriptions to prevent the exposure of his shallow pretenses, and tells his gaping victims that his medicines cost ten dollars per ounce and more, and that he sends to New York, Boston and foreign countries for much of it. He is the discoverer and sole proprietor of the never-failing cancer remedy and world-renowned cure for consumption. He treats pimples, boils and local skin eruptions as cancer. He sets a high price upon his work, and always gets one-half in advance, and, if possible, a bankable note for the remainder.

No age, sex, or condition in life is safe from the wiles of this scoundrel and mountebank. He is master of all the arts by which he can get a hold upon the unfortunate and suffering, and when they are once in his power he is as merciless as a pirate. He will undertake a case of consumption at the brink of the grave, will collect money in advance, and rob widows and orphans with the promise of doing something that he knows he can not do.

He is, in brief, professionally an ignoramus, naturally sharp, cunning, cruel, a thief, a cowardly robber and a merciless pirate, a murderer and a villain so black and damnable that the English language, in its utter weakness, fails to furnish words with which to paint him.

Compared with such a man, thieves, garroters, burglars and train-robbers become decent and respectable. It requires courage of a certain kind to burglarize a house or a bank, and it requires courage of a much higher order to rob a train; but it does not require any courage at all to rob a sick man. It requires nothing but a heart devoid of pity, and a nature supremely selfish and regardless of the rights and interests of others. Sustained by the fact that no law exists by which he can be punished, such a villain, after having won the confidence of his victim by his specious promises, takes the last dollar or the last piece of property, and enjoys his ill-gotten gains to his heart's content, while there is no one to "molest or make him afraid."

As before remarked the old "Jim Crow" doctor does not do a great deal of harm except among his own kind—the ignorant. I have heard gentlemen in the profession say that they thought this class of so-called doctors a necessity—that they take the ignorant and non-paying classes off the intelligent and competent physicians hands. There may be something in this when we look at it from a purely practical standpoint. But, I am not willing to admit that ignorance is necessary anywhere in this life. I am more especially disinclined to admit that ignorance is necessary to deal with the sick and the afflicted. Ignorance is not a crime and can not, therefore, be legally punished. If it could be the infliction of the death penalty through the intervention of a quack doctor would be rather severe, to say the least. But, I still insist that, so long as these ignorant fellows are permitted to work slaughter through their ignorance and incompetence then it were better that this slaughter be confined to those who are the least benefit to the world. Let us save the good and the useful if we can not save all.

I have seen and heard enough funny things concerning these ignorant quacks to fill a volume. Here is one:

In a small town where I once practiced there was an old fellow who was quite innocent in his way except for the murders he committed in trying to practice medicine. He had not the slightest idea of anatomy, physiology or pathology, and was just as innocent of any knowledge concerning the therapeutic value and action of drugs. He had a nose that had suffered from *rosacea* so long that it looked like an old, haggled and chewed up beet, one of his eyes was of the fried egg variety; but he always maintained an air of respectability by wearing a frayed plug hat.

He was always slipping in by the back door of the drug store and holding consultations with one of the clerks. This clerk really made out and filled most of the doctor's prescriptions for him after the doctor had detailed the symptoms in the case. This was, no doubt, better for the patient, for the clerk was sure not to recommend or use any dangerous drugs, while the doctor, if left to himself, might do so.

One of our physicians overheard the following conversation between a facetious drug clerk and this quack, while the clerk was helping him on one of his prescriptions:

"OH, YES, I HAVE CURED THAT TOO."

"Clerk: "Doctor, I suppose that you have performed a great many surgical operations in your time."

"Quack: "Oh, yes, a great many.

"Clerk: "Doctor, I have long since desired to find a surgeon who has performed a certain operation—an operation which has only been performed a few times, I believe."

"Quack. "What operation is it?"

Clerk: "It is the operation of *abdominal digitalis!*"

"Quack. "Oh, yes, I have done that operation

twice; but the doctors in this town will not give me credit for it."

"Clerk: "There is another operation that I wish to ask about (and I have no doubt that you have performed it), and that is *aortic regurgitation.*"

"Quack: "Yes, I have done that too, over at —— town. Oh! I tell you, it's an awful bloody operation."

After all of my experiences with quacks and, after a good deal of observation and devoting much thought to the consideration of the matter I feel constrained to say that the honest men in the medical profession would have destroyed him long ago, if the public and the press had permitted them to do so.

The general reader may not be prepared to believe this; but it is true nevertheless. I will furnish a case or two in proof. There came to the town where I then lived several years ago, one of the brazenest and most blatant advertising quacks that I ever saw. He took up fully one half of the local advertising space of the best local paper, and, besides this, issued a half-sheet each morning. He was Dr. P. Walter Connecktie (this will do for a name) "*late* of London," *late* of the Hospitals of New York City, *late* of Charity Hospital, New Orleans" etc. etc. In short he was the *late* Dr. Connecktie. Ah, reader, look out for these *late* fellows. The doctor who is "*late*," from half a dozen places will *soon* be *late* from your town, just as soon as he gets all the money that the credulous and gullible are ready to part with. The "*late*" doctor is never so "*late*" that he does not get a part of the money that all the fools have in the course of his travel. This fellow took in the ducats from every direction—foolish, weak and sick people paying $25 to $100 for a single prescription. Our medical society finally had him arrested, as he had failed to register according to law. When he went before the justice he was told that if he could show a diploma from a reputable school he would yet be permitted to register it and would not be fined. He stated, with much blandness, that he had a diploma, but that it was at the house of his brother, in Louisiana, and his brother usually went duck hunting about that time of year, and it would be difficult to get it, so he preferred to pay his fine! After this he did his practice through a local quack who had registered, and, in four weeks, took away from the little town *over three thousand dollars.* This fellow wore a plug hat and fire escape whiskers, drove out in a fine buggy behind a pair of spanking grays each afternoon and was an object of wonder and admiration to every fool in town, and yet he couldn't have located the liver at three guesses if his life had depended on it.

Soon there came another fellow. He was one of the lecturing kind. He would lecture one night to ladies, the next to men alone, and the next to a mixed audience. I went around one night out of curiosity. I found him to be, in person and manner, a sort of cross between the "single footed exhorter" at a revival meeting and the hand shaking politician. He was a voluble, oozy, sloppy, tearful fellow—one of those men who could easily overflow his banks in the dryest season on very short notice.

His subject this night was "Human Kindness." He

treated it about as an ordinary one horse preacher would have done, and, after he got himself properly wound up he told the following story, said he:

"My friends, we are, very few of us, as kind as we should be; and many of us neglect our duty to the poor and deserving. I will relate an incident which will illustrate this point. When I was young I had a very dear brother. He was one of the noblest and best boys I ever saw. He and I always played together and what was the joy of one was the joy of the other, and what was the sorrow of one was shared by the other. But we grew to manhood and went out into the world, each to work out his own fortune. Our inclinations led our paths far apart. While he was yet young he sickened and died in a town in Ohio. I was far away and could not be present to drop a tear on my beloved brother's bier."

At this point I noticed that several handkerchiefs went up to eyes to wipe away tears. He went on:

"But I always desired to see the place where my beloved brother slept. This desire haunted me everywhere I went. Finally I was in that part of Ohio lecturing; and, being near this town, I took the train on a Saturday and arrived there at night. I put up at the hotel; but I could not sleep, for I was near the ashes of the brother I had loved so much. The next morning I arose and after breakfast, I went to church as I always do when I have an opportunity." Here the most pious people looked at each other and nodded as much as to say, "that's the kind of a doctor I like."

He continued: "After dinner I prepared to visit the grave of my poor, dead brother. While I was getting ready the bell of one of the churches tolled the funeral knell. I naturally asked who was dead, and from a person who knew the facts I elicted the following remarkable story: Several years previous to this time there had come to this town a steady and intelligent mechanic, bringing with him his wife and children. They were good, religious people, but, unfortunately, through evil association, the husband contracted the drinking habit. He went from bad to worse until, finally, his little savings were all gone and he was such a hopeless and degraded drunkard that he could not procure work. At last he died in the gutter and filled a drunkard's grave. His family were left helpless and destitute, but the brave Christian mother toiled on, doing whatever she could find to do and lovingly keeping the little flock together. At last, from sheer want little Willie died, and after him little Anna, and finally little Johnny. There were none left now but the brave mother and little Mary; and, finally that dread disease, consumption, seized the poor mother and the bell that I heard, tolled her funeral knell.

I went out to the cemetery, and, after a little search I found my brother's grave. I knelt down and reverently thanked the Lord that he had permitted me to find the spot where the bones of my dear brother and the companion of my youth rested."

More tears here and, hence, more handkerchiefs.

"I sat down," he continued, "and let my mind revert

to the time when as boys this brother and I wandered over hill and dale and gathered the wild flowers and laughed in our boyish glee, unmindful of what the future had in store for us, and unmindful of the fact that our little feet which trod—"

Here the doctor broke down and got out his own handkerchief, while there was general weeping and blowing of noses. The reference to "little feet" drew my attention to the doctor's, and I noted that they were now almost as large as fiddle boxes! After violently blowing his nose he resumed:

"While I was sitting there, and just as the sun was sinking in the west, a funeral cortege wound its way slowly into the grave-yard. There was no hearse—only a common wagon—and only a few mourners. There was one poor, little, ragged and half starved girl—about twelve years old, whom I felt sure was little Mary. She was the only real mourner and she was weeping as if her little heart would break. They went to that part of the grave-yard which I knew was the "Potter's Field," and there laid the poor form to rest, and then they departed. I still sat, watching the sun as he sank to rest, and thinking of the unhappiness that is brought into the world by strong drink, until the dusk of evening was upon me, when I arose to go. As I did so I heard a choking, sobbing sound in the direction of the new made grave. I quickly wended my way thither and there, crouched upon the little mound, was the starved and ragged form of little Mary—clinging frantically to the earth that covered the form of her dear mother;

left alone in the world to starve and die, with no one to help her, and no one to love."

Here the "doctor" slopped over again and went for his handkerchief—in which act a large part of the audience joined, while I looked around to see if I could find a rock or a rotten egg!

"I took her by the hand and gently lifted her up. After a little resistance she went with me. I took her to the hotel and had her cared for, and the next day, after getting her some new clothing, I took her to another town where I had some wealthy relatives; and at my solicitation they adopted her and gave her a splendid education, and now she is a refined and Christian lady— one of the noblest and best in the state of Ohio."

At the conclusion of the story those who had been drawing on their lachrymal sacs gave their noses a final squeeze and the doctor went on to another part of his subject.

As the audience went out I met two excellent and kind Christian ladies—both friends and patrons of mine—whose eyes showed evidence of having been recently subjected to a severe mopping. One of them asked:

"Doctor, don't you think Doctor Gullus is a good man?"

"No," I answered, "I dont think he is."

"Why, doctor, what makes you say that?"

"Well," I answered, "because no good man is a liar and this fellow is. He is one of the worst I ever saw, because he lies about things which ought to be held as sacred."

"Why, doctor, what makes you—

"Wait," said I, "we can't talk here. Will you do me the kindness to call at my office tomorrow? If you will I will explain myself."

They both promised; for, in addition to having their curiosity aroused, I had some right to make demands on their time, for I had slept in chairs in both of their houses, and held my finger on the pulse of the little one when the issue was doubtful.

True to their promise they came the next day. After upbraiding me for my hard-heartedness and apparent rudeness the night before, they demanded that I should tell them what I meant.

"Now, dear friends," I began, "you heard that story about the little girl, did you not, and noted every point in it?"

Yes, they thought they had.

"Did you notice anything inconsistent in the story?"

No, they didn't think they had.

"Well, now," said I, "listen. We will suppose that this terrible tragedy took place in this town. You two ladies were among those who visited this family in all their poverty and terrible afflictions. You were with the mother in the last death agony, and held poor, little, starved and ragged Mary's hand when the last earthly prop was swept from under her. You were in the funeral cortege that went to the "Potter's Field," and, after laying the poor, wasted form away, you turned around in the dusk of the evening, and left poor little

Mary lying on her mother's grave, and you—two good Christian ladies—marched back to town! Mary is left, not only out in the world, but out in the cemetery, half-starved and poorly clad and night coming on. Do you believe such a miserable lie as this concerning *any* of the people of *any* town in Ohio? I am not an Ohio man; but I desire to come to their defense. I know it is not true, and were I an Ohio man I should egg that scoundrel before he leaves town, or I would make him swallow his hypocritical lie. Why, the Hottentots, the wild Indians of the plains, would not be guilty of such an outrageous thing!"

They looked at each other for awhile and one of them spoke:

"Jennie, I guess we made miserable fools of ourselves."

The other assented and added:

"Oh, I could just take a stick and break his head."

A woman always gets mad if she finds that she has cried at the wrong time!

"Well, what made him tell such a story?"

"Because he knew that there were a great many people who would make miserable fools of themselves," I answered.

And he did know. These fellows know human nature like a book—better than you and I, reader.

We had him arrested and he beat us. Why? Because the public and the press were almost unanimously against us. He had subsidized the one and "bamboozled" the other. He went away taking with him about $4,000 of fools' money, and at the next town a poor, weak woman, who had left her family and followed him from town to town, committed suicide because of the hopelessness of her love for this gentle and tender—robber.

THE END.

OTTO FLEMMING
1009 ARCH STREET
PHILADELPHIA, PA.

Manufacturer of Electric Apparatus, for use in Electro-Therapeutics, Gynæcology and Surgery. Stationary and Portable Apparatus for Faradic and Galvanic Currents, or Galvano Cautery. Milliampere Meters, Current Controllers. Applying Electrodes in all varieties. Repairing.

AN IMPORTANT NEW WORK
  JUST PUBLISHED

The Practical Application of Electricity in Medicine and Surgery,
By Dr. R. W. ST. CLAIR, M. D.

Cloth, 12mo, 236 pages, about 70 illustrations.

What has already been said of this most excellent work, a copy of which should be in the hands of ever practitioner:—The *Times and Register*, of January 31, 1891, speaks of it as follows: "Throughout, Dr. St. Clair's work is filled with practical hints It reminds us of Munde's Minor Surgical Gynæcology in many respects. What is included under the name of 'experience' is what this book supplies to the novice. To any of our readers who intend to buy a battery, but have never used electricity, or paid any special attention to this potent agent, we would say, 'Procure Dr. St. Clair's book and read it before you invest in this expensive apparatus.'"

Copies mailed prepaid to any address, on receipt of price, $2.00

Address, R. H. ANDREWS, M. D.,
Editor and Proprietor of The Medical Summary

P. O. BOX 1217, PHILADELPHIA, PA.

"YALE" SURGICAL CHAIR.

The only Chair in which all the movements known to modern surgical and gynæcological work are combined in a single chair; new and valuable features that no other chair possesses. It is simple in mechanism, strong in construction, beautiful in design and easily understood and operated. Send for large Catalogue.

Fig. XVII—Dorsal.

Fig. I—Normal.

A few of the positions are: normal, reclining, semi-reclining, horizontal, ¾ length, dorsal, Sim's right or left lateral, oblique, dorsal with hips raised, side tilt, raising or lowering, chloroform narcosis, rotating, etc., etc.

Fig. IX—Chloroform Narcosis.

GOULD DENTAL CHAIR.

A new invention, giving new positions heretofore unknown in a Dental chair and which make it to-day the most popular operating chair on the market; strong, light, firm, simple to understand and easy to operate, and at a price within the reach of every dentist. Send for Catalogue with prices.

Fig. II—Normal.

Fig. VII—Highest Position

Fig. XIV—Chloroform Narcosis

Canton Surgical and Dental Chair Co.,
62, 64 and 66 East Seventh Street,
CANTON. OHIO.
Manufacturers of Gould Dental Chairs, "Yale" Surgical Chairs, Fletcher Fountain Spittoons Wilcox Spiral Dental Engines, Duplex Cord Dental Engines, Etc., Etc., Etc.

PONCA COMPOUND

A Uterine Alterative Especially Affecting the Mucous Surfaces.

INDICATIONS:
- Metritis,
- Endo-Metritis,
- Subinvolution,
- Menorrhagia,
- Metrorrhagia,
- Leucorrhœa,
- Dysmenorrhœa,
- Ovarian Neuralgia,
- Threatened Abortion,
- Suppressed Menses,
- Painful Pregnancy,
- After-Pains.

"Ponca Compound exercises a decided and specific alterative action upon the uterine tissues as also a general tonic influence upon the Pelvic Organs:—It has a tendency to absorb plastic deposits, to regulate the vascular supply, to relieve congestion, to tone up the nerve forces, to regulate the bowels, and to remove spasmodic conditions. In most instances it eradicates the principal influences that cause and keep up engorgements, displacements, etc., and can always be relied upon as the chief factor in bringing about normal conditions."

EACH TABLET CONTAINS EXT. PONCA, 3 GRS.; EXT. MITCHELLA REPENS, 1 GR.; CAULOPHYLLIN, ½ GR.; HELONIN, ¼ GR.; VIBURNIN, ¼ GR.

Ponca is a small plant growing on the south-western prairies and is used by the Indian women for troubles of the uterus and its appendages, on account of a strong alterative action.

100 TABLETS WILL BE MAILED UPON RECEIPT OF $1.00

TONGALINE

Possesses a peculiar affinity for viscid secretions, neutralizing and eliminating them through the natural channels. It is diaphoretic, laxative, anti-septic, anti-neuralgic, and anti-rheumatic, hence is

INDICATED IN
- NERVOUS **HEADACHE**,
- Rheumatism,
- Neuralgia,
- La Grippe,
- Sciatica,
- Gout.

HEADACHE.

"I prescribed Tongaline for a lady who has suffered exceedingly with Headache for several years. The pain is mostly confined to the top of the head, and continues often for 24 hours, unless she is thoroughly narcotized by an opiate. Tongaline was taken in doses of a teaspoonful at intervals of an hour, and the third dose relieved her entirely. There was no malaise or bad feelings of any kind following its use. Other physicians here speak very highly of their experience with Tongaline."

THOMAS H. URQUHART, M.D.,
Hastings, Neb.

IT CONTAINS TONGA, EXT. CIMICIFUGÆ RACEMOSÆ AND THE SALICYLATES OF SODIUM, PILOCARPIN AND COLCHICIN.

SEND FOR CLINICAL REPORTS.

MELLIER DRUG COMPANY,
109 & 111 Walnut Street, ST. LOUIS.

Doctor—

IF YOU WANT TO KEEP IN LINE WITH THE PROFESSION SUBSCRIBE FOR THE

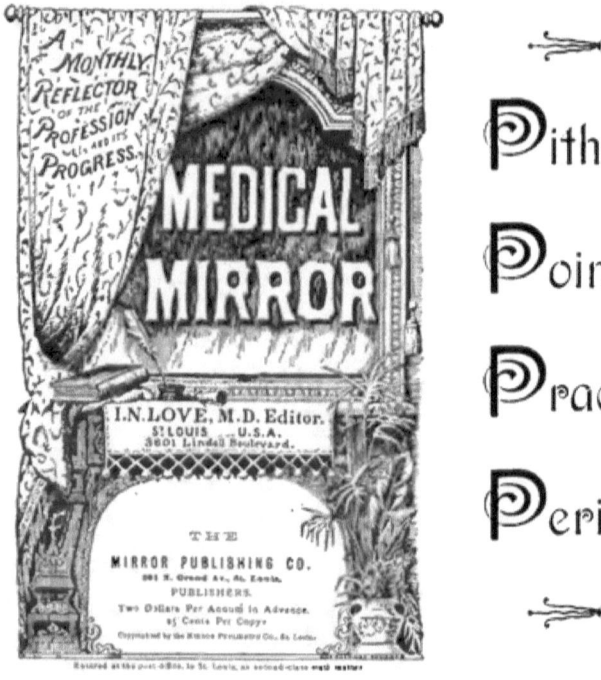

Pithy
Pointed
Practical
Periodical

Helpful alike to the BUSY and the UNEMPLOYED DOCTOR.

Prof. W. W. Dawson, of Cincinnati, Ex-President of The Amer. Med. Ass'n, says: "The MEDICAL MIRROR is the terscst, brightest, best and juiciest Medical Journal which comes to me—I do not relinquish it till I have read it completely through."

Subscription Price, $2.00 a year, in advance

ADVERTISER

Pharmaceutical preparations, food products—anything needed by the DOCTOR in his work—should be reflected in the MIRROR advertising pages, which the Doctors read for a record of the PROGRESS OF PHARMACY.

ST. LOUIS—a half million of inhabitants—a distributor of supplies to a larger territory in return tributary to it than any other city in America.

Over two-thirds of the profession of St. Louis are subscribers to the MIRROR.

The MIRROR is a national journal—large circulation in all the States, but the teeming States of the West and South are its special field.

For advertising rates apply to

MIRROR PUBLISHING CO.,
301 N. Grand Avenue, St. Louis.

⇢ E PLURIBUS UNUM ⇠

This cut does not represent the Honorable Chauncey M. Depew, making an after-dinner speech; it is not Grover Cleveland on "The Campaign of Education," nor yet is it the editor of

DANIEL'S TEXAS MEDICAL JOURNAL.

It is not a Pathological Specimen of any kind. It is Dr. Merryman's idea of E Pluribus Unum, or ye Medical Profession—many in one—all

Clamoring to subscribe for the celebrated TEXAS MEDICAL JOURNAL, the champion of LEGITIMATE MEDICINE and the defender of the dignity of professional character; that has done more for the Texas profession than all other agencies combined. The fearless and outspoken advocate and defender of the CODE OF OUR FATHERS, and the "TERROR OF QUACKS."

"The best medical journal in the south." (Memphis Med. Monthly.)
"The most intensely original journal that comes to our table; always fresh and interesting." (Sanitarian.)
It is a "Daisy," a "Jewel"; as fresh and sparkling as the most enterprising journalist could wish for. (St. Joseph Medical Herald.)
"The editor is a sharpshooter with a pen." (Homœopathic Journal.)
"The editor is to be congratulated on the scientific value of its contents." (Gaillard's.)
(Scores of such opinions of the press are on record.)

is the Official Organ of the leading District Medical Societies.
Among its Collaborators are

M. SWEARINGEN, M.D., State Health Officer of Texas.
T. D. WOOTEN, M.D., President Board of Regents, State University.
Professors PAINE and HADRA, of the Texas Medical College.
Professor BETZ, of Heilbron, Germany, etc.

Edited and published monthly at Austin, Texas, by
F. E. DANIEL, M.D., late Secretary Texas State Medical Association
Twice elected.   Twice resigned.   After five years' service.
Subscription price, $2.00 per year.   The Best Advertising Medium in Texas.
Send for Rates.

Now don't all speak at once, like that hydra-headed fellow at top; but send in your subscriptions SLOWLY, so as to give our book-keeper time to SPEND THE MONEY. Address
DR. F. E. DANIEL, Austin, Texas.

A Brief Summary of Hypodermic Medication, and its Advantages.

A PAMPHLET CONTAINING THE MOST RECENT SUGGESTIONS ON THE TECHNIQUE OF HYPODERMIC MEDICATION; SAMPLES OF OUR

Soluble Hypodermic Tablets, S. & D.'s

WHICH ARE SOLUBLE IN COLD OR WARM WATER AND ALWAYS READY FOR INSTANT USE; AND A SAMPLE BOTTLE OF

Ergotole, S. & D.'s

A CONCENTRATED PREPARATION OF ERGOT, SPECIALLY PREPARED FOR HYPODERMIC USE, WILL BE SENT TO ANY PHYSICIAN FREE OF COST.

Hypodermic Syringes, S. & D.'s

WHICH ALLOW THE MAKING OF A SOLUTION IN THE SYRINGE, ARE SENT AT THE FOLLOWING PRICES:

LEATHER-COVERED CASE, TWO TUBES OF TABLETS $2 50
METAL CASE, TWO TUBES OF TABLETS 2 50
METAL CASE, FOUR TUBES OF TABLETS 3 50
FLEXIBLE LEATHER CASE, AS SHOWN BY CUT 3 50

SHARP & DOHME BALTIMORE, MD.

ESTABLISHED 1860

THE FIRST RAW FOOD EXTRACT
(Introduced to the Medical Profession in 1878.)

BOVININE

THE VITAL PRINCIPLES OF BEEF CONCENTRATED

Containing 26 Per Cent. of Coaguble Albumen

AN IDEAL FOOD.   PALATABLE.   KEEPS PERFECTLY.

BOVININE consists of the Juices of Lean Raw Beef obtained by a mechanical process, neither heat nor acid being used in its preparation. The nutritious elements of lean raw beef are thus presented in a concentrated solution, no disintegration or destruction of the albumen having taken place. The proteids in solution amount to 26 per cent. of the weight of the preparation, and give to it the great dietetic value it possesses in all conditions where a concentrated and readily assimilable food is needed.

BOVININE is easily digested and COMPLETELY absorbed from the intestinal tract, thus furnishing an extremely valuable nutrient in Typhoid Fever, after surgical operations in the abdominal regions, in all diseased conditions of the intestinal tract characterised by ulceration or acute and chronic inflammation, and in diarrhoeic complaints.

BOVININE, containing as it does all the nutrient properties of lean raw beef in a highly concentrated form, furnishes to the Medical Profession a reliable and valuable aid to treatment in Phthisis, Marasmus of both young and old, in all wasting diseases, in continued fevers, and in supporting treatment.

BOVININE, on account of its BLOOD-MAKING PROPERTIES is *especially* of service after surgical operations, in cases of severe injuries attended with great loss of blood, and in the peurperal state.

BOVININE, for rectal feeding, is unsurpassed in excellence, having been used for weeks continuously with no irritation or disturbance resulting. The most satisfactory results from its use as an enema are obtained by adding to each ounce of *BOVININE* ten grains of Pancreatic Extract and two ounces of water. This should be well mixed and injected slowly. No preparation of opium is necessary in the enema.

SAMPLES will be furnished to any member of the Medical Profession free, carriage paid, upon application to the company.

PREPARED ONLY BY
The J. P. Bush Manufacturing Co.,
CHICAGO & NEW YORK, U. S. A.

DEPOT FOR GREAT BRITAIN:

32 SNOW HILL,   LONDON, E. C.

HUMMEL AND PARMELE
MEDICAL JOURNAL ADVERTISING

A. L. HUMMEL, M. D.
612 Drexel Building
PHILADELPHIA

CHAS. ROOME PARMELE
19 Park Place
NEW YORK

| GOUT

CALCULI

RHEUMATISM

AND ALL

URINARY

DISORDERS | **"GARROD SPA"**
(Lithia-Potash Water)

Compounded from most reliable scientific sources. Uniform in composition. Agreeable of taste.

CONTAINS MORE LITHIUM BICARBONATE
in a pint than any natural water in a gallon.

SEND FOR PAMPHLETS
TO
DR. ENNO SANDER
SPECIAL AGENCIES :   ST. LOUIS, MO.
R. E. RHODE, 504 N Clark Street   CHICAGO
JOHN D. PARK & SONS . . . . . . CINCINNATI
MEYER BROS. DRUG CO. . . . . KANSAS CITY
RENZ & HENRY . . . . LOUISVILLE
RICHARDSON DRUG CO. . . . . . OMAHA
W. S. THOMPSON, 703 Fifteenth Street
                             WASHINGTON, D. C. |

www.ingramcontent.com/pod-product-compliance
Lightning Source LLC
Chambersburg PA
CBHW050846300426
44111CB00010B/1147